Cool Capitalism

Cool Capitalism

JIM McGUIGAN

www.plutobooks.com

First published 2009 by Pluto Press
345 Archway Road, London N6 5AA and
175 Fifth Avenue, New York, NY 10010

www.plutobooks.com

Distributed in the United States of America exclusively by
Palgrave Macmillan, a division of St. Martin's Press LLC,
175 Fifth Avenue, New York, NY 10010

Copyright © Jim McGuigan 2009

The right of Jim McGuigan to be identified as the author of this work
has been asserted by him in accordance with the Copyright, Designs
and Patents Act 1988.

British Library Cataloguing in Publication Data
A catalogue record for this book is available from the British Library

ISBN   978 0 7453 2640 5   Hardback
ISBN   978 0 7453 2678 8   Paperback

Library of Congress Cataloging in Publication Data applied for

This book is printed on paper suitable for recycling and made from
fully managed and sustained forest sources. Logging, pulping and
manufacturing processes are expected to conform to the environmental
standards of the country of origin. The paper may contain up to
70 per cent post-consumer waste.

10 9 8 7 6 5 4 3 2 1

Designed and produced for Pluto Press by
Chase Publishing Services Ltd, 33 Livonia Road, Sidmouth EX10 9JB, England
Typeset from disk by Stanford DTP Services, Northampton, England
Printed and bound in the European Union by
CPI Antony Rowe, Chippenham and Eastbourne

To the memory of my grandfather, James Patrick McGuigan, who started me on this course.

CONTENTS

Preface and Acknowledgements   xi

Introduction: On 'Cool'   1

1 **The Spirits of Capitalism**   9
    The Old Spirit   9
    The New Spirit   19
    Capitalism Transmogrified   31

2 **The Great Refusal**   45
    Rebellious Autonomy   47
    Picasso, Rivera and Kahlo   58
    Cool Art and Business   72

3 **Consumer Culture**   83
    Conspicuous Consumption   86
    Mass Consumerism   99
    Cool Seduction   108
    Commodity Fetishism and Mobile Privatisation   116

4 **Market Values**   129
    Neoliberal Discourse   132
    Enterprise Culture   140
    Creative Industries   149

5 **Working Life**   166
    Emotional Labour   168
    Individualisation   175
    Generation Crisis   188

6	**Anti-Capitalism Revisited**	197
	Cool Brands and Sweated Labour	199
	One No and Many Yeses	205
	Limits to Capitalism	216

| *Notes* | 230 |
| *Index* | 268 |

Everything relates to everything else.
David Harvey

PREFACE AND ACKNOWLEDGEMENTS

This book consists mainly of cultural analysis and ideology critique, less so of political economy. It is concerned with certain aspects of the culture of capitalism that are prevalent today. Of necessity, however – since the book is about capitalism – the cultural processes explored here cannot be detached entirely from economic and political processes. Capitalism was never considered so legitimate and taken for granted as a virtually natural state of being as it has been over the past 30 or so years. Consequently, it might be thought, capitalism hardly needs justifying. Yet, in a significant sense, it is constantly justified according to the terms and referents of everyday life both by necessity and by apparently free choice. Still, there are reasons for criticising capitalism, as a great many people are now becoming aware. To call its justification, however deep-seated, into question is to call into question capitalism itself. This book is principally about a curious feature of how capitalism is legitimised today – the extraordinary incorporation of dissent – and how debilitating that is for both opposition and, indeed, for justice. In the absence of dissent that is genuinely disconcerting, however, capitalism is allowed to get away with murder, and not only metaphorically speaking.

In writing about these matters, I have drawn upon the knowledge and advice of many people, only a few of whom will be mentioned here since I cannot remember the source of every nugget of wisdom for which I am personally indebted. Mick Billig for straightening me out about formal logic; Jackie Dingly-Jackson for explaining the significance of the Japanese Knotweed plant; Jan Flaherty on money and youth; Mike Gane for tolerating my purportedly redundant delusions; Martyn Lee for checking that I wasn't completely wrong about consumer culture; Ruth Lister for suffering my ultra-radicalism; Jo Littler for confirming in her work that I might be thinking along the right lines; Christopher

McGuigan for the insight of youth; Angela McRobbie for worrying about some of the same things as me; Graham Murdock for always making sure that I wasn't too stupid; John Richardson for checking that I didn't say anything too politically incorrect about *The Apprentice*; Chris Rojek for originally suggesting the idea of writing a book about this subject; Dominic Wring for sharing my angst about these matters; and Laurie and George Salemohamed for being very nice. As usual, I am grateful to Lesley and Jenny for putting up so patiently – especially Lesley – with my constant diatribe against the iniquities of capitalism. The general approach I have taken is very much inspired by the work and example of Trevor Griffiths and Doug Kellner, which has taught me a great deal about dialectical thought. Also, I would like to thank Tom Lynton for his excellent work on the cover.

The work for this book was largely completed before American sub-prime mortgage defaults led to a credit crunch, an international financial crisis and a recession turning into what is likely to be a lengthy depression on a worldwide scale. This, no doubt, has rekindled awareness of the deeply flawed political economy of global capitalism. However, at the time of writing, the cool culture of capitalism still persists as a powerful feature of ideological hegemony throughout the Earth. It will take a while before that pervasive set of assumptions and practices are called properly into question. This book is dedicated to such questioning.

Leamington
March 2009

INTRODUCTION: ON 'COOL'

Cool capitalism is the incorporation of disaffection into capitalism itself. 'Cool' is the front region[1] of capitalism today for those who are seduced by its cultural appeal and especially for those who aspire, mostly in frustration, to the greatest fruits of a capitalist civilisation. For capitalism to command hearts and minds, it is necessary to mask out its much less appealing back region, manifestations of which are perpetual sources of disaffection. For the sake of capitalist legitimacy, such disaffection must be assuaged: hence the role of 'cool' in translating disaffection into acceptance and compliance. What is 'cool'? Before exploring that question, I should say something about how I was prompted to write on these matters.

A few years ago, around the turn of the millennium, I was struck by two American TV ads. (I cannot remember which brands they were selling nor have I sought to find out since it is of no consequence, and I have anyway no desire to contribute to the advertising effort.) The first ad involved a young man seeking to persuade his boss, an older man, of the virtues of a new computer system he wants him to buy for the office. He repeatedly describes the system as 'cool'. The expression on the boss's face is one of deep scepticism concerning the young man's peroration. Eventually, however, the young man observes that the new system will save the company money, whereupon the older man replies, 'cool'. The second ad featured Dennis Hopper as a middle-aged business executive driving a sleek automobile across an American wilderness. This footage is inter-cut with footage of Hopper's younger, hippy self riding a motorcycle in the 1969 movie, *Easy Rider*. In both cases, the ads featured the relationship between a younger and an older man. The first ad showed the younger man convincing the older man that a new computer system was 'cool'.

At the end of the second ad, Hopper burns off his younger self when he accelerates past him. It brought to mind the old adage that if you are not a socialist at 20 you do not have a heart, but if you are still a socialist at 30 then you do not have a brain. It is a fitting ideological coda to the twentieth century.

Since the early 2000s I have been collecting similar references to 'cool' either in the actual use of the word or in signs somehow redolent of sentiments associated with it. For instance, in 2001, Switzerland's ambassador to Britain became concerned about the negative impact internationally of aspersions cast upon his country's reputation, such as stories about the banking of Nazi gold. In order to demonstrate that Switzerland was cool he decided to invite graffiti artists to adorn the walls of the underground car park in the London embassy. One of these artists was to become highly renowned and indeed bankable – the elusive, Bristol-born artist who calls himself Banksy. His principal graffiti for the Swiss embassy, which remains on the wall next to the car park's exit, is a montage of 21 copies of a picture of Lenin with a Mohican haircut and the legend, 'Vulture Capitalists'. This and other examples of Banksy's work at the embassy are now said to be worth a million pounds.[2]

In 2004, Hill & Knowlton (China) Public Relations Co. Ltd. conducted a 'China Cool Hunt' survey of students in Beijing and Shanghai. The market research evidence showed that Chinese students value 'cool', whatever that means, and they associate it with leading Western or Westernised brand companies, most notably Nike, Sony, Adidas, BMW, Microsoft, Coca-Cola, IBM, Nokia, Samsung, Ferrari and Christian Dior.[3] 'Cool' has travelled a long way, from the West coast of Africa to the Americas and around the whole world – as far, in fact, as 'communist' China.

It is generally agreed among commentators that the notion of 'cool' came out of Africa. The American art historian Robert Farris Thompson traces its sources to the Yorubaland coastal region of modern-day Nigeria. Although origins do not legislate for current meaning and significance when tracing the genealogy of discourse,[4] nevertheless, it is interesting to know something of origination if only to marvel at how the meaning of words tends to alter subtly over time, and possibly even become inverted. The word *itutu* means 'composure',[5] an important quality in battle, especially in a hot climate. The denotation may refer to 'composure' but there is a broader set of connotations best summed up by the term 'cool'. In studying Yoruban art and ritual, Thompson argues that 'coolness' is a 'trait which grants a person the power to incarnate the destiny of his tradition'.[6] He studied 'the semantic range of the concept, "cool" in thirty-five Niger-Zaire languages, from Woloff of Senegal to the Zulu of South Africa' and notes that in Africa 'coolness is an all-embracing positive attribute which combines notions of composure, silence, vitality, healing, and social purification'.[7] Coolness is associated with personal power and courage: 'A cool person does not hide.'[8] It is enacted in the dance and in the clarity of the singing voice. Thompson talks of 'the striking African custom of dancing "hot" with a "cool" unsmiling face'.[9] Coolness is also evident in style of walking and bodily movement generally, exemplified today in black American '*bopping* ... a mode of asserting strength of self, broadly dovetailing with portions of the African mode of "looking smart"'.[10]

Thompson was alert to the connections between an ancient tradition and a modern vernacular, the performance of the young Yoruba warrior and the expressive lifestyle of the cool cat on the city streets of the United States.[11] The slave trade in Africans, abducted from the West coast and the hinterland, transported across the perilous sea in appalling conditions to the Americas, during which many were lost on the way, is a shameful episode of early capitalism with a complex historical legacy that has been described as 'the Black Atlantic'.[12] It is a history of suffering and abuse, which has left a deep and abiding trace, not only in terms of injustice but in the response of African dignity under pressure, the culture of American cool. As Dick Pountain and David Robins observe, 'In Africa Cool belonged to the realm of the sacred, but once it transported to America it evolved into a kind of passive resistance to the work ethic through personal style.'[13] Furthermore, they suggest: 'The slave trade mingled African hedonism with New

World Puritanism, inducing a moral ambivalence that survives into modern Cool.'[14]

Since the abolition of slavery and long before the flowering of the civil rights movement in the 1960s, the most evident site of cool in the United States (and not only in the past but to a significant extent still) was in black music and style, most notably in mid-twentieth-century jazz culture.[15] This was focused intensely around the bebop maestros and their sullen rebellion, where the word 'cool' figured as part of an in-group lexicon that was to develop into a popular argot that would be adopted increasingly by whites, eventually spreading from the dissident margins into the mainstream of youth culture by the late twentieth century. The site of African-American culture is crucial, but not exclusively so, for the sentiments associated with cool, if not always for the word. The word and its associations are not fixed in meaning and, in any event, it is frequently said to be uncool, if not impossible, to try to pin down a definition of cool. However, in their survey of cool rules Pountain and Robins do identify three essential traits of the 'cool' persona, 'namely narcissism, ironic detachment and hedonism'.[16] These traits can certainly be found in a succession of youthful subcultures since the Second World War. Take narcissism, for instance. Self-regard, fastidious concern with style, and what could readily be construed as offensive deportment are typical of young men who may otherwise have had little to show off about. There was a Gallic version among the post-war Parisian existentialists, dressed in black, Gauloises cigarettes hanging languidly from their lips, obliged to act out anti-bourgeois nonconformity in every free choice, condemned to freedom in an inauthentic world. It was not very cool to become too heated about politics, however, like some decidedly uncool Stalinist. The *zazou* subculture of French youth during the occupation of the early 1940s was a related, though less intellectual, manifestation of petit-bourgeois narcissism with an edge of cool irony.[17] Incidentally, the term 'zazou' derived from Cab Calloway's jazz slang, which was further embellished by Slim Gaillard's scat singing.

Ironic detachment, the second cool trait identified by Pountain and Robins, is the appropriate stance, a don't care attitude in conjunction with disgust at the system – 'whatever', with its sneer and feigned indifference. Punks and their progeny constituted an extreme branch of the ironic tendency. A subterranean lifestyle, hedonistic pleasure-seeking – the third trait – and illicit drug-taking are all manifestations of cool. Some genuinely dropped out, but the hippies of the late 1960s and early 1970s were usually weekenders, harbingers of the present-day hedonistic mainstream, characterised by unruliness and binge-drinking – behaviour also deemed cool – among teenage girls and young women as well as youthful males.

The adoption of black style, demeanour and sentiment by whites goes back a long way, at least as far as Norman Mailer's 'white negro' and hipster style of the 1950s.[18] There is, of course, a downside to cool, particularly for young black males, as documented by Richard Majors and Janet Mancini Billson in their sociological study, *Cool Pose: The Dilemmas of Black Manhood in America*: 'coolness may be a survival strategy that has cost the black male – and society – an enormous price'.[19] Although not confined to black men in urban poverty, cool is very prominent in that context. It expresses black masculine identity and pride in the ghetto. It enables the black man to manage anger in oppressive circumstances, facilitating 'poise under pressure'.[20] A core element of the downside is a sense of 'compulsive masculinity', damaging to both male and female relationships. Cool pose is creative but also destructive, representing a peculiar homology with the driving force of capitalism itself, even though black American men, with a few notable exceptions, are not great successes in capitalist America. The problems of gang culture, druggy lifestyle and disorganised sociality figure much larger than the realisation of the American Dream in the lives of young working-class black men – and, indeed, of black women too – characterised by an incipient nihilism.[21] Comparable problems exist among young whites enthralled by the cult of cool, in the disorganised working-class neighbourhoods of de-industrialised inner cities and outer suburbs.[22]

Shorn of its black context, however, cool floats free, available for the articulation of both resistance and incorporation, and, over time, traversing from one to the other. Today, the word 'cool' seems to be on the lips of every youngster in Western and Westernised culture, signifying very little – not much more than 'good' or 'okay' – and adopted with insouciance by their parents. While that may be an innocent end-point, it is not the whole story, which is about how a culture of disaffection crossed the political landscape, arrived at the opposite side, and neutralised dissent along the way. A key study in this respect is the book version of Thomas Frank's doctoral thesis, *The Conquest of Cool*.[23] According to Frank, the '60s in the United States went down in history as a decade of rebellion when the counter-culture[24] challenged the dominant culture at its very heart. Yet, in truth, the counter-cultural challenge effectively – and ironically – refreshed the culture and political economy of corporate America, thereby contributing to its survival and flourishing. The conventional distinction between 'conservatives' and 'liberals' rather misses the point of the deeper cleavages in American society. The division between rich and poor is starker than that between Democrat and Republican, and has become more so.[25] Seen in retrospect, the '60s rebels, turning over redundant shibboleths, were the saviours rather than the gravediggers of corporate America. As Frank remarks, 'rebel youth remains the cultural mode of the corporate moment, used to promote not only specific products but the general idea of life in the cyber-revolution'.[26] Incidentally, Peter Biskind has put forward a similar argument specifically concerning the 'movie brats' who came to prominence in the 1970s, effectively saving Hollywood. The likes of Francis Ford Coppola, Peter Fonda, Dennis Hopper, Bob Rafelson and Bert Schneider presented themselves as dangerous rebels but wound up giving Hollywood a cool makeover, hence boosting long-term profitability.[27]

Business was eager to integrate rebel ideology into its corporate practices, to 'revolutionise' management. Entrepreneurs welcomed the counter-cultural challenge into the corporation since it accorded with their own thinking on the deficiencies of organised capitalism. This involved breaking with 1950s conformity, the robotic American way of life that critics, humanistic and social-scientific, had incessantly attacked: the 'organisation man', the 'one-dimensional man', and so on. Business needed a shot of daring imagination that broke with the old ways. As it happened, 'By the middle of the 1950s, talk of conformity, of consumerism, and of the banality of mass-produced culture were routine elements of middle-class American life.'[28] Furthermore, 'the meaning of "the sixties" cannot be considered apart from the enthusiasm of ordinary, suburban Americans for cultural revolution'.[29] A consensus was already forming for the historic shift into cool capitalism, the marriage of counter-culture and corporate business, which has survived the high divorce rate ever since.

Frank is unusual among cultural analysts in that he reads management texts in order to discern the principles of corporate America and of what I am calling cool capitalism.[30] During the 1950s and '60s, there was increasing disquiet in management circles about the organisation man's lack of creative flair. A key tool of the newer management philosophy was to become 'market segmentation', which differentiated between taste and lifestyle categories, assuming social heterogeneity rather than homogeneity in a diverse population. Consumer subjectivity became the object of attention for this new school of management. It was assumed that the customer had become 'hip', in a quaint old term, to what was going on in this forerunner of cool business discourse. Although such language made an early appearance in the story related by Frank, for stretches of time it lay fairly dormant until revived triumphantly in the 1990s. In the longer historical view, then, the counter-culture turns out to have been a moment in the rejuvenation of middle-class and corporate America. The 1990s saw 'the consolidation of a new species of hip consumerism', in Frank's words, 'a cultural perpetual motion regime in which disgust with the falseness, shoddiness, and everyday oppressions of consumer society could be enlisted to drive the ever-accelerating wheel of consumption'.[31] At the same time, business became 'funky',[32] having shed its reputation for bureaucratic conformity. Simultaneously, the longing for another world has diminished for the young, to be replaced by the longing for cool commodities and their fetishistic properties.

Frank's account is American-centric – in many respects justifiably so – but in this book the claim is advanced that cool capitalism is now a too deeply entrenched and pervasive phenomenon to be limited to the particular history of how US capitalism turned cool. The more recent period under consideration here has witnessed the transition from mid-twentieth-century organised capitalism to neoliberal capitalism on a global scale. At the same time, communism has collapsed and social democracy has been eclipsed. This book is concerned with capitalism in its cultural aspect and begins by considering how the Protestant ethic of earlier capitalism was superseded by a much more hedonistic ethic. The transformation was greatly aided, as Frank notes with reference to the American counter-culture, by cultural opposition to capitalism, and is yet more markedly exemplified for me by the incorporation of 'the great refusal' of art in general into the capitalist ideology and market practices associated with the alleged panacea of 'creative industries' presented as offering solutions to the problems arising from the collapse of manufacturing and heavy industry in what used to be the 'advanced' capitalist nations, and the devolution of such work to cheap labour markets around the world. The attendant shift from production to consumption in culture and economy has seen the 'democratisation' of consumerism in wealthy countries and the growth of immense consumer aspiration in poorer countries. These developments are described with reference to processes of cool seduction and enhanced commodity fetishism in a privatised way of life where communication technologies play a vital role.

Although this book is concerned with the cultural aspects of capitalism, it is important not to treat them in splendid isolation from economic and political processes, and in particular the way in which neoliberal ideology has exerted market reasoning over all practices and colonised the everyday life of late modernity. The effects on working lives and well-being through the lifecycle are severe for many in an insecure and excessively individualistic culture. There are, however, sources of resistance: a renewal of anti-capitalist and oppositional practice that, nowadays, cannot be regarded separately from the struggle over resources in a crisis-ridden environment.

1
THE SPIRITS OF CAPITALISM

This chapter looks at how capitalism has been conceptualised since the nineteenth century. The very notion of capitalism as a civilisation was formulated in German sociology after Karl Marx had studied the capitalist mode of production in comparatively advanced industrial Britain. Early debate concerning capitalism turned on issues of political economy and culture, particularly circulating around the argument that ascetic Protestantism was conducive to capitalist activity. Such values are no longer much associated with capitalism, which has now developed a distinctly hedonistic cultural aspect and, indeed, a 'cool' tone. The cultural face, legitimisation and justification of capitalism make up the core topic of this chapter, tracing developments during the twentieth century from the socialist challenge in the mid century up to the apparently total hegemony and legitimacy of capitalism that prevails in the world today.

The Old Spirit

Marx was extremely impressed by capitalism. In *The Communist Manifesto* of 1848 he wrote in such glowing terms about the civilisation that was being constructed by the bourgeoisie that Marshall Berman was prompted much later to ask, 'What have the bourgeoisie done to deserve Marx's praise?'[1] The architects of capitalism, the bourgeoisie, had liberated the creative capacity of human beings. This was represented concretely on the grandest scale by enormous building projects to facilitate the expansion of production and trade, though these were not exactly novel historically. Most important, however, was the bourgeois push for perpetual change. Marx famously characterised the driving force of capitalism with considerable eloquence:

> Constant revolutionising of production, uninterrupted disturbance of all social conditions, everlasting uncertainty and agitation distinguish the bourgeois epoch from all previous ones. All fixed, fast-frozen relations, with their train of ancient prejudices and opinions are swept away, all new-formed ones become antiquated before they can ossify. All that is solid melts into air, all that is holy is profaned, and man is at last compelled to face with sober senses, his real conditions of life, and his relations with his kind.[2]

Even after the collapse of Soviet communism, towards the end of the twentieth century, Marx was still fêted for his grasp of capitalism's world-historic significance and his extraordinary percipience about the process of globalisation[3] – not only by erstwhile Marxists but by ideologues of capitalism as well.

In the first volume of Marx's *Capital*, the only one prepared for publication by Marx himself and published in his own lifetime, he sought to formulate a scientific analysis of how capitalism worked. The analysis was based, as Marx always put it, on the 'English' case. The analysis was grounded in historical evidence that does not necessarily warrant the abstraction of general criteria of universal validity, a temptation which tended to guide and possibly misguide many subsequent 'Marxists'. Marx was 'scientific' in his analytical procedure, unlike his idealist predecessors in German philosophy and some of his own followers.

Marx aimed, in the earlier and more technical part of the first volume of *Capital*, to account for the determination of value in the capitalist mode of production, incorporating the already well-established argument that value derived from labour, distinguishing between use value and exchange value, and tracing the process whereby capital extracts surplus value from labour. The capitalist mode of production only really gels with the formal subsumption of labour under capital on a scale sufficient for the whole process of surplus-value extraction to operate systemically.[4] Marx insisted upon this because capitalism did indeed exist sporadically in all sorts of manifestations before its formation as the dominant mode of production in Britain during the nineteenth century – for instance, in Italian banking from the Renaissance. Marx was interested in understanding how capitalism operated maturely, as it happens, not with some academic debate over 'origins' as such. Though he did, of course, examine the role of the enclosures, capitalist agriculture, imperial conquest and commerce as well as the industrial revolution and early factory system in the formation of British capitalism, which was undoubtedly in the vanguard when Marx was writing in the mid nineteenth century.[5]

Marx's technical analysis of the production and circulation of value shows that an ostensibly equitable set of arrangements – 'a fair day's wage for a fair day's work' – conceals a systematically unequal relation between capital and labour. The worker is, in effect, only partially remunerated, sufficient at best to sustain subsistence, for the labour power expended in doing the job. The unremunerated portion is the source of surplus value and, ultimately, of profits that are either distributed as dividends to shareholders or ploughed back into capital accumulation. This is an endless and dynamic process in which the extraction of surplus value depends upon the rate of exploitation, such that the capitalist is motivated constantly to increase it by whatever means possible: lengthening working time, replacing labour with machines, and so on. On the surface, the activities of the capitalist are reasonable and, indeed, 'rational', yet they conceal a deeply unreasonable exploitation of human capacities and possibilities beneath the surface. Marx uncovered this dirty secret of capitalism in technical argument concerning the mode of production – the contradictions between the forces of production (labour, technology, etc.) and the relations of production (time–work discipline, unequal ownership of the means of production, coercive measures supported by the powers of the state, etc.). It was difficult to keep the secret hidden from critics and reformers, as testimony in the British government's own blue books revealed. Marx drew upon such official reports for empirical substantiation of his general arguments concerning the inhumanity of capitalism. This was demonstrated by evidence of dreadful conditions of employment that undermined claims to the historical superiority of bourgeois 'civilisation'.

So, Marx praised capitalism but he also, more consequentially, criticised it in no uncertain terms and looked to surpass it. Other early students of capitalism were less interested in exploring the prospects for surpassing the new mode of production but concentrated, instead, on understanding how it came about and became legitimised. In his account of capitalism, and in accord with his 'materialist conception of history', Marx had placed a great deal of emphasis on material factors and much less on 'ideas'. His early work challenged Hegel's idealist historicism in German philosophy, whereby the 'spirit' of an age was thought to define its character and development. By contrast, Marx went on to study the actual conditions of the age in the terms of political economy, of which ideas were a part but not the whole story.

The nascent discipline of sociology, however, was not so willing to ditch the legacy of German idealism. The likes of Werner Sombart, for instance, insisted that capitalism had a spiritual aspect which was neglected by Marx and his followers.[6] There was an unavoidably political context to the intellectual dispute over capitalism, since Marxists wanted a socialist rather than a capitalist society and at certain times – from the late nineteenth century and throughout most of the twentieth – it looked as though they might have their wishes fulfilled. The early sociologists were not so politically motivated in a direct sense, though they were far from innocent of politics however much they talked of 'objectivity'. Max Weber argued that the Protestant ethic in its Calvinist version had an elective affinity with the spirit necessary for developing capitalism in its modern, rational and most legitimate form. Weber himself was well aware that his thesis could be taken as a deliberate rebuttal of 'the materialist conception of history', and probably intended it to be so, although this is denied by some recent commentators. There is no necessary incompatibility, however, between the Marxist and the Weberian accounts of early capitalism.[7] In fact, Weber's thesis may even be seen as complementary to Marx's more rounded analysis since it illuminates the ideological dimension of capitalism, a dimension that Marx certainly acknowledged.

By the early years of the twentieth century, Marxism had made great political advances, especially in Weber's own country of Germany. Following Engels's interpretations and promotion of Marx's thought after the latter's death in 1883, a great many Marxists had adopted a rather more economically deterministic view of history than Marx himself had probably held. At the turn of the century, such economic materialism had become a kind of orthodoxy that, arguably, over-simplified Marx's own complex and unfinished theorising, which was, nevertheless, in any event wide open to differences of interpretation.[8] Orthodox Marxism of this kind, particularly in Germany, claimed that historical change was derived entirely from economistic class struggle and the movement of material forces. Ideational forces (beliefs and cultural values), on the other hand, were merely secondary emanations, in effect, furnishing ideological legitimacy for the prevailing order. Weber called this view 'one-sided'. As a sophisticated social theorist, Weber claimed to be offering a multi-dimensional account of the emergence and development of capitalism.

However, in his famous thesis, *The Protestant Ethic and the 'Spirit' of Capitalism* (originally published in a journal in two parts in 1904–5 and republished in revised form as a book in 1920), Weber concerned himself solely with ideational forces, in particular, 'the Protestant ethic'. This was consistent with his evolving theory of meaningful action, which was to become so influential in the kind of sociology that attributed great significance to culture, not least of which was Talcott Parsons's ambitious synthesis of classical social theory in structural functionalism, the American perspective that came to dominate sociology in the mid twentieth century.[9] Incidentally, it was Parsons who first published an English translation of the revised version of Weber's thesis in 1930.[10] This translation was the one used by Anglophone readers for 70 years until new translations into English of the first and second versions appeared at the beginning of the twenty-first century.[11] Although the second version is a mature work, reflecting Weber's own more developed social theory, there is rather little difference between the versions in English, (although there is greater interpretative accuracy of German words in the latest

English translation of the first version that eliminates Parsons's American domestication of the revised text).

In both versions Weber carefully dissects the various strains of nonconformist Protestantism. He does not explicitly discount the Anglican Church's residual Catholicism, although this is taken for granted, but he is at considerable pains to dismiss Lutheranism as the kind of Protestantism that was conducive to the development of modern, rationalistic capitalism. He places great emphasis on the Swiss theologian John Calvin's doctrine of predestination that so influenced Presbyterianism, the Puritans who emigrated to North America in the early seventeenth century, the Methodism that emerged in Britain over a century later, and European continental Pietism. Calvin's doctrine of predestination was extremely harsh. He argued that God was all powerful, and whether believers would go to Heaven or Hell was already decided at birth. The Elect were chosen by God before they had the opportunity to do good work or to sin. Such a view was deeply offensive to Roman Catholicism and its offshoots, which held out the prospect of repentance and forgiveness for sinners. The Calvinist Protestant's fate was predestined: nothing could be done about it. The psychological effect on the person was, in practice, the opposite of what might have been expected, in Weber's argument. Instead of throwing up their hands in despair, Calvinists were inclined to prove their election to the next world through meaningful action in this one.

This orientation translated into a particular approach to work, especially for the entrepreneur but also for the God-fearing worker. Weber noted other orientations associated with capitalism, such as greed and love of riches, which had not been prohibited in the Catholic Italian states. Adventure capitalism, banking and mercantilism, however, were not sufficient for the development of a highly rational and methodical way of doing business, the fundamental 'spirit', in Weber's estimation, that facilitated a robust and resilient capitalist system for producing and circulating commodities efficiently.

The early Protestant capitalists were motivated by an ethical orientation, to demonstrate their election, according to Weber, and not just to make money for its own sake, though money was undoubtedly a serious consideration. The eighteenth-century precepts of Benjamin Franklin – 'time is money' and so forth – represented the spirit of capitalism in its nascent state and, no doubt, influenced capitalist development in North America. It is not difficult to see the ideological appeal of the Protestant-ethic thesis in Parsonian sociology from the 1930s onwards since it indicated a direct line of descent from the New England Puritanism of the seventeenth century to the capitalist American Dream in the twentieth. For Weber, the values of Puritanism – deferred gratification and the like – had an affinity with the rational process of capital accumulation and shaped typical bourgeois principles of conduct, including meticulous book-keeping. Weber himself recognised that the subsequent development of capitalism did not necessarily articulate such Protestant ethics, but these very precepts had become deeply ingrained in the culture of capitalism, irrespective of the religious affiliations of its agents.

Weber's thesis was always problematic in relation to Marx's 'English' case since Calvinist Protestantism was a much more pronounced feature of Scottish than of English culture, where Anglicanism retained Catholic roots. Still, Scottish intellectuals like the political economist Adam Smith were at the heart of the eighteenth-century Enlightenment in Britain and their influence was great in England, and not only in Scotland. There was also a strong dissenting tradition in England that dated from the Civil War and before, and, indeed, that was residually present in the culture of Northern industrial capitalism. As R.H. Tawney remarked rather tellingly, 'Puritanism was the schoolmaster of the English middle classes.'[12] Of course, Weber himself had been motivated in the first instance and stimulated in his enquiries not so much by the 'English' case at all but by the German experience, where he noticed that Protestants rather than Catholics were most active in developing capitalism.

It can hardly be missed, then, that Weber attributed an ethical motivation for capitalist activity that transcended purely pecuniary motives, whether or not he was accurate on the specific details of national conditions. That the development of capitalism was motivated by ethics is an argument with which Marxists would normally disagree. Weber's legendary debate with 'the ghost of Karl Marx' may not, however, have represented an insurmountable theoretical difference. Weber also emphasised the importance of material factors and denied that he was positing a one-sided idealism that gave precedence to culture over economy against a one-sided materialism that reduced the former to the latter. Yet Weber certainly admired British capitalism and liberal democracy – so, the 'English' case did matter for him. Although also an admirer of charismatic authority as well as rational-legal authority, he was hostile to Bismarck and to Kaiser Wilhelm. Weber participated in the writing of the Weimar constitution and was keen to install firmly something approximating liberal democracy in Germany following the disaster of the First World War. Moreover, he had visited the United States in 1904 and was duly impressed by its dynamism. Like the good Protestant – though Lutheran – bourgeois he was, Weber defended capitalism on ethical and rational grounds at a time when the threat of socialism and communism was on the rise. He feared that 'the iron cage' of rational bureaucracy would disenchant the capitalist world but, to his mind, a bureaucratised socialism would be worse.

Parsons, in his later work, built a sociological system that placed cultural values at its heart, especially 'the central value system' cherished by capitalist America. This was spelt out in his typology of 'pattern variables'.[13] The typology was directly relevant to and incorporated into the kind of development theory that aimed to modernise underdeveloped countries along capitalist lines. As Jan Nederveen Pieterse comments, in the 'modernization scenario laid out in Talcott Parsons' "pattern variables" ... modernization is defined as a movement from particularism to universalism, from ascription to achievement, from functional diffuseness to functional specificity, and from affective roles to affective neutrality'.[14] The values of universalism, achievement, functional specificity and affective neutrality clearly echo the rational spirit of Weber's Protestant ethic. Weber himself had devoted much of his work to comparative study of world religions and forms of legitimate authority, implicitly in order to account for why capitalism had developed in some places and not others, under cultural conditions conducive to capitalism or not, as the case may be.[15] His own persistent distinction between 'Orient' (Eastern traditionalism) and 'Occident' (Western modernity) had affinities with other early European sociological distinctions – such as Tönnies's community/society and Durkheim's mechanical solidarity/organic solidarity – governed by a general binary opposition between 'tradition' and 'modernity' that was associated with the classic sociological problem of accounting for the transition from the former to the latter. And for Weber, mainstream European sociology, and subsequently hegemonic American sociology as well, modernity was capitalist modernity, 'the spirit of the age'.

In a speech of January 1936, Joseph Schumpeter, the economic sociologist, posed the question, 'Can Capitalism Survive?'[16] His answer was immediate and succinct: 'No, ladies and gentlemen, it cannot'. This summary judgement must have been alarming for his audience at the United States Department of Agriculture Graduate School in Washington, DC. Schumpeter posed the question again in his distinguished book, *Capitalism, Socialism and Democracy*, originally published in 1942 during the darkest days of the Second World War. His answer then was equally blunt, though he justified it at much greater length. Do not get the idea that Schumpeter was hostile to capitalism: far from it. Born in Moravia in the Austro-Hungarian Empire in 1883, Schumpeter was educated in Vienna, worked as a lawyer and businessman, served briefly and unsuccessfully in the Austrian coalition government after the First World War as finance minister, failed as a banker and turned to a full-time academic career, eventually winding up at Harvard in the early 1930s. He knew his Marx but was no Marxist; and was acquainted with Weber, who was a more significant influence on his thought. Like Weber and other Germanic intellectuals Schumpeter admired strong leadership, a penchant which was to be given a terrible shock by the rise of Hitler. Commentators tend to characterise Schumpeter's politics as similar to those of British Toryism. Interestingly, however, he not only answered the question of whether capitalism would survive in a negative manner, he also posed the question of whether socialism would work and answered it in the affirmative.[17]

Now, it is astonishing that someone of Schumpeter's ilk should have been so negative about capitalism's fate and positive about the prospects for socialism. In fact, he did not like socialism either as an idea or in practice, though he probably did see it as somehow inevitable. A great many other non-socialists did so as well in the middle years of the twentieth century. Schumpeter was always very positive about the spirit and practice of capitalism, echoing Marx's vision of solids melting with his renowned notion of 'creative destruction', described in *Capitalism, Socialism and Democracy* as 'the central fact about capitalism. It is what capitalism consists in and what every capitalist concern has to live in'.[18] As in Marx's characterisation, the emphasis is on dynamism and perpetual change, as capitalism careers about, building things and then knocking them down in order to put something else in their place. Unlike Marx, however, Schumpeter had no reservations about the unqualified good of creative destruction. At the heart of the matter, for him, was the daring and innovative entrepreneur:

> [T]he function of the entrepreneur is to reform or revolutionize the pattern of production by exploiting an invention or, more generally, an untried technological possibility for producing a new commodity or producing an old one in a new way, by opening up a new source of supply of materials or a new outlet for products by reorganizing an industry and so on.[19]

While that figure may have gone out of fashion in Schumpeter's day, he (and sometimes she) was to make an heroic comeback a few decades later.

According to Schumpeter, the poor prospects for capitalism were not so much to do with the threat of Soviet communism (in fact, he showed more interest in 'English' labourism after the Second World War) but more to do with something like the internal contradictions of capitalism (echoes of Marx again). Mid-twentieth-century monopoly capitalism was so bureaucratic that it was not a congenial setting for the heroic, risk-taking entrepreneur of the old school to flourish. Moreover, following the Depression, state intervention – even in the US under Roosevelt

– was turning capitalism into a kind of socialism from within. Schumpeter also played around with what he called 'the theory of vanishing investment opportunity',[20] a theory which neoliberal capitalism was to disprove, however temporarily, in the closing decades of the twentieth century with digitalisation, the Internet and intensified globalisation.

Adding insult to injury, in Schumpeter's account, capitalism was no longer popular. He remarked, 'the capitalist process produced that atmosphere of almost universal hostility to its own order'.[21] Furthermore, 'unlike any other type of society, capitalism inevitably and by virtue of the very logic of its civilization creates, educates and subsidizes a vested interest in social unrest'.[22] Artists and writers are forever attacking the system; and the system pays for them to do so. Schumpeter had no great liking for critical intellectuals. They were the gravediggers of capitalism.

How much Schumpeter really believed in his negative prognosis for capitalism is open to debate. Whether or not he intended it to be so, it seems most likely that he was predominantly read as issuing a warning – that capitalism was in grave peril and something must be done about it so as to turn back the Reds from the gates of the citadel.

The New Spirit

Writing in the 1970s, Daniel Bell, the eminent American sociologist, was worried about what he called 'the cultural contradictions of capitalism'. Although Bell described himself as 'a socialist in economics, a liberal in politics, and a conservative in culture',[23] like Schumpeter, he was not a critic of capitalism in principle. He had long passed from a youthful Trotskyism to what was widely regarded as a 'neoconservative' position in his mature years. Yet, similarly to Schumpeter, Bell's encounter with Marxism had left him with a distinctly dialectical mode of reasoning in which he appreciated the collision of opposing forces and sensed possible outcomes that were not, in his opinion, conducive to capitalism. Even so, he had already declared 'the end of ideology'[24] and announced confidently 'the coming of post-industrial society',[25] all of which suggested that capitalism was, apparently, doing rather well.

Bell agreed with Weber's Protestant account of the origins of capitalism. The Protestant ethic, in its classical version, is ascetic in a manner that is entirely consistent with rational calculation and capital accumulation. From such a point of view, excessive consumption and pleasure-seeking wastes wealth and results in an indigent way of life. Ideally, capitalism must be associated with moral rectitude. However, Bell remarked gloomily, 'the ascetic element, and with it one kind of moral legitimation of capitalist behaviour, has virtually disappeared'.[26] In this, Bell was not simply reacting to the impact on social conduct of 'the Sixties' but to a deeper and longer term erosion of capitalist attitudes and justifications. In effect, he identified two other sources of contradiction in addition to 'the counter-culture': modernism and mass consumerism.

The argument about Modernism, with a capital M in Bell's usage, is a complicated one. And, indeed, 'Modernism' itself is a complex abstraction referring to an enormous range of practices albeit most closely associated with European artistic movements of the late nineteenth century through to the mid twentieth. Bell relies on suggestive if rather simplifying generalisations about Modernism. For him, it involves 'a rage against order', 'the eclipse of distance' and 'preoccupation with the medium'.[27] According to Bell, Modernism's adversary is 'the bourgeois worldview'. Curiously, however, the bourgeois worldview and Modernist culture both value individual freedoms. But their ideal embodiments of 'the free self' are quite different: 'paradoxically, the life style that became the image of the free self was not that of the businessman'.[28] Modernism, instead, retains the Romantic ideal of the rebellious bohemian, in effect, the artist rejecting orderliness, seeking immediate sensation, and calling into question codes of representation. These values flow into a more generalised hedonism, which is not the exclusive preserve of alienated artists.

Modernism as a revolt of intellectuals against the capitalist system, Bell notes, is now established routine for 'the cultural class', but its political challenge is, at the same time, exhausted due to the eclipse of socialism whilst, also simultaneously, popular hedonism is on the rise. 'The Protestant ethic and the Puritan temper', 'codes that emphasized work, sobriety, frugality, sexual restraint, and a forbidding attitude to life',[29] have been blown away by the exponential growth of mass consumerism during the twentieth century. It is important to appreciate the sheer mundanity of this development in the United States for, after all, it is American culture and society with which Bell is primarily concerned: 'The greatest single engine in the destruction of the Protestant ethic was the invention of the installment plan, or instant credit.'[30] The whole culture has become motivated by instant gratification. As Bell puts it: 'The cultural transformation of modern society is due, singularly, to the rise of mass-consumption, or the diffusion of what were once considered luxuries to the middle and lower classes in society.'[31] Moreover, 'The seduction of the consumer has become total.'[32] The problem, in Bell's estimation, is that this shift from asceticism to hedonism leaves capitalism with scant moral justification in the Weberian sense.

During the '60s, the assault of Modernism and the rise of mass consumerism were topped off by a set of counter-cultural values that became very popular; most notably, in Bell's account, by the so-called 'democratization of culture' that dispenses with judgement as to worth. Anything goes in this new regime; nothing is sacred; anyone's opinion is as good as anyone else's. What was Bell's solution to the terrible malaise he had diagnosed? Back in the 1970s, he called for a return to tradition and a revival of religion, thereby confirming his deepest conservative impulses. In spite of his doubts concerning prophecy in the social sciences, Bell's call would seem to have been heeded if not literally heard. It is most profoundly exemplified by today's 'clash of fundamentalisms', in Tariq Ali's resonant phrase,[33] which includes not only political Islam's attack on the United States as the godfather of global capitalism but its defence in the form of the fundamentalist Protestantism that put Bush the Second in power and kept him there.[34]

Bell recognised that the evolving conjuncture was a new kind of capitalism. Having dispensed with the rectitude and moral justification of the Protestant ethic, however, the legitimacy of capitalism was, Bell thought, now cast into doubt. In this, he was wrong. As we shall see, the new spirit did not so much generate an irresolvable contradiction but, instead, contributed to a fresh and ebullient resolution. Capitalism has gone through a kind of spiritual renaissance, according to French sociologist Luc Boltanski and management theorist Eve Chiapello. Their book, *The New Spirit of Capitalism*, is a monumental study of the transformation of capitalism in its organisational and ideological aspects since the 1960s.[35] Originally published in 1999, *The New Spirit of Capitalism* traces developments in the period 1965–95. Today, Boltanski and Chiapello remark, the very term 'capitalism' is seldom used even by critics. Back in the 1960s and '70s, it was a key concept of critical social science. The comparative silence about 'capitalism' since then has, however, coincided with dramatic transformations in capitalism itself, both economic and cultural. Criticism of capitalism has been silenced when it might have been most vociferous. How is this curious turn of events to be explained?

Boltanski and Chiapello do not simply claim that the old spirit of capitalism has been superseded by a new one. In fact, they identify three spirits of capitalism. The first is very much the one identified by Max Weber at the beginning of the twentieth century and mourned by Daniel Bell in the 1970s. The ascetic spirit is closely associated historically with liberal capitalism, free trade, family business and heroic entrepreneurship, also documented by the late-nineteenth-century novel as well as classical German sociology. While they state that the subject of their book is '*ideological changes that have accompanied recent transformations in capitalism*',[36] Boltanski and Chiapello do not offer a professedly Marxist analysis of capitalist ideology. Instead they draw on the Weberian definition of capitalism as endless accumulation by peaceful means that is justified by cultural/spiritual values as a necessary supplement. The problem with the first spirit of capitalism is that it lost its justificatory force when confronted by economic crisis and socialism in the first half of the twentieth century. The emergence of what has, among various nominations, been called 'organised capitalism',[37] the era of monopolies and the welfare state, was the dominant form of capitalism from the mid to late twentieth century. It featured strong trade unions and quasi-socialistic justification in wage bargaining, welfare benefits and social reform generally. It is even recalled today as a kind of socialism in practice.[38] It was most certainly constructed, at least in part, by the socialist challenge to capitalism that so much worried Schumpeter in the 1930s. As Boltanski and Chiapello note: 'The spirit of capitalism is precisely the set of beliefs associated with the capitalist order that helps to justify this order and, by legitimating them, to sustain the forms of action and predispositions compatible with it.'[39] It is not at all surprising, then, that organised capitalism in its welfare-state mode should be misrecognised in memory today as 'socialism', since the present state of affairs is so very different. Its enemies always did call it 'socialism'. Its dominant feature was 'security' in the sense of concessions won from capitalism by the organised working class, concessions that have now been either withdrawn or heavily diluted.

In Boltanski and Chiapello's account, the new spirit which has superseded this interim spirit is associated with notions like 'network'[40] and 'connexity'.[41] Such a characterisation – if not exactly the spirit – of the new capitalism has affinities with Manuel Castells's extrapolation from the properties of computer networking to a theory of generalised sociality in 'the information age',[42] though Boltanski and Chiapello themselves are sceptical of what can easily be construed as techno-hype and the analytical fallacy of technological determinism.

Boltanski and Chiapello skirt around the Marxist debate over ideology, especially the rigid distinction between 'science' and 'ideology' in the Althusserian 'detour of theory' and its subsequent unravelling in post-structuralism.[43] Rather more problematically, they do without a critical concept of ideology as distorted communications motivated by unequal power relations. At the risk of sliding into relativism, Boltanski and Chiapello treat ideology as the means of legitimisation or, more precisely, justification for a given state of affairs, for instance, in the successive 'spirits' of capitalism. These justifications are represented in their scheme of things with regard to idealised 'cities', which, it has to be said, is not the most satisfactory feature of the thesis.

The city, in this abstract sense, is founded upon a sense of justice. In order to engage commitment from people 'the city' must appeal to some compelling principle of just conduct and the common good. In *The New Spirit of Capitalism*, Boltanski and Chiapello identify no less than seven such cities: the first six being the *inspirational city*, the *domestic city*, the *reputational city*, the *civic city*, the *commercial city* and the *industrial city*. Each of these cities of justice/justification may animate different spirits of civilisation in various historical mixes. And, in the case of the capitalist system, justifications typically have to be borrowed from religion, as in the original spirit of capitalism, or from somewhere else, such as socialism in the case of organised capitalism. Although not providing the only justification, the industrial city is closely associated with the second spirit of capitalism and the promise of widespread prosperity and distributive justice. The seventh city, which is most closely associated with the new spirit of capitalism, is the *projective city*.[44] Neo-capitalism, and people charged with its new spirit, are project-oriented, whether, for instance, in the typical case of a portfolio worker moving between projects in a network of connexity or in a project such as the urban regeneration of a de-industrialised city by cultural leverage (my example). It is important to appreciate that Boltanski and Chiapello's typology of cities of justice is just that: a Weberian set of ideal types, not an empirical generalisation about the history of cities or a model readily applicable to the parlous state of many cities in poorer parts of the world today.[45]

For Boltanski and Chiapello, capitalism, in whatever phase, is an 'absurd system' since wage earners are obliged to surrender labour power to exploitation and accept a life of subordination to the rich and powerful. So, capitalism has to come up with some cunning justifications for how it operates in face of what should be such a blatantly obvious complaint. Why do people accept it? The best source of justificatory refreshment for the capitalist system, according to Boltanski and Chiapello, is, paradoxically, the enemy – that is, the critique of capitalism itself. If capitalism can respond effectively to justifiable criticism, incorporate and neutralise the force of the counter-argument and cool out disgruntled people, then it is in business, so to speak.

To flesh out the ideology of the projective city and the new capitalist spirit, Boltanski and Chiapello conduct a survey of mainly French management texts from the 1960s to the 1990s. Typically, such literature is addressed to *cadres*, managerial workers. Such literature tends to be organised around problems, solutions and rejections. From the 1960s there emerges a critique of hierarchy in business organisations and what Boltanski and Chiapello describe as a 'transition from control to self-control' in the rhetoric of management inscribed in these texts.[46] There is increasing emphasis on autonomy in managerial occupations and the 'employability' of the *cadre* who seeks 'fulfilment through a multitude of projects'.[47] The value of security as a test of justice associated with the second spirit of capitalism is increasingly superseded by a rhetoric of autonomy and associated values that echo critical discourses of the late 1960s and 1970s. Boltanski and Chiapello provide a list of

> qualities that are guarantees of success in this new spirit – autonomy, spontaneity, rhizomorphous capacity, multitasking (in contrast to the narrow specialization of the old division of labour), conviviality, openness to others and novelty, availability, creativity, visionary intuition, sensitivity to differences, listening to lived experience and receptiveness to a whole range of experiences, being attracted to informality and the search for interpersonal contacts – these are taken directly from the repertoires of May 1968.[48]

Such qualities are not only different from the original spirit of capitalism described by Weber but are also very different from qualities associated with the second spirit in the era of organised capitalism. And Boltanski and Chiapello are no doubt correct in linking them to May '68 and all that. These values were espoused by various sections of the French Left, from the cultural revolt of the Situationists, through student protest and onwards to workers' action supported by Maoists and Trotskyists. None of it had much to do with the official Communist Left that was so implicated in organised capitalism through orderly trade-union bargaining. Here, we come across one of the main weaknesses – or, perhaps, strengths – of Boltanski and Chiapello's whole thesis: its specific focus on France. They are clearly illuminating processes that are not peculiar to France. For example, the mainly French managerial literature they examine quite evidently represents, or is at least strongly influenced by, Anglo-American management theory. The Paris *événements* were distinctive yet by no means internationally isolated moments of public protest in the late 1960s. Boltanski and Chiapello are critical of loose notions like 'globalisation' and rationalise their more concretely national point of reference accordingly whilst also making no generalising claims beyond the French case. Still, the question arises, are they talking only about France? I think the answer has to be no.

A key feature of their thesis concerns the role of critique in the transformation of capitalism and its 'spiritual' justification.[49] They distinguish between two kinds of criticism: the *artistic critique* and the *social critique*. These two critiques draw upon different sources of indignation. With regard to the artistic critique, indignation is felt particularly concerning the *disenchantment*, feeling of *inauthenticity* and generalised sense of *oppression* associated with capitalism. On the other hand, the social critique evinces indignation at *poverty* and *inequality* plus the *opportunism* and *egoism* characteristic of the capitalist system.[50] The artistic critique gives rise to demands for autonomy, liberation, authenticity and singularity. The social critique of exploitation in capitalist society calls for labour movement solidarity to bring about greater equality and fairness.[51] Both kinds of critique were present in France during '68 and the immediately following years. And both wrung concessions generally, and particularly in the workplace. The social critique and its values had already played a significant role in the transition from the first to the second spirit of capitalism. Organised capitalism was, in effect, disciplined by values of social justice. The social critique also, in the early years, played a role in the eventual transition from the second to the third, 'new' spirit of capitalism; but, as it turned out, in practice the artistic critique had much more of an impact in bringing about the present culture of capitalism, which is so 'spiritually' different from the first and second cultural configurations of capitalist society.

In France, the emphasis on labour flexibility and the concomitant casualisation of labour were given a huge boost during the period of socialist government in the 1980s. In effect, the artistic critique was absorbed by elite *cadres*. As Boltanski and Chiapello put it: 'Autonomy was exchanged for security.'[52] While these developments were experienced as liberating by some, Boltanski and Chiapello are inclined to stress the downside, such as the pressures of multitasking, the weakening of trade unionism and the individualisation of wages, which may have suited many *cadres* but were not to the benefit of the lower orders: 'Unqualified blue-collar workers are ... most affected by unemployment and job insecurity.'[53] Their conditions of work were heavily undermined, furthermore, by outsourcing that exacerbates problems of insecurity and poor pay.

While all this was happening, the ironic success and recuperation of the artistic critique was accompanied by the enfeeblement and failure of the social critique, especially a loss of conviction in its indignation at exploitation and call for class solidarity. Yet, since the 1980s debacle, Boltanski and Chiapello discerned signs of hope in a revival of the social critique in the late 1990s:

> We believe that, following the disarray of the 1980s, we are currently witnessing a period of revival of critique of this sort. Of the two forms of critique that were constructed in the nineteenth century – the *artistic critique*, which elaborates demands for liberation and authenticity, and the *social critique*, which denounces poverty and exploitation – it is the latter that is showing a new lease of life, however hesitant and modest it may currently be. Moreover, there is nothing surprising about this if we remember that when the fallout of the 1960s protest wave came, from the mid-1970s onwards, the fate of the two critiques was very different: whereas themes from the artistic critique were integrated into the discourse of capitalism, so that this critique might seem to have been partially

satisfied, the social critique found itself nonplussed, bereft of ideological props, and consigned to the dustbin of history.[54]

However, the newer articulations of social critique dispensed with the concept of *exploitation* and tended to replace it with a notion of *exclusion*. This is so not only in France. Including the excluded is cardinal terminology for the European Union's social programmes. In Britain, when New Labour was elected in 1997, it immediately set up a Social Exclusion Unit. In the British case, however, the term being erased by the new discourse was not so much 'exploitation' – which was always anyway used much less in Britain than in France – as 'inequality'. The term 'excluded' now covers a vast array of marginalised and subordinate groups from not-quite-polite to say 'backward' and 'degenerate' regions, encompassing disparate ethnicities and including deprived women, the disabled, the long-term unemployed and so forth, and hardly ever defined in terms of a shared class interest, except perhaps as a disorganised 'underclass'. The object of social policy according to this rhetorical regime is 'inclusion'. Boltanski and Chiapello usefully comment on the consequences of a discourse of exclusion/ inclusion for the older discourse of class exploitation:

> Unlike the model of social classes, where explanation of the 'proletariat's' poverty is based upon identifying a class (the bourgeoisie, owners of the means of production) responsible for its 'exploitation', the model of exclusion permits identification of something negative without proceeding to level accusations.[55]

As Alex Callinicos points out in his commentary on *The New Spirit of Capitalism*, 'Exploitation is a relational concept.'[56] Although the rhetoric of 'inclusion/exclusion' is actually rather more relational than, say, 'poverty', it is not so relational in a critical sense as 'exploitation'. Inclusion is not usually said to be at the expense of the excluded whereas exploitation definitely refers to a questionable relation between those who do the exploiting and those who are exploited. Boltanski and Chiapello argue that the relatively non-relational concept of exclusion – as opposed to the relational concept of exploitation – has an affinity with the network model of society characteristic of the new spirit of capitalism within which nobody is to blame for the suffering of others. This is exemplified in Manuel Castells's much admired work on 'the rise of the network society' in 'the information age', where he only ever speaks of exclusion and never of exploitation.[57] Boltanski and Chiapello draw out the implications of these contrary ways of conceptualising inequality for movements that bear the revived social critique:

> One of the difficulties encountered by the new movements is the transition from the notion of exclusion – whose compatibility with a representation of the world in terms of networks we have noted, together with the fact that it pertains to a 'politics of sentiment' – to a theory of exploitation that would make it possible to relieve the 'excluded' of the burden of unilateral individual responsibility or inexorable fatality, and thus establish a link between their lot and that of the better-off, particularly those who occupy privileged social positions. Such an operation would make it possible to flesh out the responsibility of the latter, and constitute a better guarantee for the most deprived, than mere appeals to 'big-heartedness'. Moreover, transformation of the theme of exclusion could facilitate identification of the new causes of exclusion over and above a lack of qualifications, which is the explanation most frequently advanced at present.[58]

Boltanski and Chiapello are interested in restoring the link between indignation at poverty and indignation at egoism. As they say, 'A theory of exploitation must demonstrate that the success and strength of some actors are *in fact* attributable, at least in part, to the intervention of others, whose activity is neither acknowledged nor valued.'[59] It is necessary to use a term like 'indignation' (the same word in both French and English), then, instead of the term 'resentment' – favoured by the political Right and occasionally adopted in error by Nietzsche-influenced Leftists – which suggests mere envy. 'Indignation', as the *Oxford English Dictionary* puts it, refers to 'scornful anger at supposed injustice'. Boltanski and Chiapello point out, for instance, that in 'a connexionist world' mobility through physical and mental space is a defining quality of 'great men' (*sic*) whereas fixity in place is typical of 'little people' (*sic*): 'Great men do not stand still.

Little men remain rooted to the spot.'[60] This 'mobile/immobile differential' is relational; the mobility of some is facilitated by the immobility of others. It is a sad fact that *'the misfortune of little people makes for the good fortune of great men'*.[61] Boltanski and Chiapello slam home the point:

> The demand for autonomy and the individualistic ideal of self-begetting, of self-realization as a superior form of achievement, which represent the dominant values in a connexionist world, contribute to rendering those who are comfortable in networks largely inattentive to indebtedness as a legitimate source of social bonds.[62]

According to Boltanski and Chiapello, 'the ideal type of the great man in a projective city' is 'the *network-extender*'.[63] Sebastian Budgen offers a helpful illustration of the type: 'dressed-down, cool capitalists like Bill Gates or "Ben and Jerry"'.[64]

Boltanski and Chiapello also consider the prospects for reviving the artistic critique in the twenty-first century but, rather than delving into that discussion at this point, here it is best to register the summary propositions of their thesis, central to which is *the absorption of the artistic critique into a rejuvenated capitalism* in the late twentieth century, that has brought about a distinctly 'new spirit':

1. Capitalism needs a spirit in order to engage the people required for production and the functioning of business.[65]
2. To be capable of mobilizing people, the spirit of capitalism must incorporate a moral dimension.[66]
3. If it is to survive, capitalism needs *simultaneously* to stimulate and to curb insatiability.[67]
4. The spirit of capitalism cannot be reduced to an ideology in the sense of an illusion with no impact on events in the world.[68]
5. Capitalism has a constant tendency to transform itself.[69]
6. The principal operator of creation and transformation of the spirit of capitalism is critique (*voice*).[70]
7. In certain conditions, critique can itself be one of the factors of a change in capitalism (and not merely in its spirit).[71]
8. Critique derives its energy from sources of indignation.[72]

As Callinicos has pointed out, from an avowedly Marxist position, Boltanski and Chiapello's conception of critique as corrective rather than radical is problematic.[73] This is because critique in the corrective sense is forever incorporated and serves to refresh that which it challenged; a rather tragic fate indeed, and probably not what was intended.

Capitalism Transmogrified

Boltanski and Chiapello's work begs the question of whether 'spiritual' justification of present-day capitalism is merely a novel legitimisation for a persistent capitalism or connected to a new kind of capitalism. In philosophical terms, this concerns the relation between representation and the thing itself. To put it perhaps too simply as an either/or question: is 'network', for instance, a specifically ideological figure or, beyond signification, an actually existing material reality?

It is possible that the very same thing may be signified in quite different ways, as when an old product is given a superficial makeover in order to hoodwink the customer. However, it is probably wiser, with regard to the problem in hand, to assume that there is a more substantial relation in the general case between a changed representation, a 'new spirit', and the thing itself. After all, it has been commonly agreed since Marx that a defining feature of capitalism is changeability, that it does not stay the same but is forever in flux, renewing itself and, in effect, transmogrifying. The OED defines 'transmogrify' as 'to transform, especially in a magical or surprising manner'. We are concerned here with accounting for how recent capitalism has established an extraordinarily pervasive legitimacy in what might be considered 'a magical or surprising manner', that is, with the emergence of cool capitalism. When looking at capitalism, however, it is safest to assume that there is both continuity and change, that something fundamentally capitalist persists – an economic system founded upon exploitation and the endless pursuit of accumulation – but undergoes various transformations over time. In fact, there is a long history of speculation on and analysis of the transmogrification of capitalism in which disputes occur over whether such transformation is total, in the sense of giving rise to something beyond capitalism, or partial, in the sense of being a modification of capitalism but not its supersession. Such speculation and analysis is not confined to the Marxist tradition and the endlessly deferred breakthrough into something actually resembling the ideals of 'socialism' or 'communism'. There has also been considerable speculation on the matter among commentators basically favourable to capitalism and, indeed, fiercely opposed to Marxism.

A key issue here concerns the separation of ownership and control that, it was argued, began most consequentially in the era of organised capitalism. In 1932, the American business writers Adolf A. Berle and Gardiner C. Means published a very influential book, *The Modern Corporation and Private Property*.[74] They contended that there was an increasing separation of ownership and control in the modern business corporation. The era of the family firm, when ownership and management were in the same hands, was passing. In its place, salaried managers were controlling the means of production and shareholders – a much more widely dispersed set of people than in the past – sat back and collected the dividends that managers decided to distribute to them. Characteristic of such theoreticians of change, Berle and Means believed they had spotted an emergent tendency, the early stage of a process that with the passage of time would become extremely significant. The implication was that the interests of managers and shareholders were no longer identical and might possibly begin to diverge sharply. Most obviously, shareholders might be greedy for higher dividends in the short run whereas managers might wish to reinvest more in order to reap higher profits in the longer run. That would, in one sense, just be good business but it could also, at least in theory, represent the self-interest of propertyless managers in boosting their own rewards – salaries, pensions, shares in the firm, and the like. Such an outcome, however, would hardly be detrimental to the firm.

Over the following decades, Berle in particular drew out some of the implications from the original thesis.[75] This involved, for instance, research on share ownership regarding large individual and family holdings of capital, 'popular capitalist' dispersal of share ownership among the wider population, and the rise of institutional investors, most especially pension funds, which made capitalism look and act very differently from the image of robber barons exploiting their downtrodden workers. Moreover, managers were responsible people who might be as motivated by the social good in general as by profit-making. Here we see the origins of a latter-day notion of 'corporate social responsibility'. Such themes fed into the formation of 'management science' and the ascent in social standing for managers and the profession of management, comparable to lawyering and doctoring, in the United States and elsewhere. Berle and Means not only propagated an American ideology of good capitalism and worthy managers, they influenced, for instance, post-Second World War Labour governments in Britain, including the 1945 Attlee government and the 1964 Wilson government that placed great emphasis on modern technocratic expertise in managing capitalism.[76] It is also important to register, however, objections to the separation of ownership and control thesis that have been made over the years.[77] It is highly debatable to what extent managers' interests and orientations diverge from shareholders large and small, and there is considerable evidence of similar social origins and shareholding between senior managers and large-scale investors, not to mention the inaccurate inflating of the value of a company on the stock exchange in order to serve the interests of both managers and investors (as in, for instance, the Enron scandal of the early 2000s).

The Berle and Means thesis was rather benign in tone. It was soon given a chilling reiteration in James Burnham's much more ambitious book, *The Managerial Revolution*, written at the beginning of the Second World War.[78] Burnham, yet another ex-Trotskyist – who also went on to admire Nazi Germany and the Stalinist Soviet Union in succession – argued that the managers, vaguely defined in his scheme of things, were becoming the new ruling class not only in Europe and Eurasia but also in his own homeland of the United States. Burnham claimed his thesis was a disinterested work of social science in which theory conformed to factual evidence and eliminated wishful thinking. He argued that Marxists were right to assume that capitalism would not survive, an assumption that was held not only by Marxists around 1940 – as we have already noted in the case of Schumpeter. However, Marxists were mistaken in believing that socialism or communism would succeed capitalism. The Soviet Union provided the clearest empirical evidence to support the thesis. Although capitalism had been destroyed there, it had not been replaced by socialism, defined as control over the means of production by the masses. Control over the means of production was in the hands of the Communist Party and its industrial managers. This was nothing like socialism.

Burnham also sought to refute the Marxist argument that the National-Socialist state in Germany was a degenerate solution to the economic crisis on behalf of capitalism. There, similarly to the Soviet Union, party bureaucrats and their appointed industrial managers were in control. Roughly the same thing was occurring in the US under the 'New Deal' regime of F.D. Roosevelt, though as yet less comprehensively developed. Control over the means of production was passing from capitalists to managers. So, the managerial revolution was a universal phenomenon of advanced industrialism. At the same time, three power blocs were forming in the world as a result of the managerial revolution, centred respectively on the United States itself, Germany and Japan. At the beginning of the war Burnham thought the Nazis would win but by the end of it he was applauding the victorious Soviet Union. Not someone, then, whose gambling tips you would want to bet your house on.

George Orwell wrote a devastatingly critical essay on Burnham's managerial revolution thesis.[79] He commented, for instance, on Burnham's predilection for making long-term predictions based on currently short-term trends that were very quickly proved wrong. In this respect, Orwell had identified a common feature of managerial thought under an enduring capitalism – extravagant and probably erroneous prophecies extrapolated from current events that might not prove especially consequential – though he may not have realised he was doing so himself. Orwell also commented upon Burnham's slavish devotion to power and cult of the powerful. Today, we might call him 'a power junky'. This is also a persistent feature of managerial thought, exemplified in daily panegyrics to the likes of Bill Gates and Steve Jobs.

Still, a problem of naming remains. There is a particular line of thought that is especially relevant to the problem of naming the cutting-edge kind of society, which is largely associated historically with the idea that 'industrialism' is the major category, not capitalism. In fact, use of the term 'industrialism' precedes 'capitalism'. From the industrial revolution of the late eighteenth century, speculation about its significance for civilisation as a whole became commonplace. Saint-Simonian socialists and early sociologists in France had no word for capitalism but were very concerned with the social impact generally of what we would now call 'industrialisation'. In Britain, Thomas Carlyle spoke of 'industrialism' from the 1830s.[80] Use of the term 'industrialism' has often been used since then to mask over or marginalise debate concerning the defence and critique of 'capitalism'. In such a discourse it was routine for many years to talk of 'industrialists' instead of 'capitalists' so as to eliminate the lingering pejorative connotations of the latter term. And, during the Cold War between the capitalist West and the communist East, some American sociologists talked in a more conciliatory tone of a 'convergence' of the two systems due to their common industrialism.[81]

Anthony Giddens has pointed out that both terms are valid since 'capitalism' refers to an exploitative system based upon the extraction of surplus value whereas 'industrialism' has distinctive properties of its own that are analytically separable from 'capitalism'.[82] Although industrialism developed within the framework of capitalism, it is not reducible to capitalism. The communist states of the twentieth century were industrial and not ostensibly capitalist (though even that is debatable). Industrialism uses inanimate sources of power to work upon and transform nature, and it creates artificial environments. This has resulted in the production of both great wealth and enormous environmental damage. Green politics seek to check the damaging effects of industrialism, capitalist or otherwise. Leaders of newly industrialising countries, especially in Asia, claim to be keen on matching the standards of living that already exist in the older industrialised countries of the West. In spite of arguments about a transition to so-called 'post-industrialism' in places like Britain and the United States, industrialism, in this sense, is growing rather than diminishing in the world.

A host of nominations omitting the word 'capitalism' have succeeded one another over the years. In rich countries 'industrialism' began to be displaced by 'post-industrialism' from the 1960s, and a succession of other 'posts' followed, most notably 'postmodernity'.[83] As late as 1993, management guru Peter Drucker was still talking about 'post-capitalist society'.[84] These formations have been called, for instance, the 'information society', the 'knowledge society' and the 'network society', all of which, in one way or another, recall Burnham's 'managerial society', now zoomed up by new developments in information and communication technologies.[85] These ideas mostly emanate from US schools of management and social science.

Peter Berger's book of 1986, *The Capitalist Revolution*, was refreshing because it indicated that talking explicitly about 'capitalism' instead of using an obfuscatory label was legitimate once again. On the brink of communism's implosion in Eastern Europe – though nobody was actually predicting such an imminent and momentous turn of events at the time – Berger sought to demonstrate the superior performance of Western capitalism in comparison with the record of Soviet communism and communist China, amassing a mountain of data on, most significantly, standards of living and freedom of expression. As he argued quite rightly:

> Like many widely held views, the notion of capitalism as conservative is misleading. On the contrary, from its inception capitalism has been a force of cataclysmic transformation in one country after another. Capitalism has changed every material, social, political, and cultural facet of the societies it has touched.[86]

The defence of capitalism's past record has now been superseded by celebration of its dynamic future-orientation in present-day rhetoric, for instance, with regard to the emergence of what has been named 'cultural capitalism'.[87] Jeremy Rifkin, an American business-school professor, argues that '[c]ultural production is beginning to eclipse physical production in world commerce and trade'.[88] Rifkin's cultural-capitalism thesis is a variant, then, on the old 'post-industrialism' theme propounded by Daniel Bell in the 1960s; and, like Bell, Rifkin is interested in the cultural implications of a transformed capitalism. Straight away, it should be registered that the strengths and weaknesses of the cultural-capitalism thesis replicate those of its precursor, the post-industrialism thesis. As Raymond Williams remarked in the 1980s:

> The society that is now emerging is in no sense 'post-industrial'. Indeed, in its increasingly advanced technologies, it is a specific and probably absolute climax of industrialism itself. What is often meant is the declining relative importance of manufacturing, which is due to follow agriculture into being a small minority sector of employment. The decline itself is real, in some societies, though even there its assessment is confused by tendencies in the export of manufacturing, within a world capitalist system, to countries with much lower labour costs and little or no working-class organisation.[89]

Since the 1970s, US business has devolved much of its manufacturing to Third World and newly industrialising countries, leaving a 'rust belt' in its own previously manufacturing areas. Detroit in Michigan, for example, remains the business centre for much of the American motor-vehicle industry but the actual manufacture of cars and trucks goes on elsewhere, particularly down in Mexico where wages are much lower than in the US. The American working class has experienced massive de-industrialisation over the past 30 years, hardly relieved by culture-led urban regeneration schemes that have been called 'landscapes of deception'.[90] Where there used to be a job in the local automobile factory, you are lucky now to be working in an out-of-town shopping mall or in an office downtown where the vehicle business's management is based. You might, of course, merely be there to clean the mall or the office. This is all 'service' work, much of it as physically demanding as factory work.

The exponential growth in cultural production need not be denied, but the claim that physical production is no longer very important in the world economy is utter nonsense. It looks like that only from the vantage point of an American business school where future *cadres* of high-tech capitalism are being trained. Rifkin claims that cultural capitalism is an 'experience economy' in which customers seek and are supplied with pleasurable experiences rather than things. Access to experience, not ownership of property, is the motivating force for consumers. In this sense, cultural consumption is paramount in the 'transition from industrial to cultural capitalism'.[91] Whereas Boltanski and Chiapello emphasise the transformation of work associated with the new spirit of capitalism, Rifkin, similarly to Bell, emphasises hedonistic consumption, though his text is addressed probably first and foremost to the apprentices of what I would call 'cool capitalism'.

Rifkin's *The Age of Access* is a curiously ambivalent and, indeed, internally conflicted book. It is divided into two parts. Part I is entitled, 'The New Capitalist Frontier'; Part II, 'Enclosing the Cultural Commons'. The frontier metaphor is apt in that the first half of the book sets out an exciting and inspiring scenario for the young capitalist to take off into. The metaphor of a cultural commons, derived from the common land of pre-capitalism, being enclosed by the capitalist seizure and commodification of everything, problematises the whole process and links up with various sources of criticism: green politics, anti-capitalism, and so on. In this, Rifkin's *The Age of Access* is characteristically cool capitalist and may even be considered a bible of cool capitalism. Cool capitalism is largely defined by the incorporation, and thereby neutralisation, of cultural criticism and anti-capitalism into the theory and practice of capitalism itself. Two chapters in particular exemplify the double-sided coin of 'cultural capitalism': 'The Weightless Economy' from the first part of the book; and 'The New Culture of Capitalism' from the second half. Rifkin declares at the beginning of 'The Weightless Economy':

> The physical economy is shrinking. If the industrial era was characterized by the amassing of physical capital and property, the new era prizes intangible forms of power bound up in bundles of information and intellectual assets. The fact is, physical products, which for so long were a measure of wealth in the industrial world, are dematerializing.[92]

The evaluation of national wealth is no longer represented by the weight of traded commodities but, instead, in symbolic meanings through the magic of financial dissociation from the exchange of things.

Dematerialisation is pervasive and takes many different forms, even including, for instance, the irrelevance of face-to-face office space for mobile executives who can nowadays communicate with colleagues via wireless laptops and cell phones from anywhere at anytime. Yet more importantly, businesses these days also seek to minimise their physical inventories while simultaneously providing 'just-in-time' delivery to customers. Digital distribution of music in the cultural arena is a perfect example of dematerialisation in putting shops out of business and rendering the physicality of the CD obsolete. Ideally, contemporary enterprises would prefer to conduct all their business entirely in cyberspace instead of physical space. Money too has been dematerialised as digits on a VDU, compared to the materiality of paper money the value of which was once underpinned by precious metal. Another feature of weightlessness is decline in ordinary savings and the growth of consumer borrowing and debt. In this 'new era ... holding property, in all of its various forms, becomes less important than securing short-term access to commercial opportunities'.[93] This is true of both consumers and companies, according to Rifkin. Increasingly, consumers and companies prefer to lease rather than to buy. For the consumer, leasing a car with all the services attached becomes more attractive than buying a car. Companies lease facilities rather than lumber themselves with physical assets that may quickly go out of date in a fast-changing economy. They divest themselves of the material means of production and outsource for products and services.

As Rifkin notes, 'outsourcing has become the organizational centrepiece of an emerging network economy'.[94] Outsourcing is fundamental to current systems of manufacture. In this respect, Nike is an exemplary company. It is 'for all intents and purposes, a virtual company'.[95] In reality, it is a research, design and marketing outfit. The actual manufacture of sportswear is outsourced to factories around the world, including 'anonymous manufacturers in Southeast Asia', whose employment practices, working conditions, long hours and low pay would not normally be acceptable in the United States (though there are also enclaves of sweatshop labour located in the US itself, for instance, in South-Central Los Angeles). Rifkin remarks, disingenuously: 'This new type of network approach to doing business, with its emphasis on nameless suppliers to produce the physical products, can sometimes result in the exploitation of workers.'[96]

The most valuable assets today are intangible, argues Rifkin. Physical, tangible property matters much less than the informational template. In this respect, Microsoft is the classic case. It deals in patented software. Great wealth, in point of fact, derives from *ownership* of intellectual property, the cardinal form of intangible property, which somewhat contradicts the thesis of a transition from ownership to access as the distinguishing feature of the age. Policing valorisation, though, can be irksome for intellectual property holders, when unscrupulous pirates rip off American corporations around the world. Additionally, Rifkin stresses the general growth of 'informational', 'cultural' and 'creative' industries in the global economy. These industries influence all industry in raising the importance of intellectual property and meaningful design,[97] thus, it might be inferred, universalising Adorno and Horkheimer's condition of 'the culture industry'.[98] Interestingly, however, Rifkin noted in 2000 that 'new information-based industries – finance, entertainment, communications, business services, and education', still made up only 25 per cent of the US economy.[99] Even in the United States, cultural capitalism was not quite so advanced at the beginning of the new millennium as one might have supposed. The prophetic signs, however, were there to read in the runes. The life-science companies, for instance, were patenting life itself, our very genes.

Again, from a distinctly American-centric point of view, Rifkin discerns a neat identity between the newer ways of doing business and the attitudes and desires of consumers. The locus of such an identity is the marketing category of *lifetime value* (LTV). Rifkin explains it thus in the first chapter of the book, 'Entering the Age of Access':

> The top fifth of the world's population now spends almost as much of its income accessing cultural experiences as on buying manufactured goods and basic services. We are making the transition into what economists call an 'experience economy' – a world in which each person's own life becomes, in effect, a commercial market. In business circles, the new operative term is 'lifetime value' (LTV) of the customer, the theoretical measure of how much a human being is worth if every moment of his or her life were to be commodified in one form or another in the commercial sphere. In the new era, people purchase their very existence in small commercial segments.[100]

And, later, in a chapter entitled 'Commodifying Human Relationships':

> The new idea in marketing is to concentrate on share of customer rather than share of market ... Marketing specialists use the phrase 'lifetime value' (LTV) to emphasize the advantages of shifting from a product-oriented to an access-oriented environment where negotiating discrete market transactions is less important than securing and commodifying lifetime relationships with clients.[101]

The new marketing model has a notion of *R (relationship) technologies* in order to 'control the customer', as Rifkin puts it. He does not, however, say to what extent customers are actually controlled – or, perhaps we should say, 'seduced' – by R technologies. Here, Rifkin opens up issues concerning the dynamics of consumer culture as a feature of cultural capitalism that he does not himself resolve and that, no doubt, call for further investigation. For him, the LTV marketing model is as yet an avant-garde phenomenon. Like other prophets of capitalist transformation, then, Rifkin is picking up on the early symptoms, developmental trends that may – or may not – prove to be of great general significance in the future.

Rifkin helpfully summarises the key terms of the transition from 'industrial capitalism' to 'cultural capitalism' in 'the age of access':

> The birth of a network economy, the steady dematerialization of goods, the declining relevance of physical capital, the ascendancy of intangible assets, the metamorphosis of goods into pure services, the shift in first tier commerce from a production to a marketing perspective, and the commodification of relationships and experiences all are elements in the radical restructuring going on in the high-tech global economy as part of humanity begins to leave markets and property exchange behind on its journey into the Age of Access.[102]

As it transpires, Rifkin himself is not entirely happy with these developments. There is a downside – or, rather, several downsides – to cultural capitalism. This is spelt out in the second part of the book, 'Enclosing the Cultural Commons', and introduced by the chapter entitled, 'The New Culture of Capitalism'. Rifkin describes 'the new cultural economy' as 'a world of symbols, webs and feedback loops, connectivity and interactivity, in which borders and boundaries become murky and everything solid begins to melt'.[103] Surely, we have come across that final phrase before.

In the age of 'access' the operations of cultural capitalism commodify the arts and lived culture. Rifkin extols the residual value of art as 'the most sophisticated medium of human expression' and notes '[t]he oppositional stance of the arts',[104] its bohemian and critical qualities that until recently typified its place in society. He seems to regret the closing of the gap between art and capitalism by which, arguably, the arts are absorbed into capitalism and critical distance is lost. It is not only that capitalism reduces the independence of art but that it also seeks to encompass the whole of lived experience as well as artistic culture. All of this is captured by the metaphor of enclosing the cultural commons. Capitalism is enclosing actual public space – with, for instance, the private shopping mall replacing the town square – whilst also enclosing virtual space and the sites of informational and cultural communication.[105]

Later in the book, Rifkin discusses the depletion of cultural resources by their incessant mining, paralleling the ruthless and unsustainable exploitation of nature:

> Not surprisingly, as cultural production becomes the high-end sector of the economic value chain, marketing assumes an importance that extends well beyond the commercial realm. Marketing is the means by which the whole of the cultural commons is mined for valuable potential cultural meanings that can be transformed by the arts into commodified experiences, purchasable in the economy.[106]

Further on, he says: 'The culture, like nature, can be mined to exhaustion.'[107] Rifkin discusses, for instance, the phenomenon of world music as a gigantic cultural mining and commodification of difference. He also notes that 'Countercultural trends have been particularly appealing targets for expropriation by marketeers.'[108] In this respect, Rifkin also comments upon the role of 'cool hunters' among cultural intermediaries.

Against both the state and the market, Rifkin extols civil society and 'third sector' organisation where ordinary sociality is formed and where the wellsprings of trust and meaning are located. He has pointed out that there are over a million not-for-profit organisations in the US that generate between them over 600 billion dollars of annual revenue.[109] Many non-commercial organisations in the third sector are cultural in the narrow sense of, say, arts companies; the rest are cultural in a broader sense, such as churches.

For Rifkin, there is a struggle for cultural diversity twinned with the struggle for bio-diversity. He claims to be sympathetic to the movement for social justice, which has also been called the 'anti-capitalist', 'anti-corporate' and 'anti-globalisation' movement, amongst other things. Such movements represent 'a cultural backlash to globalization', in Rifkin's opinion.[110] In all this, he declares himself in favour of culture against commerce, though he recognises that such a position is also potentially reactionary as well as resistant, that is, potentially fertile ground for backward-looking forms of fundamentalism.

From a political point of view, then, there is a certain schizophrenia in the cultural-capitalism thesis, at least in the way it is formulated by Jeremy Rifkin. In representing its dynamism and future promise, Rifkin identifies but also exaggerates significant trends in capitalist culture today. His argument can in some ways be seen as complementary to Boltanski and Chiapello's thesis on the new spirit of capitalism. Theirs is a much more measured and carefully documented treatment. They emphasise the legitimacy of/justification for the new capitalism, especially regarding work and career orientations. Rifkin is less concerned with the legitimacy of capitalism in spite of his rhetorical gestures towards anti-capitalism. For him, so it appears, the legitimacy of or justification for the newer kind of capitalism is scarcely in doubt. His whole thesis points towards the consumer's engagement with cultural capitalism, and in that sense it complements Boltanski and Chiapello's thesis.

If we want to understand the new culture of capitalism – here, 'cool capitalism' – it should be examined from both the production and the consumption moments in the circuit. In fact, capitalism has a history of consumption as well as production that contributes to the characterisation of its different phases or 'spirits'. Moreover, while it is important to register the succession of capitalist modes of production and consumption, it should also be noted that each successive spirit remains in play simultaneously and, to a degree, remains in contestation, despite the current dominance of 'the new spirit of capitalism'. Boltanski and Chiapello have argued that the rejuvenation of capitalism has much to do with the incorporation of critique, at different times social and cultural. That recognition is built into Rifkin's thesis, which I regard as a profound statement of cool capitalism insofar as it simultaneously both incorporates and quite possibly neutralises critique.

2
THE GREAT REFUSAL

Herbert Marcuse described art as 'the Great Refusal – the protest against that which is'.[1] This is a Romantic view of art and one that is deeply embedded in the Western tradition of culture and society. The Romantics rebelled against early industrialism, its mechanical rationality, its inhumanity and, indeed, its rape of nature. They sometimes evinced conservative nostalgia for a lost 'golden age' and, at the same time, looked forward to a more humane future when strongly felt emotions and imaginative flair would triumph over the grim rationality of the industrial grind. Romanticism was also a reaction to the excesses of Enlightenment Reason and was marked by the hopes and disappointments of the French Revolution towards the end of the eighteenth century. The Romantic ideal of the rebellious artist became dominant in the nineteenth century. Art was thus seen as a critical counterpoint to the civilisation that was brought about, in effect, by the emergence of industrial capitalism and the intellectual convulsions associated with it.

Marcuse himself was an old Romantic, in both his Hegelian philosophy and aesthetic critique of 'one-dimensional man'. For him, 'the aesthetic dimension'[2] offers resistance to the one-dimensionality of a 'technological society' that had resulted from late industrialism. Like his Frankfurt School compatriots, Theodor Adorno and Max Horkheimer,[3] Marcuse tends to be dismissed today as a cultural elitist who was hostile to modern technology. Marcuse, however, was not hostile to technology as such. His actual complaint concerned the development and use of technology to control and discipline people in their working lives and their 'free time'. This did not preclude the possibility of socially useful technology designed to liberate rather than dominate.

For Marcuse, the 'Great Refusal' of art was represented not so much by its realistic content as by its unrealistic form. In this sense, he went against the privileging of realism in Marxist aesthetics and favoured avant-garde formalism instead. The binary opposition of form and content deployed by Marcuse is, however, far too simplistic and misleading. Even Marcuse recognised that the content of Gustave Flaubert's *Madame Bovary* articulated an unacceptable mode of conduct, according to bourgeois conventions in nineteenth-century France; and it was that content, as well as the naturalistic style of writing, which made it radical, a notable example of the Great Refusal. *Madame Bovary* enunciated a new 'structure of feeling', to use Raymond Williams's term, which indicates an inextricable connection between form and content.[4] Quite rightly, however, Marcuse noted that artistic alienation is different from the social alienation identified by Marx: it has to do with the intellectual transcendence of prevailing conditions. However darkly pessimistic it may be (as in Samuel Beckett's novels and plays, cited by Marcuse), the work of art's refusal of the present offers the promise of a better future. Refusenik art may break with the rules of easy communication in order to expose a lack of communication.

Marcuse railed against what he called 'neoconservative' critics who had, in their turn, attacked the critique of a debased mass culture that was so prominent in the 1950s and was critical common sense at the time.[5] These neoconservatives defended the populist incorporation of the oppositional potential of art into everyday life, thereby obliterating its critical force. Populist denial of aesthetic discrimination destroys 'the Great Refusal'. As Marcuse put it in the early 1960s:

> Today's novel feature is the flattening out of the antagonism between culture and social reality through the obliteration of the oppositional, alien, and transcendent elements in the higher culture by virtue of which it constituted *another dimension* of reality. This liquidation of *two-dimensional* culture takes place not through the denial and rejection of the 'cultural

values' but through their wholesale incorporation into the established order, through their reproduction and display on a massive scale.⁶

And, further on:

> Prior to the advent of this cultural reconciliation, literature and art were essentially alienation, sustaining and protecting the contradiction – the unhappy consciousness of the divided world, the defeated possibilities, the hopes unfulfilled, the promises betrayed. They were a rational, cognitive force, revealing a dimension of man and nature which was repressed and repelled in reality. Their truth was in the illusion evoked, in the insistence of creating a world in which the terror of life was called up and suspended – mastered by recognition.⁷

These observations on the alienating power of art and its incorporation into a dulled, happy consciousness are far too totalising, a feature of Marcuse's Germanic style of idealist philosophising. Some art may have been – and may still be – like this, but a great deal of art has never articulated the refusal. Were he still alive, Marcuse would no doubt say that such conservative art is not 'real art', which again is too sweeping and rhetorically vacuous. Although I personally disagree with Marcuse's general perspective,⁸ I nonetheless believe that his observations do, with considerable insight, identify and place in question a discernible trend that is much more advanced now than when Marcuse was writing. In this chapter, then, the dialectical process of refusal and incorporation is traced in particular cases with regard to the work, reputation and fate of Pablo Picasso, Diego Rivera and Frida Kahlo; the complex and ever closer relation between art and business; and the exemplary instance of cool capitalism represented by the phenomenon of 'Young British Art'. To begin with, however, it is necessary to investigate how art ever came to be considered the 'Great Refusal' in the first place.

Rebellious Autonomy

Art is meaningful yet is also a situated social practice enabled and constrained by historically specific cultural, economic, political and, indeed, technological conditions. The artist produces meanings but the artist also has to eat. Culture and economy, at least in this basic sense, are always intimately connected together. In the ideal type of a feudal society, artists barely exist. In medieval Europe, they were mainly seen as craft workers, no more or less significant than, say, carpenters. By the Renaissance, however, the artist was emerging as the master craftsman (they were always men, with only a few female exceptions appearing on the margins of cultural production) who organised his workers to help him fashion artistic representations and decorations for spiritual and temporal authorities, the church, aristocracy and monarchy. That something like an artist, distinct from a craft worker, emerged in Renaissance Italy, which was a prelude to capitalist modernity, makes sense, since the artist only really comes into being with the advent of capitalism. The early bourgeoisie very quickly joined the aristocracy as constituting a public for art. They tended to demand domesticated images and family portraits to adorn the bourgeois home. Rembrandt was very clear about the terms of the transaction between himself and his seventeenth-century customers in the Netherlands. His use of materials and time were calculated precisely and included in the price for the commissioned work.[9] By this time, then, the artist was already not only a producer but also a small trader in the marketplace of mercantile capitalism.

In 1635, the *Académie française* was established to police art in France, thereby indicating a shift in power over the arts from church to state. During the eighteenth century, further developments, in both Britain and Germany as well as in France, contributed to a secularisation of the arts, signified by the institutionalisation of criticism and the birth of modern aesthetic theory,[10] both of which would come to mediate – and, to an extent, compete with – the operations of art and literary markets. Patronage – ecclesiastical and political – declined, and artists and writers lost a certain kind of security of employment. Their growing intellectual individualism was complemented by their social positioning as economic individuals selling their wares on the open market. The image of the artist that still prevails in Western culture, in however mystified a guise, derives from the late eighteenth- and early nineteenth-century Romanticism that was notably theorised in German philosophy and practised in English poetry. The artist is here a lone figure with a special gift, a superior imagination that enables him or her to see and depict what the rest of us miss. Sometimes such a figure is cast as a misunderstood genius suffering for his or her art. So, the artist may be a courageous and controversial educator of the senses and the sensibilities. The Romantic artist is also thought to be a critic of society and perhaps, as Shelley put it, an 'unacknowledged legislator' as well. This ethereal figure is not only an idealist illusion but is also manifested materially in typical though often degraded form as the representative of an alternative way of life: that of the bohemian, an autonomous rebel living in a space separate from the mainstream.

Elizabeth Wilson has traced the history of the bohemian from Paris in the 1830s and '40s to the present day. While the British called Roma and travellers 'gypsies', the French called them 'bohemians'. The connotations are obvious enough. However, the bohemian stood for more than a marginal nuisance to respectable society. According to Wilson, 'Bohemia is the name for the attempt by nineteenth and twentieth-century artists, writers, intellectuals and radicals to create an alternative world within Western society (and possibly elsewhere).'[11] The bohemian is a myth in Barthes's sense,[12] neither quite true nor false, a bearer of ideological meanings. Wilson herself traces the 'legend', sensible as she is of the gulf between representation and reality. For her, the bohemian is an ambiguous figure, caught up in countervailing forces, trying to live a life on the outside while looking in sceptically, a life that may be quite impossible to sustain. The bohemian wants to be 'authentic' in an inauthentic world. This very often involves shocking and outraging respectable society, but that, at the same time, depends on respectable society's willingness to be shocked and outraged. In one sense, bohemians were the beneficiaries of the disruption and apparent freedoms unleashed by capitalism. However, as Wilson remarks wryly, 'the new freedom was for some the freedom to starve'.[13] The bohemian hated the bourgeoisie yet depended upon them for money, not only on proceeds from the sale of work but also on handouts from well-to-do but disgruntled fathers and sympathetic relatives. If, however, the bohemian actually became a success in the marketplace, this was in effect a kind of failure. To be accepted by respectable society, thereby succumbing to incorporation into the foul world of the bourgeoisie, was living death for the bohemian rebel.

Ambivalence ran through the succession of modern art movements associated with Bohemia from the mid nineteenth century and into the twentieth century: realism, naturalism, impressionism, cubism, and so forth. Each movement challenged academic art, was at first rejected by the academy and, eventually, usurped the old academy and became the new one, in a dialectic of refusal and incorporation. Some bohemians even became rich. The bohemian districts of Paris – Montmartre and Montparnasse – were frontier zones for the alternative way of life. Through the course of the nineteenth and early twentieth centuries similar place-based cultures of dissidence formed elsewhere, for instance in Greenwich Village on Manhattan and Soho in London. While these places may have been cheap and congenial habitats for artists, writers and their like, they were to have a wider appeal, not least to business people attracted by the bohemian ambience. Sharon Zukin traced this gentrification process in New York from the 1960s onwards in her celebrated study, *Loft Living*.[14] Bohemians were pioneers of an exciting way of life in rundown parts of the city, quite different from the dreary suburbs. Many of them could not afford to stay there, however, once the bourgeoisie had moved in and colonised the space. This is one evident feature of the tragic fate of Bohemia in which the despised bourgeoisie always seem to win out in the end.

Nevertheless, Bohemia is a serially reiterative phenomenon. Wilson cites, for instance, the post-Second World War succession of youthful subcultures that were connected to Bohemia, from the Parisian existentialists, through the New York beats, San Francisco hippies and London punks to whatever form it takes at present. Bohemians have been pioneers in the art of living that, on going mass-cultural, loses its critical force as a viable alternative. If everyone is doing it, there is no rebellion involved; time to move on. Historically, notes Wilson, the various iterations of Bohemia offered a place of comparative freedom for women, though men were most typically the dominant figures, often idealising women as muses while keeping them in a subordinate position. Sexual experimentation and 'perverse' orientation were features of a libertarian habitus that rejected dominant norms. Furthermore, Bohemia displayed greater openness than did mainstream society to differences of ethnicity and 'race' even during the nineteenth century. In the twentieth century, Bohemia prefigured the loosening of social mores and greater cosmopolitanism that is now associated with the new spirit of capitalism.

The prototypical bohemian was Gustave Courbet, from a comfortably off but not rich bourgeois family in the countryside who took Paris by storm around the time that Paris was also being hit by the storms of revolution and counter-revolution in the period 1848–51, ending in a monarchist *coup d'état*.[15] He was a realist in painting who flouted academic norms yet won a medal at the Salon held on the Champs-Élysées in the summer of 1849, the showcase for officially approved art. So, he had certain advantages, not least of which was official recognition by the Salon in spite of his support for anarchic socialists inspired by the Proudhon of 'property is theft' in 1848.

Marx wrote about the events of 1848 in his *Eighteenth Brumaire of Louis Bonaparte*, where he reminded the reader of Hegel's observation on recurrence in history: 'He forgot to add, the first time as tragedy, the second as farce'.[16] If the original French Revolution from 1789 had ended tragically, its subsequent manifestation in 1848 was farcical. During that year the interests of the bourgeoisie separated sharply from 'the people', the peasantry and the nascent industrial proletariat. Subsequently, republican and democratic advances were turned back and the monarchy was restored. While the bourgeoisie favoured a modernisation of politics, the cost of peasant and working-class emancipation was much too high a price for them to contemplate. A similar separation had occurred in Britain with the 1832 Reform Act that emancipated bourgeois men and nobody else, followed by the angry emergence of the first British labour movement represented by Chartism, the demands of which were eventually realised only after tragic failure in the 1840s.

When the tide was turning against the Left in the aftermath of 1848, Courbet retreated to the countryside to paint his most controversial works: *The Stonebreakers* (1849) and, especially, *Burial at Ornan* (1849–50). Courbet's work was not only attacked by critics of the 1851 Salon, it was also praised. Opinion was divided along political lines. *Burial at Ornan* was extremely unsettling for those members of the urban bourgeoisie who had only come off the land themselves in the past couple of generations. They idealised the countryside as a socially undifferentiated and traditional background to the modernity of the city. The trouble with Courbet's rather ugly painting of black-coated men at a rural funeral is that these figures are indisputably bourgeois according to the dress code of the day. This brought to the surface a hidden history, that of the bourgeoisie's transition from the country to the city and its fear of rural as well as urban unrest. The urban bourgeoisie had not themselves been peasants for quite some time; their interests and those of the peasantry were not the same. This was an alarming truth to announce when rural workers had for a brief moment threatened insurrection. As T.J. Clark remarked in his study of Courbet:

> We begin to see why Courbet's imagery was so profoundly offensive in 1851. That was the year, more than any other, when the myth [of social unity in the countryside] was most needed and most under threat. At the very moment when the political domination and social confidence of the bourgeoisie were in doubt, rural society seemed about to spawn its own conflicts. Worst of all, at the heart of that conflict, the focus of peasant hatred, was an object whose very existence was unthinkable to the Parisian bourgeois, a profound embarrassment to his own identity – the *bourgeois de campagne*. He existed and he was hated; nor did he exist as a result of an heroic act of will; he had, it seemed, evolved; at times he could even be unconscious of his bourgeois status and its demands. One day he could wear the black dress-coat; the next, the peasant smock.[17]

Courbet not only pasted the bourgeoisie; he was arrogant with it too. This is clearly represented in his painting of 1854 that was exhibited at the World Exposition, *The Meeting*.[18] It depicts Courbet himself with a knapsack on his back, staff in hand, encountering his patron, Alfred Bruyas, and the patron's servant on a country lane. The patron greets the great artist with due deference and the servant casts his eyes down in the face of pure genius. Courbet's cockiness is signified by his pointed beard, pointing haughtily at these supplicants. *The Meeting* is a striking representation of bohemian self-identity, its independence from and, indeed, swaggering stance towards the bourgeoisie. The bohemian – a radical in art and in politics – is seen as utterly self-assured. Courbet was vilified for this kind of thing, and ridiculed for what was seen as his failed politics for the rest of his life. Moreover, in his person he swelled up from the beautiful young man of the early portraits to become a bloated drunkard, a victim of bohemian excess, and spent his last years after his prominent role in the 1871 Paris Commune in exile in Switzerland.

However, it is important to recall the remarkable way in which Courbet's art around 1850 addressed politics directly, fearlessly and, to some extent, consequentially, in a manner that is almost inconceivable now. To appreciate how brief a moment that was and how the connection between art and politics became so much more complex and convoluted during the second half of the nineteenth century, we must turn to Pierre Bourdieu, the great French sociologist of culture, for clarification.

Bourdieu treats both culture and politics as games played out on separate though occasionally overlapping force fields. The political field has precedence over the cultural field; and cultural producers are in a position structurally subordinate to economic and political power. Bourdieu's book, *The Rules of Art*, in effect analyses the emergence of a relatively autonomous cultural field in nineteenth-century France and tracks its contradictions and historical development. At first, this is explored through a reading of Flaubert's *Sentimental Education*, which is itself a meditation on the emergent cultural field and the manoeuvres of participants in Bohemia. The structural subordination of artists and writers is mediated by both 'the market' and 'lifestyle and value systems'.[19] Bourdieu himself is primarily concerned in *The Rules of Art* with the literary sector of the cultural field whilst also recognising its overlaps and interactions with the visual art sector. He notes, for instance, that the Salon's function in this play of force was not so much to include but to exclude, to keep the unacceptable out. The internal logic of the cultural field, however, reverses the logic of the economic field, at least in the mid nineteenth century, in that the value of culture is not supposed to be reducible to financial value.[20] It established the principle of a 'pure aesthetic', ostensibly unsullied by pecuniary considerations. That, of course, is an ideological distortion and displacement since, at the same time, art was becoming a valuable commodity of bourgeois society, in fact, a store of wealth for collectors. Nevertheless, contest on the field of cultural production was fought not over money but over claims concerning symbolic worth, and was subject to the unequal distribution of power. This resulted in political struggle over art at a greater distance from political struggle proper than when Courbet was at his peak.

According to Bourdieu, the 'literary and artistic field' was constructed in opposition to the '"bourgeois" world'.[21] There were two kinds of bohemian identity within the field: 'proletaroid intellectuals' and 'penniless bourgeois'. Both related to the market in symbolic goods with ambivalence. They evinced *'moral indignation* against all forms of submission to the forces of power or to the market'.[22] Politically, however, bohemian culture bifurcated after the cataclysm of 1851. Disillusionment set in and some departed from Courbet's 'social art', turning instead to 'art for art's sake', the extreme form of Kantian aesthetic autonomy.

Charles Baudelaire is the seminal figure in the movement away from overt political commitment in the direction of aesthetic detachment, enunciated at the end of the 1850s in his influential essay, 'The Painter of Modern Life'.[23] There, Baudelaire invented the *flâneur*, a figure sometimes translated into English as 'the dandy'.[24] Baudelaire's strolling aesthete observes the life of the city, high and low, and merely seeks, thereby, to capture the sensations, the pulse and the imagery of modernity. If you read Baudelaire carefully, you will see that the *flâneur* is an aristocratic figure in style and affectation rather than a man of the people, albeit perhaps down at heel, actually holding the populace in some contempt and regarding women in a sexist manner, which was, it has be said, scarcely anachronistic for his time.[25]

Still, similarly to the social critic, the aesthete maintained antipathy and distaste for officially approved 'bourgeois art', and, in theory, anything tainted by the bourgeoisie. In this sense at least, fastidious aestheticism, like socialism, was oppositional, albeit unlikely to bring bourgeois society to its knees, as the politically active would always jibe. A tradition of bohemian politics in the literary and artistic field survived, however, long into the next century and was presaged by Emile Zola's more or less specifically French invention of 'the [public] intellectual' around the Dreyfus Affair at the end of the nineteenth century, speaking out on matters of urgent public interest – thereby forging an historical link between Voltaire in the eighteenth century and Sartre in the twentieth.

Bourdieu identifies the mechanisms of autonomisation in the cultural field of mid-nineteenth-century France:

> The movement of the artistic field and the literary field and the literary towards a greater autonomy is accomplished by a process of differentiation of the modes of artistic expression and by a progressive discovery of the form which is suitable for each art or each genre, beyond the exterior signs, socially known or recognized, of its identity.[26]

The process was played out prototypically by the battle between academic art and the avant-garde from the 1860s onwards in Paris, best exemplified by the story of Edouard Manet and the impressionists, and in particular how they were refused and then incorporated, eventually becoming part of the academy. It is vital to appreciate the institutional context of the story, not only its political hermeneutics.[27]

In broad terms, we are here addressing the institutionalisation of cultural innovation and the consecration of art in bourgeois society during the formation of fully fledged capitalism. In the 1670s the French Royal Academy of Painting and Sculpture established a biennial exhibition that came to be known as 'the

Salon'.[28] At first only members of the Academy were allowed to exhibit. This restriction was lifted in 1791 as a consequence of the Revolution. The institution of the Salon survived the vicissitudes of politics over the years and by the mid nineteenth century was a popular bourgeois spectacle of summer in the city, sponsored by the state. Artists were motivated to put their work forward to the Salon in order to gain a public for it and to obtain governmental commissions, particularly necessary prior to the full development of a capitalist market in art. Jurors were appointed by the state, and they selected work according to established academic criteria of aesthetic value, the techniques of which were taught at the École des Beaux-arts. In the early to mid nineteenth century such criteria included rules concerning historical profundity and personal dignity; historical subjects and elite portraits were the favoured genres, while landscape and still-life, fated to be popular genres of impressionism, were considered less important. Such academicism was increasingly called into question by new movements in the arts.

Manet observed many of the conventions of academic art and received official approval and public commissions, exhibiting at the Salon on several occasions before as well as after the refusal of *Le déjeuner sur l'herbe* in 1863.[29] In that painting, he depicted a nude woman sharing a picnic in the countryside with two young bucks. Incidentally, by 1863 the submissions to the Salon had become enormous numerically, resulting in a very large number of rejections; so Manet's refusal was by no means exceptional, though he was widely regarded as a very fine artist while most of those refused probably were not. As George Heard Hamilton notes: 'In 1863 the number of artists excluded by the jury grew so large that the government was compelled to open an exhibition of the rejected works, the famous Salon des Refusés, an expedient tried again on a smaller scale and then abandoned.'[30] That there was a Salon des Refusés at all, housed in the very same building as the Salon itself, is an extraordinary occurrence. I am tempted to say, 'only in France'. The dialectic of refusal and incorporation is a much broader and more complex institutional process than this governmentally organised incorporation of the refused, yet the fact that it happened is an exceptionally concrete exemplification of the process. Although the Salon des Refusés was a temporary operation, tried only twice, institutional change followed. Eventually the jurors were selected entirely from the ranks of professional artists, no doubt reflecting the power structure within those ranks, which recognised to an extent that the permanent revolution of artistic innovation now beginning could not be directed by the state nor effectively resisted by it. In effect, power over art was passing from the state to the market, with the emergence of private dealers and a healthy bourgeois market for Manet's followers and successors, especially the impressionists.

As Belinda Thomson remarks, 'Manet, to a certain extent, subverted ... academic conventions; the impressionists broke away from them wholeheartedly.'[31] So did the market. In 1865 Manet was back in the Salon with an even more controversial picture than *Le déjeuner sur l'herbe*; this time with his *Olympia*, painted two years earlier. Again, Manet both observed and subverted established academic conventions. The painting referred to the egregious tradition of the nude in European painting, a sort of sanitised pornography. Often the models for such work were prostitutes, as was the model for *Olympia*. So what was it that upset his critics so much? Clark is probably right to suggest that it had something to do with class.[32] This prostitute was working class rather than transcoded as *déclassé*. The more serious problem for the critics, however, and one that they could hardly enunciate, was that Olympia was *naked*. She was not just a nude. Manet's earthiness offended refined taste; so did the inclusion of a negress, albeit as a servant, and a black cat reference to Manet's comradeship with that other reprobate, Baudelaire.

France was defeated in war by the Prussians, who effectively stopped at the gates of Paris after a symbolic parade through the city. The revolutionary uprising of the Paris Commune was put down brutally by the state. But the art world, in Howard Becker's term,[33] rolled on and constituted what became its typical *modus operandi*. The eminent Manet had one-man exhibitions and the 'Anonymous Society of Painters, Sculptors, Engravers, etc.' put on an independent exhibition in 1874 that became known as 'the first Impressionist Exhibition',[34] followed by others into the 1880s with progressively less shock effect. By the end of the century, impressionism was officially approved art and the bourgeoisie felt safe enough to put its pretty pictures on their walls. The autonomous process of artistic innovation, refusal and incorporation was underway, and would last until the erosion of artistic and, indeed, intellectual autonomy towards the end of the twentieth century, about which Bourdieu complained so bitterly in his later years.[35]

Picasso, Rivera and Kahlo

During the twentieth century, the relation between art and politics became ever more fraught, though later in the century it suddenly ceased to matter very much, if at all. The Russian Revolution of 1917 heralded the creation of a new kind of society, a communist society that was supposed to surpass capitalism. Communism, it was assumed, would produce a different kind of person. To refashion humanity, the arts and media of communication were recruited to the cause. In the 1920s, experimentation was allowed to flourish, most impressively in cinema,[36] but, once Stalin gained control, experiment was frowned upon, usually dismissed as 'formalism' and reviled as 'counter-revolutionary'. Instead, the great bourgeois traditions of art were to be sustained and imbued with socialist content. The deadly prescription of 'socialist realism' was imposed.[37] Nazi cultural policy had certain similarities to Soviet policy in the arts and media. It too demanded positive images and representations of healthy people building the new society.[38] Modernist work, with its often grim negativity, was denounced as 'degenerate'.[39]

The unfolding tragedy of Soviet communism was, paradoxically, accompanied mid century by great enthusiasm for its revolutionary promise in capitalist countries, not least amongst artists. Art produced by left-wing and professedly 'communist' bohemians for the marketplace thrived in the 'decadent' West, leaving behind an impressive legacy. Little of the art that was produced in the East under 'actually existing socialism' is remembered with such awe-struck devotion today. We only need to mention a few outstanding names of Western artists on the communist Left, such as Pablo Picasso, Diego Rivera and Frida Kahlo. For the most part, such artists did not tow the Moscow line, though occasionally they got tangled up in it due to membership of 'the Party'. Their work is better understood in connection with the dialectic of refusal and incorporation characteristic of the capitalist art world in the mid twentieth century rather than confined exclusively to a communist commitment under the comparatively 'free' conditions of the capitalist West.

Writing about Picasso in the 1960s, Marxist art critic John Berger remarked, 'Picasso is now wealthier and more famous than any other artist who has ever lived. His wealth is incalculable.'[40] The legend of Picasso as the greatest artist of the twentieth century was firmly established by the 1950s; and, from then until his death in 1973, Picasso was fêted not only for his art but also for his opulent lifestyle on the Cote d'Azur. He had become a canonical – albeit still living – artist and a world-famous celebrity, whose very signature made a scribble valuable. However, even Picasso could not have anticipated that his signature would eventually become a marque on a car thanks to the commercial nous of his descendants. Picasso was rich long before the 1950s. From an early age his work found wealthy buyers and in 1930 he was able to purchase a chateau in his adopted country of France.

How did this child from the lower reaches of the Spanish bourgeoisie and a card-carrying member of the French Communist Party become so rich and famous? Was there not a contradiction or two here? Berger's book, *The Success and Failure of Picasso*, eschews common-sense moralism; his is not a critical discourse on 'champagne socialists' but a serious attempt to explain the phenomenon of Picasso. For Berger, Picasso must be understood in the context of the 'dualism ... at the very heart of the bourgeois attitude to art. On the one hand, the glory and mystery of genius; on the other hand, the work of art as a saleable commodity.'[41] Picasso was fascinating because he was a gifted enigma, difficult for anyone to fathom, the bearer of an old Romantic myth. That he was also spectacularly successful in the fine-art market made him yet more fascinating, a wonder to behold.

Well into middle age, Picasso showed little or no interest in politics, though he had been touched by Catalonian anarchism as a very young man, before he set off on his journey to fame and fortune in Paris at the turn of the century. His attitude was closer to 'art for art's sake' than to 'social art'. Timothy Hilton says that 'Picasso never really had a social eye.'[42] Even when painting a beggar, Picasso was largely uninterested in the social problem. He was, however, passionately interested in the aesthetic problem of representation, and in this respect he was indeed a revolutionary. He became famous with *Les Demoiselles d'Avignon* in 1907. Like Manet before him, Picasso depicted prostitutes not as refined nudes but as naked women plying their trade, in this case with cynical disregard for the bourgeois punter. The most radical feature of the painting, however, was its borrowing from African 'primitive' art, fashionable in Paris at the time. Hilton comments: 'Picasso's use of black art may be swiftly summarized. It meant masks instead of faces, striation rather than modelling, and the employment of totem- or dervish-like figures and outlines to give a *frisson* quite alien to the European tradition, and the more startling because of its evident derivation outside that tradition.'[43] Picasso was an early avatar of cool.

He went on, with Braque, to invent cubism, an entirely new way of looking at the world and representing it, going beyond mere photographic realism to an analytical interrogation of the composition of things and their perception. Cubism is generally regarded as the most significant moment in the history of European art since the Renaissance. Perspective gave way to perspectivalism, different ways of looking. As Berger observes in his essay on cubism, the 'aim was to arrive at a far more complex image of reality than had ever been attempted in painting before'; and, he claims, 'All modern design, architecture and town planning, seems inconceivable without the initial example of cubism.'[44] The ascent of cubism as the most positive and intellectually daring of modern art movements was ended abruptly in 1914 with the onset of the First World War. Post-war art movements – expressionism, surrealism, etc. – were either nihilistically disposed or merely disengaged from any kind of utopian project. By the 1930s, when he was regarded as a sell-out by his cubist collaborators, Picasso's work was increasingly focused upon the meaning of ancient archetypes and symbols – the Minotaur and so on – rather than cutting-edge problems of representation. This is hardly surprising if Berger's thesis that Picasso was a 'vertical invader' is correct:

> Picasso was a vertical invader. He came up through the trap-door of Barcelona on to the stage of Europe. At first he was repulsed. Quite quickly he gained a bridgehead. Finally he became a conqueror. But always, I am convinced, he has remained conscious of being a vertical invader, always he has subjected what he has seen around him to a comparison with what he brought with him from his own country, from the past.[45]

Picasso was nostalgic for a simpler way of life that had been lost with the fanciful passing of Rousseau's mythical noble savage. In a sense, Picasso's radicalism was motivated by a Romanticism that bordered on reaction, but this did not cause him to fall into the arms of Franco's fascists, who wanted to turn the clock back in Spain from a modern and democratic republic to a priest-ridden autocracy. He refused their advances and agreed to become titular Director of the Prado when its collection of great art from the past was endangered by the fascists' indiscriminate bombardment. And, when the republican government invited him to contribute to the Spanish pavilion at the Paris Exposition, he gladly accepted the commission to paint a mural, thereby making it crystal clear whose side he was on in the civil war that was tearing his country apart. In effect, Picasso was politicised by events.

When, at the beginning of 1937, Picasso accepted the commission for the expo, which was to be held in the summer, he did not know what his contribution would be.[46] In the meantime, he produced his most overtly political work, a savage attack on General Franco in the form of a satirical cartoon strip, *Songe et Messonge de Franco* (*Dream and Lie of Franco*). Then the Luftwaffe bombed the Basque town of Guernica on the afternoon of 26 April 1937. 1,645 civilians died and 889 were seriously injured. Berger comments: 'Guernica was the first town ever bombed in order to intimidate a civilian population: Hiroshima was bombed according to the same calculation.'[47] In effect, fascist brutality in Spain had decided Picasso's subject matter for his mural. What else could it be?

Guernica is a monochrome combination of cubist rhetoric, Spanish symbolism and a pessimistically humanitarian response to the horror of modern warfare when non-combatants are on the frontline. It had no great impact at the expo itself, though it did draw criticism from the Left. Socialist and communist critics found *Guernica* obscure in style and lacking any sign of resistance or call to arms. It had not yet become the greatest work of political art of the twentieth century. The subsequent history of *Guernica* was chequered, but its significance grew as an affront to warmongers. The painting went on loan to the Museum of Modern Art (MOMA) in New York and stayed there until after the deaths of both Picasso and Franco, when it eventually wound up in Madrid. It did not *return* to Spain, since it had never been there. Back in 1939, the retrospective Picasso exhibition that featured *Guernica* at MOMA had cemented Picasso's already substantial reputation in America, his indisputable place in the canon of modern art and, indeed, ensured the market value of anything he produced. In a sense, *Guernica* revived Picasso's reputation as the greatest modern artist, a reputation he was to live off for the rest of his life while producing mainly inconsequential work.

Nelson Rockefeller – the American business tycoon (of the Standard Oil dynasty) and Republican politician – was so impressed by *Guernica* that he asked Picasso if he could have a tapestry copy made of it, to which the artist agreed. When Rockefeller died, his wife gave the tapestry to the United Nations Building in New York, where it now hangs. On 5 February 2003, Colin Powell made a last-ditch attempt there to obtain UN approval for the United States' planned invasion of Iraq. It was thought judicious on this occasion to cover up *Guernica* with a blue shroud, no doubt because its message was still so manifestly evident and would upset the viewing public by implying that their representatives were being asked to give consent to what Picasso had condemned so eloquently.⁴⁸

When he painted *Guernica*, Picasso was not yet a communist. He joined the French Communist Party in 1944, inspired by the heroic role it played in the Resistance to the German Occupation rather than by the truths of historical materialism. As the Cold War between the United States and the USSR developed, he became an outspoken figurehead for peace in various activities and events promoted by the Soviet Union. For this reason, he was denied a US entry visa in 1950. Whether or not Picasso was simply what had been dubbed in the 1930s a 'useful idiot' acting for Stalinism, like several other Western intellectuals at the time, it is worth quoting his stated motives for becoming a communist:

> Have not the Communists been the bravest in France, in the Soviet Union, and in my own Spain? How could I have hesitated? The fear to commit myself? But on the contrary I have never felt freer, never felt more complete. And then I have been so impatient to find a country again: I have always been an exile, now I am no longer one: whilst waiting for Spain to welcome me back, the French Communist Party have opened their arms to me, and I found there all whom I respect most, the greatest thinkers, the greatest poets, and all the faces of the Resistance fighters in Paris whom I saw and were so beautiful during those August days; again I am among my brothers.⁴⁹

There is no reason to believe that he was insincere. Picasso even painted a portrait of Josef Stalin on his death in 1953.

Another famous artist who also committed to communism in the middle of the twentieth century was the Mexican muralist, Diego Rivera. Although younger than Picasso by five years, Rivera exceeded him in fame, at least in the Americas, if only for a brief moment during the early thirties. Rivera's one-man show of January 1932 at MOMA in New York – seven years before Picasso's legendary show at the same venue – attracted a great many visitors and more than any previous exhibition held there.⁵⁰ The show included Rivera's *Frozen Assets* (1931), his condemnatory depiction of human misery beneath the soaring skyscrapers of Manhattan.

As a young man, Rivera had spent several years completing his apprenticeship in Paris, where he came under the sway of Picasso. For a while, he was a second-generation cubist. His eventual break with Picasso was, in a sense, a Mexican declaration of independence from the tutelage of Spain.[51] It was more than that, however, since Rivera's politics related much more directly to his art than did Picasso's in that period. This is exemplified by Rivera's cubist-style painting of 1915 entitled, *Zapatista Landscape (The Guerrilla)*, signifying admiration for the outlaws who contributed to the Mexican Revolution of 1910, which was a democratic rather than a communist revolution. Post-revolutionary Mexico, however, did open up space for left-wing politics and, indeed, for the cultural politics of Rivera and his fellow muralists, who decried the 'bourgeois' easel-painting practised by the likes of Picasso.

On his election to the Mexican presidency, General Alvaro Obregón made the university rector in Mexico City, Jose Vasconcelos, minister of education. Vasconcelos knew and saw great promise in the young artist, Diego Rivera. He also wanted to cultivate *mexicanidad*, a sense of Mexicanness, in a largely illiterate and peasant population. This might be facilitated to some extent, so he imagined, by public art that represented the Mexican people, their heritage and their struggle against Hispanic imperialism, ideally in the form of murals on the walls of public buildings. Vasconcelos called Rivera back from his European sojourn, but when he realised that Rivera had no idea how to paint murals a government grant was procured for the artist to return to Europe to study fresco painting, the work of Giotto and others, from the Italian Renaissance. Rivera, always a very good student, learnt swiftly and was soon the leading muralist in Mexico.

A huge, strong man and a quick worker, in 1923 Rivera covered 17,000 square feet of the Ministry of Education's walls with Mexican images that, according to Pete Hamill, 'continue to be used today as book jackets, album covers, and posters; they represent Mexico to the world, and in some ways, to Mexicans themselves'.[52] Hamill remarks further:

> The masterworks of Diego Rivera were created by a man of growing political convictions. It was as if the return to Mexico had given him the confidence to express his beliefs about society – a confidence not possible in countries where he was not a citizen – and those beliefs were strongly Marxist. The emergence of Rivera as a communist was quite sudden; during the long years of expatriation, he had little to say about such theories. In Mexico, he quickly surrounded himself with passionate, strong-willed communists like Guerrero, and made friends with many others, most of them younger than he was. The maker of public art and the Marxist partisan emerged at almost the same time.[53]

In 1922, Rivera joined the tiny Mexican Communist Party, which was committed to Leninist principles. In 1927 he visited the Soviet Union and only had good things to say about it. He had become the Mexican Party's leading figure not just because of artistic standing but also due to considerable political nous. Rivera's comrades turned on him, however, because of his acceptance of government commissions, and they forced him to preside over his own expulsion from the party in 1929. By this time, while enjoying the irony of his self-expulsion, Rivera was sympathetic to Leon Trotsky, who had been banished from the Soviet Union by Stalin a couple of years previously. In the following decade, Rivera joined the Trotskyist Fourth International, arranged asylum for Trotsky in Mexico, and for a while hosted him at Frida Kahlo's family home. Rivera was later to fall out with Trotsky, however, possibly due to the latter's affair with Kahlo. He was even suspected of complicity in Trotsky's assassination at the hands of a Stalinist agent in 1940. In the 1950s, after Kahlo's death, Rivera begged his way back into the dyed-in-the-wool Stalinist Communist Party of Mexico, which he, following Kahlo, regarded as a return 'home'.

Of the three communist artists under consideration here, Rivera was easily the most ideologically committed Marxist. This did not stop him accepting lucrative commissions from gringo capitalists as well as the Mexican government. In 1930 he painted a mural in the luncheon club of the San Francisco stock exchange. And although in his native land Rivera had romanticised the Mexican peasantry, he was hugely impressed by the sheer industry of the North American worker and the *industrialism* of *industrial* capitalism. So, it was not too difficult to take money from Henry Ford's son, Edsel, to paint murals celebrating industrial production in Detroit, the 'Motown' of black America. His *Detroit Industry* murals at the Detroit Institute of Arts, with their celebration of the heroic worker, outdid in artistry and matched in aesthetic orthodoxy the slavish 'socialist realism' demanded by Soviet cultural policy. Of course, at this time, in the depths of the Great Depression, US capital was on the brink of making serious concessions to the American working class. Roosevelt's New Deal, incidentally, also included government commissions for radical artists. That the leading Marxist artist in the world worked directly in the service of capitalist philanthropy during the 1930s, adorning municipal palaces with paeans to Fordism, was not so contradictory as it might now appear. There were, however, limits to how far Rivera could go in this line of business.

In 1933, along with Picasso and Henri Matisse, Rivera was commissioned to paint murals in the Rockefeller Center at the RCA building in New York. Picasso and Matisse dropped out, so Rivera was left all by himself to paint the pretentiously titled *Man at the Crossroads Looking with Hope and High Vision to the Choosing of a New and Better Future.* He put Lenin in the picture, although the Bolshevik leader had not been included in the original drawings for the mural. This was a provocation that Rivera must have known would cause trouble. The young Nelson Rockefeller, mainly to please his father, John D. Jnr., demanded that Lenin's image be painted out; Rivera refused. He was paid off and the almost finished mural was destroyed. Rivera subsequently painted a smaller version of it at the Palacio de Bellas Artes in Mexico City; so the work has not been lost to posterity. There were public protests against Rivera's treatment and the destruction of the mural, organised by a then substantial American Left in New York City, but to no avail. Before leaving New York, Rivera painted some murals at the New Workers School. Henceforth though, Rivera was no longer to be a public – albeit 'revolutionary' – artist for US capitalism. In his later and declining years, he earned much needed money from portrait commissions of rich gringos, a private and rather less iconoclastic form of bourgeois art. In any event, the mural's days as the pre-eminent form of public art had passed. The cinema took its place.

Diego Rivera was a big man in every way: tall and stout, he painted large murals and, at one time, his reputation was enormous. It has now been eclipsed by that of his diminutive wife, Frida Kahlo. Following a bus crash in her teens, in which an iron bar speared her pelvis and vagina, Kahlo took up painting in bed-ridden convalescence. She had already suffered from polio in childhood. Never able to bear a child, her physical incapacities worsened as she aged, resulting in several operations that caused more problems than they solved. To alleviate the pain, she became dependent on drugs and alcohol. Kahlo died aged 47 in 1954, quite possibly at her own hand. Kahlo's paintings are mostly small in scale, especially the bed-ridden ones, and there are only around 150 in all, produced over a career of nearly 30 years. Although Kahlo had originally approached Rivera (a much older man and already an acknowledged master) during the mid 1920s for an expert opinion on her paintings, she did not take herself very seriously as an artist until the late 1930s. In her painting of 1931, *Frida Kahlo and Diego Rivera*, he carries the signs of his trade, brushes and palette; she, dressed in traditional red-and-green costume, holds his hand demurely, representing herself as the little wife. He is heavy and solid, with his feet planted firmly on the ground; she is light, her dainty feet looking as though they are almost floating on air. The present reversal of their respective standing in art history would have amazed them both.[54]

As Oriana Baddeley remarks in the guidebook to the 2005 Kahlo exhibition at Tate Modern in London: 'Frida is both a star – a commercial property complete with fan clubs and merchandising – and the embodiment of the hopes and aspirations of a near-religious group of followers.'[55] Collected by Madonna and the subject of a Hollywood biopic courtesy of Miramax,[56] Kahlo had by the early twenty-first century become a cool icon of feminism effectively retrieved from the fetid clutches of communism. She was a communist too, but little was said about that in 2005.

Her paintings were fetching $5 million a shot. Moreover, as the feature film *Frida* suggested, her life was at least as fascinating as her art. In my opinion, the movie is, up to a point, a faithful selection from and representation of the knowledge about Kahlo unearthed by Hayden Herrera for her splendid biography of 1983. Edward Lucie-Smith noted the significance of Herrera's biography of Kahlo in 1993:

> During their own life times there was always an element of rivalry in Diego and Frida's relationship but Diego always seemed to have the upper hand, since Kahlo was perceived as worthy of consideration largely because of her position as Rivera's consort. Since the publication of Hayden Herrera's vivid and revealing biography of Kahlo in 1983, however, this perception has changed, and Frida's fame as a feminist heroine has increased so that it almost eclipses that of her husband. It seems likely that Kahlo would have found this development astonishing.[57]

Kahlo and Rivera were not, as it happens, rivals in art. He was her greatest fan and she admired his work greatly. Their relationship, however, was indeed turbulent. She knew of his incorrigible philandering before their marriage, which Kahlo more or less condoned until he made love to her sister. Kahlo embarked upon a succession of both heterosexual and lesbian affairs that he usually tolerated and occasionally even encouraged. They divorced and remarried the following year. In Roman Catholic Mexico, during the 1930s and '40s, Kahlo and Rivera's conduct was outlandishly bohemian. Kahlo was then in the shadow of Rivera, merely an eccentric background figure in the great artist's legend, a legend that loomed so much larger than her own during their lifetimes. Now, he is on the whole remembered as her communist dinosaur of a husband.

In spite of Frida Kahlo's latter-day fame and comparatively recent discovery as an 'old mistress',[58] there are doubts concerning her artistic excellence over which I am not in a position to adjudicate, since, arguably, there are no reliable criteria of judgement and standards of achievement to go by. Griselda Pollock says, with reference to Artemesia Gentileschi, that such an old mistress's 'fame is more a matter of notoriety and sensationalism than any real interest in comprehension'; and she notes, furthermore, that such an observation is equally applicable to Kahlo.[59] Rather than weighing Kahlo and Rivera in the balance of art-historical judgement, it is more apposite to ask historically grounded questions: first, how did their art differ from one another? And, second, why is Kahlo so much more fashionable now than the Colossus of the 1930s, Diego Rivera? With regard to the first question, Herrera makes a brilliant comparison:

> Frida's intelligence worked in a different way from Diego's. Shunning theories and overviews, she penetrated into the particular, focusing on details of clothing, faces, trying to capture an individual life. Later, she would probe the insides of fruits and flowers, the organs hidden beneath wounded flesh, and the feeling hidden beneath stoic features. From his more distanced and abstract vantage point, Rivera encompassed the breadth of the visible world; he populated his murals with all of society and the pageant of history. Frida's subjects, by contrast, came from a world close at hand – friends, animals, still lifes, most of all from herself. Her true subjects were embodied states of mind, her own joys and sorrows. Always intimately connected with the events of her life, her images convey the immediacy of lived experience.[60]

This virtually amounts to a stereotypical distinction between the feminine and the masculine imaginations, though Herrera makes no such essentialist claim.

It is generally agreed that Kahlo's best work is in self-portraiture; and there is evidence of her talent right at the beginning in the preliminary *Self-Portrait* (1926), heavily influenced by Modigliani, painted at the age of 19. *The Two Fridas* (1939), one of her larger canvases, painted at the time of the divorce from Rivera, is perhaps her greatest work. It represents the bifurcation of her failed marriage (Frida in a white wedding dress bleeding) and her Mexican spiritedness (Frida in a colourful dress, looking defiant, an independent woman). The most direct image of Frida's psychological turmoil over the divorce, however, is *Self-Portrait and Cropped Hair* (1940), where she is depicted wearing a man's suit and having cut off her long hair. When it comes to suffering, the most emblematic image is *The Broken Column* (1944), a crumbling edifice with pins of pain in an orthopaedic corset. By then, Kahlo was coming into her own as a recognised artist, having exhibited in New York and with the surrealists in Paris. A year before her death she was accorded a one-woman show in Mexico City before an adoring public, among them her former and still devoted students. Because of her leg amputation and fatal ill health, Kahlo had to be carried into the gallery in her sickbed, against the doctor's advice.

Kahlo's paintings represent, amongst other themes, her miscarriages, her disdain for the United States, and her positive identification with the popular culture of native Mexico (mistaken as surrealism by the irritating André Breton, who seems to have thought anything Mexican was surreal). Her claims to be considered a feminist 'old mistress' are manifold, and are perhaps most crudely signified in *A Few Small Nips* (1935), an ironic commentary, executed rather poorly by fine-art standards, on a man's description of how he stabbed his wife to death. This was a *retablo*, that is, a painting on metal, typical of 'naive' or 'primitive' Mexican art. Kahlo was by no means naive or primitive, although her technical skills as a painter were nothing like as professionally honed as Rivera's virtuoso displays.

The Miramax movie downplays the depth and persistence of Kahlo's communism. It seems to figure only in the earlier part of her life and is excised from the narrative of her declining later years. However, the truth is that she was welcomed back into the Stalinist fold of the Mexican Communist Party long before Rivera was re-admitted. Shortly before she died, Kahlo insisted on attending a demonstration protesting against the US role in overthrowing the Guatemalan socialist government, one of a long succession of gringo interferences in the US 'sphere of influence' south of the border. Towards the end, Kahlo had become troubled by the lack of explicit politics in her art but her efforts to overcome this were less than impressive. There is, for instance, the truly dreadful *Marxism Will Give Health to the Sick*, featuring Kahlo in her orthopaedic corset being cured by the hand of Karl Marx. When she died in July 1954, an unfinished portrait of Stalin was left on her studio easel and *The*

Internationale was sung at her funeral; inconvenient facts for a coolly feminist embrace of an old commie.

As a coda to this discussion of the affirmation of official communism by Picasso, Rivera and Kahlo, it is important to note that many other left-wing artists and intellectuals were caught up in the Cold War on the anti-communist side, unbeknownst to themselves at the time. By the late 1940s, intellectual faith in communism and Western veneration for the Soviet Union were sorely tried by revelations of the Gulag and, later in 1956, by the partial repudiation of Stalin's legacy by Nikita Khrushchev. In the 1930s, Trotsky's critique of the 'betrayal' of the Russian Revolution had contributed to the formation of an incipient 'New Left', as an alternative to both Soviet communism and social democracy. This alternative Left was a feature of the bohemian milieu in places like Greenwich Village.

After the Second World War, when Europe was in ruins, the official centre of the Western art world shifted from Paris to New York, with all the necessary ingredients to hand: a network of rebellious artists, taste-defining critics like Clement Greenberg,[61] and major institutional support from, most particularly, MOMA. Abstraction – and especially abstract expressionism – was promoted as the new avant-garde, going beyond the still representational work of not only Rivera but also Picasso. Artists like Jackson Pollock and Mark Rothko came to the fore as indigenous American geniuses able to match and surpass artists in the European tradition at their own game.

Although the Democrat President, Harry S. Truman, successor to Roosevelt, hated modern art, and the Republican politician, George Dondero, declared bombastically, 'All modern art is Communistic',[62] it turned out that in the 1950s abstract expressionism was the perfect kind of art to be recruited in defence of 'the Free World'. What could be freer than spraying paint apparently randomly on canvas, as did Pollock?[63] You would have been in serious trouble doing that kind of thing in the Soviet Union. Nelson Rockefeller (yes, him again), president of MOMA in the 1940s and '50s, called abstract expressionism 'free enterprise painting'.⁶⁴ That Pollock himself was on the Left in his youth and had been influenced by Mexican mural art in the 1930s made him ideally suited to serve as an icon for the cultural Cold War against the 'socialist realism' required of artists in the USSR.

Abstract expressionism and kindred strands of bohemian rebellion in the 1940s and '50s arose from the autonomous dynamic of the cultural field in which innovation comes out of left field; however, worldwide promotion of 'free' art and thought had to be organised in order to achieve the ideological aims of US cultural diplomacy. The Congress for Cultural Freedom, founded in 1950, was a secretive and lavishly funded front for the Central Intelligence Agency's (CIA) cultural strategy in the Cold War, the history of which has been recounted by Frances Stonor Saunders in her book, *Who Paid the Piper? The CIA and the Cultural Cold War*. Many of the facts contained in the book only surfaced sensationally after the Congress for Cultural Freedom was wound up in 1967. According to Stonor Saunders:

> At its peak, the Congress for Cultural Freedom had offices in thirty-five countries, employed dozens of personnel, published over twenty prestigious magazines, held art exhibitions, owned a newspaper and features service, organized high-profile international conferences, and rewarded musicians and artists with public performance. Its mission was to nudge the intelligentsia of western Europe away from its lingering fascination with Marxism and Communism to a view more accommodating of 'the American way'.⁶⁵

For the most part, artists and intellectuals who travelled on the Congress's gravy train did not know who exactly was paying the fare and were apparently unaware, whether in good or bad faith, that the US government was spending massively on a covert cultural policy intended as subtle capitalist propaganda in contest with the rather more blatant communist propaganda of the USSR.

Cool Art and Business

The relative autonomy of the modern art world developed according to a dialectic of refusal and incorporation, with a characteristic succession of new movements usurping the authority of older movements and eventually becoming incorporated too. As the foregoing discussion demonstrates, the autonomy of art – and of the cultural field more generally – was *relative*, never absolute. Economic and political determinations played their part in both inhibiting as well as sustaining contested progression. Incorporation, when it happened, was lucrative, and politics enlivened controversy. The question now arises of whether the dialectical tension that emerged from the mid nineteenth century and lasted through to the mid twentieth century is still in play. To put it another way, have the two dimensions of aesthetic subversion and mundane capitalist reality fused into one? Has art given in to the way things are? The discussion of visual art and communism has suggested that it was the distance from immediate politics which at least contributed to the profound success of Western artists on the communist Left compared to their easily forgotten comrades in the East. They were not so much pursuing a party line as exploring the experimental potentials of modern art. Political pressure of an overtly ideological kind is no longer so significant. With the later development of capitalism in its globalising phase, economic determination exerts much greater pressure in every walk of life, including the arts, than does politics narrowly defined.

As early as 1960, Raymond Williams declared advertising to be 'the official art of the twentieth century'.[66] This was a provocative, though prescient, remark. However, on the one hand, it was merely an observation concerning the scale of activity, referring to the sheer ubiquity of advertising and the large numbers of artists and writers employed to produce images and copy for selling products. On the other hand, Williams also wanted to say something more general about the culture:

> The structural similarity between much advertising and much modern art is not simply copying by the advertisers. It is the result of comparable responses to the contemporary human condition, and the only distinction that matters is between the clarification achieved by some art and the displacement normal in bad art and most advertising.[67]

It is interesting that Williams should have said this before Andy Warhol rose to prominence as perhaps the most influential artist since Picasso.

Warhol started out as a commercial artist turning out ads for shoes and the like in the 1950s.[68] He wanted to be taken seriously in the fine arts, however, and, on becoming a fine artist in the 1960s, was able to exercise his shoe fetishism there as well. Fredric Jameson has compared Warhol's *Diamond Dust Shoes* to Vincent Van Gogh's *A Pair of Boots*.[69] For Jameson, Van Gogh's painting is a classic work of modern art, which confers a kind of utopian dignity on manual labour. In contrast, Warhol's work, based on a monochrome photograph, silk-screened for multiple reproduction, is only a picture of dress shoes with nothing to say. Of course, it could be argued, in a common misuse of Walter Benjamin's insights,[70] that Warhol's work is inherently democratic in a mass-popular sense, and that Jameson is an elitist albeit leftist critic who is still, anachronistically, demanding heroic refusal and depth of meaning from a work of art. Jameson's exemplary comparison illustrates his general thesis that postmodernism – taking Warhol as a pioneer – is 'the cultural logic of late capitalism'. Postmodernism is characterised by Jameson as a depthless culture lacking the affectivity of modern art. Warhol himself would not have demurred. He made no special claims for his work, whilst embracing the flotsam and jetsam of mass-popular and celebrity culture.[71] His was a cool, detached and ironic pose. Warhol's work reacted, in a sense, against the *Sturm und Drang* of abstract expressionism, often regarded as the last gasp of Romanticism; though postmodernism has Romantic features too. Warhol had affinities with British pop art[72] and, although populist in intent, his work also had associations with conceptual and minimalist art, the kind of art where the art object does not matter so much as the idea. Both pop art – where the distance between art and mass culture was closed – and conceptual art – where artistry was not the point – were alternative yet companionable end games for the exhausted succession of modern art movements, after which progressive development apparently ceases and the typical rehashing of the past in recycled styles and re-combinations of elements[73] that characterises postmodern culture in general, and in particular fields such as art and fashion, gets underway in earnest.[74]

Change in the art world is related in complex and mediated ways to developments in the underlying political economy and 'spirit' of capitalism. During the nineteenth century, while ordinary members of the middle class became the customers for art, the *haute bourgeoisie* increasingly assumed the role of patron in defence of culture against the very commerce that made them wealthy enough to distribute public-spirited *largesse* to a worthy cause. By the mid twentieth century it was widely assumed that the vitality of genuine art of a higher calling could not be entrusted safely to market forces in competition with lowly mass entertainments. In the United States, private patronage was the typical mode, with its prestigious endowment and tax advantages; in Europe, public patronage was provided by central, regional and local state subsidy for galleries and museums. This was the characteristic set-up under the mature system of organised capitalism, though differing in particulars from place to place. In those circumstances, art was virtually by definition the opposite of business. Its meanings were of a quite different order to those of advertising, marketing and public relations. The great refusal of art, representing a necessary counter-point to the system, however troublesome aesthetically or politically, usually went through a process of incorporation and neutralisation. Since the 1960s, obdurate distancing has diminished and art, in one way or another, has come closer to business in general and advertising in particular. The episode of so-called 'Young British Art' in the 1990s is a case in point; it was prefigured, however, by consequential moves in the New York art scene of the 1960s.

Alexander Alberro's case study of Seth Siegelaub's dealership in conceptual and minimalist art in Manhattan exemplifies 'the new overlap of business and the arts'[75] that occurred during the 1960s. Alberro says:

> The infusion of corporate funds was a major element in the expansion of the art market during the mid 1960s. Corporate ideology in that decade

was a dynamic force, as the business world undertook dramatic transformations both of the way it operated and the way in which it imagined itself. In significant ways, corporate collectors made clear their preference for contemporary art over established work. Many in corporate practice, especially in public relations departments, imagined new, innovative art as a symbolic ally in the pursuit of entrepreneurship, a partner in their own struggles to revitalise business and the consumer order generally. Furthermore, contemporary trends in art offered the corporate patron a progressive image in the business sphere and a public sign of commitment to fresh ideas.[76]

So, there are several reasons why corporate business should embrace innovative art instead of fearing and seeking to control what was once a 'great refusal', including purchase of works for reception space and office adornment. Establishing the identity and good reputation of the corporation is the main aim, not least in the case of the tobacco manufacturer, Philip Morris's sponsorship of public art exhibitions. Chin-tao Wu has documented the various manifestations of corporate intervention in the art worlds of Britain and the United States over the closing decades of the twentieth century – when, for instance, business sponsorship, however marginal, came to be seen as a necessary supplement to basic funding provided by public subsidy so that the tail winds up wagging the dog.[77] The role of sponsorship has been controversial in European countries which have a welfare-state tradition of cultural policy and are still residually embarrassed by untrammelled capitalism. The ever closer relation of art and business is much less a matter of public controversy in the US, where the power of corporations is so closely aligned to the power of the nation. However, even there, American critics have complained about 'the corporate takeover of public expression'.[78]

While pop art was a populist move in the art game with an undeniably popular appeal, this could hardly be said of conceptual art, in which the idea is supposed to determine the thing itself, usually in a manner quite baffling to a wider public. Alberro points out that conceptual art was legitimised by a brand of art theory that denies the expressivity and craft of the artist and, moreover, depth of meaning in art, represented most notably by the critical writings of Joseph Kosuth since the 1960s. That such art has often proven to be, in effect, research and development for 'cool' advertising rhetoric is a curious phenomenon. In this corporate fusion of the art and business worlds it is seriously 'uncool' to waste words explaining the intended meanings of the artwork. The meaning, if it is active at all, is a matter of inarticulate conviction in mystifying discourse, rather like the belief that the Emperor really was wearing new clothes.

In the first instance, I think we have to see what became known as 'Young British Art' in the 1990s in reaction to the leftist art of the 1970s,[79] the excesses of 'theory' in the 1980s, and the reduction of public funding for art and culture under Margaret Thatcher's Conservative governments from 1979 and into the '90s. All of this held out the prospect of a career of principled penury for the young artist wishing to make a mark. As Angela McRobbie observed in an otherwise critical discussion of the cynical ambition typical of that generation of young British artists (YBAs), 'There has to be some way of being an artist and making a living.'[80]

The leading figure of the tendency was Damien Hirst, a sculptor of sorts whose mentor was the advertising executive, Charles Saatchi. Saatchi had opened a gallery on Boundary Road in St John's Wood, London in 1985. At a show in the gallery in 1987, Hirst had seen Jeff Koons's work celebrating consumerism. In later years, he was always to cite Koons along with Warhol and Francis Bacon as his favourite artists. In fact, Hirst and Koons constitute something of a mutual admiration society. Hirst is now an immensely rich and world-famous artist. Arguably, his talent lies not so much in art but in entrepreneurial zeal. During the mid '80s, Hirst was a student at Goldsmiths College in South East London where, although a Northerner in origin, he began dodging and diving like a stereotypical Cockney market trader, the Del Boy of the art world. In 1988, he organised a show for himself and fellow students, *Freeze*, at a warehouse in the East End. Hirst managed to attract West End dealers to the event and corporate sponsorship for the book of the exhibition. He was soon picked up by Charles Saatchi, an ad man turned 'supercollector'.[81]

Saatchi had made a considerable fortune with his brother Maurice, in the firm of Saatchi and Saatchi, during the 1970s, most famously conducting Thatcher's victorious election campaign of 1979 with the slogan, 'Labour [Britain] Isn't Working'. The company expanded by taking over other advertising agencies as it went global. It eventually overstretched itself, however, particularly occasioned by a failed takeover of the Hill Samuel Bank. The brothers were subsequently ejected from the company they had founded, whereupon they set up another successful agency, M. & C. Saatchi, which ran the Conservatives' advertising campaign for the election that they lost in 1997. The Saatchis then received commissions from the post-Thatcherite New Labour government, most notably the campaign for the disastrous Millennium Dome expo of 2000.[82]

At the time Saatchi became aware of Hirst and his mates he was switching his art collection policy from buying work by established and currently fashionable American artists, such as Koons and Schnabel, to picking up unknown work from graduating students and recent graduates in London – and, in so doing, making that work known and valuable in economic terms. His advertising executive's nose for novelty turned to the 'new' in art. In fact, he performed the hybrid role of patron, collector and dealer, later selling work collected cheaply at exorbitant prices. He even sold the early work he collected from Hirst back to the artist at a later stage in the game for £6 million.

On the surface, it might have seemed like a strange partnership – the Thatcherite advertising executive, Charles Saatchi, and the boy on the make from Leeds, Damien Hirst – but, of course, it was not. Saatchi actually bought the shark for Hirst to place in a tank of formaldehyde in 1993, the kind of thing that put him in the frame for his 1995 Turner prize, *The Impossibility of Death in the Mind of Someone Living*. When it was eventually sold in a cloudy and reduced state to an American collector ten years later for £6.5 million, Hirst agreed to do the collector a fresh one. By that time, Hirst was worth £100 million and had himself become a collector and all-round art entrepreneur with factories of art workers knocking the stuff out for him.

In the first instance, 'Young British Art' was merely the title of an exhibition that Saatchi put on at Boundary Road in 1992. Whether or not the label referred to a coherent movement remains a matter of debate. There were, inevitably, differences among the artists concerning their work and their attitudes to Saatchi. However, there was a definite disposition associated with the name, summed up by the word 'cool', used several times in Julian Stallabrass's book on the subject, *High Art Lite*.[83] The title of the book distils Stallabrass's critical perspective on the phenomenon of Young British Art: that it was a light and frothy episode, not a 'real' avant-garde of genuine consequence for art. He talks of 'high art lite in its cool, youthful, resolutely urban stance'[84] and its characteristic 'flip and cool' in-jokes that belied the apparent populism of Young British Art.[85] While registering the persistent use of the word 'cool' in the discourse around Young British Art, Stallabrass, however, never quite interrogates its ideological function, which is so much broader in significance than this transient episode in the history of art.

The apotheosis of Young British Art was the *Sensation* exhibition, *Young British Artists from the Saatchi Collection*, held at the Royal Academy in Piccadilly in 1997. This may perhaps be seen as the moment of incorporation of yet another modern artistic refusal into the mainstream. *Sensation* was indeed controversial among Royal Academicians; some resigned over it. The Royal Academy was in debt to the tune of £2 million. The razzmatazz generated by *Sensation* and the crowds that were pulled in contributed towards balancing the books. It contained work from a range of YBAs: Jake and Dinos Chapman, Tracey Emin, Marcus Harvey, Damien Hirst, Gary Hume, Sarah Lucas, Ron Mueck, Chris Ofili and Jenny Saville, to name-check the select few. Some of the work outraged sensitive members of the public. Harvey's *Myra*, a Chuck Close inspired mug-shot painting of the 1960s accomplice to child murder, Myra Hindley, made up of children's hand prints, upset the victims' surviving relatives. The Chapman Brothers' pretentiously named, *Zygotic Acceleration*,

Biogenetic, De-Sublimated Libidinal Model (enlarged x 1000), featuring young girls with penises for noses, was duly sensational. And when *Sensation* went to the Brooklyn Museum in 1999, the Roman Catholic Mayor of New York, Rudi Giuliani, tried unsuccessfully to prevent it opening because he was offended by Ofili's *The Holy Virgin Mary*.[86] Ofili, himself a practising Catholic, had used elephant dung and photographs of vaginas cut out from pornography magazines in the painting. Unsympathetic critics, like Hatton, Walker and Stallabrass, tend to doubt that attention-grabbing shock tactics of this kind represent anything like a 'great refusal' of the status quo. Yet they are undoubtedly reminiscent of the old dialectic: the first time as tragedy; the second time as farce.

Saatchi and the YBAs were experts at attracting publicity. For a brief period in the early 2000s, Saatchi audaciously moved his gallery to County Hall on the Thames, the building that had once housed the Greater London Council, abolished by Thatcher when it resolutely pursued socialist policies in the 1980s. This gesture challenged the supremacy of the state-subsidised Tate Modern that had opened to much acclaim down the river in 2000. There were, however, limits even to Saatchi's audacity. When he sought to invent new art movements, such as the short-lived 'New Neurotic Realism', his quasi-advertising confections failed to impress a public becoming jaded with Young British Art. On the left-wing of the transatlantic art world, Hans Haacke had been a persistent critic of Saatchi all along, deriding his relation to Thatcherism with *Taking Stock (Unfinished)* (1983) and the supercollector's global aspirations with *The Saatchi Collection (Simulations)* (1987).[87]

Stallabrass is gleeful about what he regards as 'the fall of Young British Art'. It had been an instance of 'a common feature of business propaganda'; that is, 'it incorporates the critiques that might be levelled against it'.[88] The cool façade of the YBA episode was fading at the beginning of the twenty-first century. Art had indeed become more like advertising and capitalist imperatives were triumphant in every sphere – but only up to a point. This downturn was partly due to the hubris and sheer arrogance characteristic not only of Saatchi but also of Hirst, who in 2000 sold his first £1 million work, *Hymn*, a gigantic version of a toy model of human physiology. With his massive earnings, he bought Toddington Manor in the Gloucestershire countryside and set about turning it into a shrine for his own art and personal tastes. And in 2007 there was the abomination of the £50 million diamond-encrusted skull. Hirst's street credibility was bound to suffer from his transformation into a bloated plutocrat, whose wealth grew out of all proportion as his pronouncements on the integrity of art's fusion with business became increasingly self-serving and vacuous. Artistic outlaws were sure to react negatively and quite possibly refuse the new dispensation. Damage had been done, however, as Stallabrass concluded gloomily in his comment on the enduring legacy of

> the outlook typical of high art lite which is to present the worst of what life has to offer with a shrug of the shoulders, to view with enjoyment but definitely not to ameliorate. This is a contradiction that is hard to see a way around: the celebration of what is cool has turned its back on the liberal and welfare values of old, and indeed with them most forms of state authority.[89]

Young British Art represented an attitude rather than a movement: an attitude that was cool with capitalist accumulation and the seductions of consumer culture; an attitude that imagined no alternative. At one level, it was merely a network of artists trying to make it, in effect, a generation of symbolic manipulators refusing anonymity and gentile poverty. As they grew older, the YBAs defined the new role of the artist as entrepreneur and flippant provocateur – embodied especially by Hirst – for aspirant young artists seeking to repeat the trick. Arguments can be had over the respective merits and demerits of each and every artist within the network but that is beyond the point of the present discussion. Some of them, concerned about their dignity as pseudo-autonomous rebels, complained and were inclined to bite the hand that fed them, most vociferously the Chapman Brothers. Ofili referred sardonically to 'Saatchi art'. And, even within the ambit of Young British Art, there were desperate dissidents, not just ungrateful children, such as Michael Landy, whose work evinced hostility to consumerism, such as in his *Closing Down Sale* installation of 1992 and *Scrapheap Services* of 1995.[90] In 2001, Landy put on an extraordinary performance in a disused Oxford Street department store, *Breakdown*, during which he destroyed all his personal possessions.[91]

Then, of course, there is the elusive Banksy, the graffiti artist who achieved notoriety in the 2000s with a renewal of social art in a satirical mode. His witty transgressions of public space posed problems for the law and the art world.[92] Again, this was a London blast from a New York past, recalling the graffiti artists of the 1970s who enraged the authorities but were also incorporated when some of their work appeared in the galleries of Manhattan dealerships. Nothing, apparently, is beyond incorporation for cool capitalism. Banksy too became incorporated, with photographs of his street work collected and displayed by none other than Damien Hirst. Still, graffiti remains a problematic object and category-busting form, even 'abject', in Julia Kristeva's term,[93] outside the law. Abjection, it would seem, is now an admissible sign for the all-consuming system.

3
CONSUMER CULTURE

At the turn of 2006/2007, *Time* magazine declared its Person of the Year to be 'You'.¹ In other years, a photograph of some illustrious individual would have been found on the magazine's cover. Bono was Person of the Year 2005, Vladimir Putin in 2007. On this occasion, however, there was a plastic mirror for the reader to gaze upon his or her own visage, thereby narcissistically retrieving the imaginary subject of 'You' from social and symbolic space. Yet, in my experience, the plastic mirror failed in its ostensible purpose. It did not reflect a self-image in plenitude – or indeed platitude – back to the Person of the Year. The plastic mirror reflected a fragmented, broken-up image, reminiscent of Picasso's cubist portraits. On the editorial page, however, there was a photograph of the editor holding up a copy of the magazine with his face reflected in the cover with crystal clarity.² It looked as though a front cover with a glass rather than plastic mirror had been mocked up in order to make the editor's photograph work for the purpose in hand.

There was another curious displacement that framed this particular issue of *Time*. The magazine complimented ordinary people for being agents of a digital democracy – few of whom however, it is reasonable to surmise, would be reading such an old-fashioned and intellectually elitist publication as *Time*. Following the lead article, attacking the 'great man' theory of history,³ there was an article entitled 'Power to the People'.⁴ The individuals featured here were mainly young bloggers and YouTubers, mostly students, with two notable exceptions, a 54-year-old former librarian from Georgia who had posted more book reviews on Amazon than anyone else, and a 45-year-old

Korean 'housewife' described as a 'citizen reporter'. Further into the issue we also learn that 'On the Web, anyone with a digital camera has the power to change history.'[5] This declaration of people power was followed by a laudatory article on Steve Chen and Chad Hurley, who had just sold their citizens' video service, YouTube, to Google for a cool $1.65 billion.[6] Were not these enterprising young men outstanding candidates over the rest of us for nomination as Person of the Year? Who exactly was being praised, then? Cool outsiders circumventing the restrictions of old media or young entrepreneurs making their first billion before the age of 30 by selling out the kind of people power they had cultivated with a new media device?

'User-generated content' was all the rage at the turn of the year from 2006 to 2007,[7] as the gift exchange of Napster had similarly been a few years earlier, before it was reined in by corporate power. The Web – or, as it has become known in this later phase, 'Web 2.0' – facilitates interactivity and peer-to-peer communications over the Net, which at first sight have usually appeared threatening to media conglomerates, especially in the music and film and television industries. In this respect, digital technology has seemingly delivered the long-held dream of media radicals for access from below to the production of meaning, rather than the ideologically passive consumption of messages passed down from above.[8] But media conglomerates could not afford to stand idly by as their powers were usurped by the innovative practices of cyber anarchy. Although these spaces of expressivity and communicative freedom were not to be closed down, they had to be brought safely within the market system of commodity circulation and be subjected to advertising. The conduit was not only a 'cool' outfit like Google. Rupert Murdoch's News Corp had already bought out MySpace in July 2006.

The issues here concerning the relations between media production and consumption are a sub-set of wider questions of consumer culture in a capitalist economy. Analytically, in approaching such questions, it is wise to steer a course somewhere between the polar extremes and countervailing forces identified as, on the one hand, cunning manipulation by corporations and, on the other hand, crafty empowerment of citizens through productive consumption, in order to explore the complex interplay of differently ordered powers in consumer culture. Manipulation and empowerment may thus be considered two sides of a delicate process whereby corporations are forced to negotiate with the unpredictable emergence of citizen-consumer activity from below in order to incorporate and neutralise potentially subversive effects of popular innovation.

Officially, the sovereign consumer is the monarch of cool capitalism. Great corporations only exist, so it is said, in order to service our every need and desire. They strive to divine our wants and then supply them. It is routine in capitalist rhetoric to attribute productive agency to consumers. The nomination of consumers/producers as Person of the Year by *Time* was flattering and, arguably, amounted to an instance of the kind of popular seduction that Zygmunt Bauman claims is the cutting edge of social control over comparatively affluent populations today.[9] Putting it another way, Yiannis Gabriel and Tim Lang remark less abstractly:

> The consumer has become a god-like figure, before whom markets and politicians alike bow. Everywhere it seems, the consumer is triumphant. Consumers are said to dictate production; to fuel innovation; to be creating new services in advanced economies; to be driving modern politics; to have it in their power to save the environment and protect the future of the planet. Consumers embody a simple modern logic, the right to choose. Choice, the consumer's friend, the inefficient producer's foe, can be applied to things as diverse as soap powder, holidays, healthcare or politicians. And yet the consumer is also seen as a weak and malleable creature, easily manipulated, dependent, passive and foolish. Immersed in illusions, addicted to joyless pursuits of ever-increasing living standards, the consumer, far from being god, is a pawn, in games played in invisible boardrooms.[10]

Consumption is an essential feature of human existence, fulfilling basic needs for, say, nourishment, shelter and clothing appropriate to the weather.[11] Consumerism, as the dominant ideological feature of late-capitalist culture, however, is much more controversial: it may be seen as the ultimate purpose of life or, alternatively, as distorting humanity's relation to the natural and social worlds. Whatever the prevailing judgement, consumerism is cultural as well as economic, that is, it is imbued with meaning. In certain cases, its symbolic significance apparently transcends its strictly economic importance. Commodities are used conspicuously to say something about social identity. Historically, consumerism and conspicuous consumption have become more widely dispersed among populations in wealthier parts of the world, and have also generated aspirations for development in poorer parts of the world. Alternative explanations for how consumer desires originate, are cultivated, sustained and transformed vie with one another in wide-ranging public debates, including contributions from psychologists and sociologists of variously administrative, disinterested and critical orientation. Most notably, the uses of newer communication technologies have been the focus of much discussion in recent years.

This chapter looks at the changing character of conspicuous consumption in both elite and popular practices, including questions of taste, pleasure, celebrity and rebel identification. It traces the construction and progress of mass consumerism during the twentieth century and examines the coolly seductive qualities of present-day consumer culture, including the technological innovations associated with mobile and privatised ways of living.

Conspicuous Consumption

The capacity to consume is fundamentally an economic matter. Yet, at a certain point, consumption becomes meaningful in excess of satisfying basic needs. At the more advanced level, it turns into a sign of distinction and an end in itself. Consumption must be conspicuous – that is, explicit – for its social magic to work, to signal to others, in effect, the consumer's worth. Consumerism in that sense has been associated historically not only with status but also with class. However, there is not always a one-to-one relation with class. It is possible to attain high status or social esteem without necessarily being economically wealthy, though in the larger scheme of things this is not as common as the association of status with 'class', either defined purely in terms of economic position or else inflected ideologically, as in 'classy', which really refers to status rather than class in the strictest sense. It should also be noted that conspicuous consumption went through a process of 'democratisation' during the twentieth century, giving rise to a mass consumerism with increasingly fine distinctions of status linked to goods and services.

At the end of the nineteenth century, the Norwegian-American economist Thorstein Veblen coined the term 'conspicuous consumption' in his book, *The Theory of the Leisure Class*. He spotted a cultural development among the rich – and especially the *nouveau riche* – in the United States that had previously been associated with the European aristocracy. The US bourgeoisie were adopting aristocratic styles and manners, as their European cousins had already done earlier in the century. In order to display their wealth and power, rich Americans projected a leisurely existence untainted by the toil of those beneath them. These people could afford luxury and liked to show it off somewhat more brashly than their European counterparts. At the turn of the nineteenth and twentieth centuries, it would have been far too vulgar even for them to have said, 'If you have it, flaunt it'; but that is exactly what their lifestyle was all about, and it functioned historically as a precursor to the celebrity culture of the present. The original leisure class, however, were much more explicitly concerned with the exclusion of others than the present-day 'democracy' of celebrity – through which anyone might have the opportunity to 'make it' in the public eye – is supposed to be. The early leisure class not only put up barriers to entry at the golf club or the polo park, they also represented models of the good life, became fashion leaders or ideals to emulate, at least in the imagination, rather like present-day celebrities in the entertainment industry such as Hollywood stars, music icons and sports personalities. As Veblen commented, 'the human proclivity to emulate has seized upon the consumption of goods as the means to an invidious comparison'.[12] Wasteful consumption was a particularly important sign of wealth and eminence. Moreover, according to Veblen, sheer extravagance is a value in its own right for the leisure class: 'The standard of reputability requires that dress should show wasteful expenditure, but all wastefulness is offensive to native taste', and 'the more rapidly the styles succeed and displace one another, the more offensive they are to sound taste'.[13]

Veblen himself was not impressed. Michael Spindler has remarked upon 'Veblen's central charge against the leisure class', namely that it was, in Spindler's words, 'hampering cultural advancement by impeding the full adjustment of society to a contemporary industrial economy'.[14] Veblen's hero was not the leisure-class wastrel but the industrious engineer. Veblen extolled the 'instinct of workmanship', craft sensibility and pride in a good job done, in contrast to the wasteful consumption of luxuries in order to impress social inferiors. Here we see in broad outline a fundamental tension in capitalist culture between the old Protestant ethic and an emerging hedonism pioneered by the rich and emulated increasingly throughout the twentieth century by the lower orders. It is a critique that gave rise to disdain for the use of 'status symbols' to attract esteem whilst at the same time such a process became a ubiquitous feature of mass-popular culture in the United States and elsewhere.

Pierre Bourdieu's celebrated *La Distinction*, published in France in 1979 and translated into English in 1984 as *Distinction: A Social Critique of the Judgement of Taste*, may be regarded as a neo-Veblenesque study of consumer culture towards the end of the twentieth century, although, 30 years later, it is already dated in a quite significant way. *Distinction* draws upon research into social patterns of taste conducted in Bordeaux and Paris during the 1960s and '70s. It tells us a great deal about the patterning of cultural consumption in France at that time. The evidence it presents, however, is less relevant now than the general approach which covers the whole field of culture from the artistic preferences of different classes to cuisine, body culture and fashion. Bourdieu's main contention is that the hierarchy of cultural tastes in society is closely aligned to the hierarchy of social classes. He also challenges the 'disinterestedness' of

Kantian aesthetics, unmasking it as ideologically interested in representing the preferences of the *bourgeoisie* – especially the *haute-bourgeoisie* – and downgrading the preferences of the *proletariat*. 'High-brow' taste in the consumption of culture – including, for instance, sport as well as the arts – is a marker of social distinction and superiority (echoing Veblen's satirical account of the leisure class at the end of the nineteenth century) rather than warranted by any objective and universal criterion of aesthetic value. In effect, Bourdieu treats cultural judgement as related to social power, especially with his analytical distinction between the 'pure aesthetic' and the 'popular aesthetic'.[15]

The pure aesthetic places great emphasis on form; hence, in the twentieth century the appreciation of, say, abstract painting. When I think of Bourdieu's conception of the pure aesthetic, I always conjure up the image of the opening of an exhibition at a fine art gallery where the participants are drinking white wine. They speak articulately with one another, sometimes in hushed tones, sometimes loudly, about the qualities of the artworks on display. They are fashionably dressed and sophisticated, though there may also be some scruffy and foul-mouthed characters around who, because they are 'artists', are licensed to be disruptive and offensive, up to a point. The popular aesthetic is quite the opposite of the pure aesthetic. It refers to the taking of a pleasurable interest, particularly in the ordinary and familiar but also in fantasy, eschewing formal refinement and stressing content over form. Widespread scepticism concerning abstract art clearly manifests the popular-aesthetic attitude: 'A child could have done that.' In contrast, preferences for soap operas with good story lines and life-like characterisation, and for Hollywood movies with great special effects and spectacular fantasy, would typically exemplify the popular aesthetic.

Bourdieu's own position shifted over the years. *Distinction* can be read as arguing that different kinds of cultural competence are merely evaluated in an unequal manner – such as classical music being thought to require greater knowledge and appreciative capacity than popular music, whereas, in truth, they are both equally valid. However, in his earlier work during the 1960s,

Bourdieu was concerned about working-class exclusion – and self-exclusion – from legitimate culture, and was sympathetic to a then current wisdom that education should compensate for the social disadvantages of class-familial background, providing working-class children with the cultural competences otherwise acquired in middle- and upper-class homes.[16] Later, his contrast between the pure and popular aesthetic seemed to reverse the hierarchical evaluation in favour of the popular over the pure aesthetic. Yet still later, in the 1990s, Bourdieu became much more concerned about how the commercialism associated with mass-popular culture was encroaching upon the arts and eroding genuinely artistic autonomy.[17]

Bourdieu's treatment of culture and class in *Distinction* is more complex, nuanced and subtly differentiated than is often understood.[18] His was, for instance, an early sighting of the postmodern scrambling of categories that problematises the established hierarchies of 'pure' and 'popular' taste. The crucial question here is: who are the taste-makers? They are typically what Bourdieu calls 'the dominated fractions of the dominant class' who have tended to be the most concerned with art and culture: artists, critics, advisors to patrons and so forth. In economic terms, they were comparatively poor but in regular social contact with the wealthy aristocracy and bourgeoisie. The rich have traditionally been less passionate about art and culture, though they were likely to own it. They would hire artists and musicians, and take advice from critics and dealers.

The number and significance of cultural intermediaries, who mediate new trends and broker cultural change for the rich and for a wider public, grew exponentially over the course of the twentieth century. These include the professions of advertising, journalism, marketing, public relations and of the modern media generally. It follows that cultural mediation and taste need to be seen in the context of various sub-groups or class-fractions that constitute the middle class. For instance, to make a gross generalisation, teachers have typically tended to be more refined in their tastes than, say, managers. And, of course, educationalists – teachers and lecturers – have played a major role in the transmission of legitimate culture. However, they are not normally the taste-makers, and with the advent of cool capitalism their role has been heavily usurped in any event. Today, there is a growth of occupations that broker taste outside the formal institutions of education. These are the cultural intermediaries of the new petite bourgeoisie. To quote Bourdieu: 'The new petite bourgeoisie comes into its own in all the occupations involving presentation and representation (sales, marketing, advertising, public relations, fashion, decoration and so forth) and in all the institutions providing symbolic goods and services.'[19] These occupations tend to be staffed either by those who, having acquired high-cultural competences, decided to exploit their advantage in this respect by mixing high and low cultures, or those without such privileged backgrounds but who are competing for distinction on an upwardly mobile trajectory by valorising popular forms, among them (in Bourdieu's words, written in the 1970s): '"middle-ground" arts such as cinema, jazz, and even more, strip cartoons, science fiction or detective stories'.[20]

The intellectual validation of popular culture that has developed since the 1960s, picking and mixing from high and low, the crossovers and convergence of forms (for instance, in multimedia), and other features of a postmodern culture, are, from a Bourdieuan perspective, driven by business and occupational interests in creating a comparatively new kind of postmodern cultural distinction. Postmodern culture, from this kind of perspective, refers to collapsing hierarchies and blurring boundaries between cultural forms, promoted by the cultural intermediaries of the new petite bourgeoisie.[21] Postmodernism is very much characterised by pastiche and irony. It is evident not only in art, literature, feature films and television but in promotional culture generally, advertising, marketing and public relations. Moreover, the blurring of editorial content and advertising in both the print media and broadcasting is perhaps the most mundane form of a postmodern aesthetic.

While Bourdieu's approach to cultural consumption has been hugely influential, there are several criticisms that can be made of it, not least being the exclusive attention to class and neglect of gender, generational, ethnic and racial differences of culture and taste. His work has been adapted mostly with regard to gender but has been used less with regard to generation and 'race'. Most important here is the argument that distinction strategies not only come from above or from petit-bourgeois fractions competing for symbolic power. They may also come from below, for instance, from younger generations and youth subcultures challenging the tastes of older generations, a fairly obvious point to make. Another significant dynamic to be identified is the influence of ethnic minority culture and, most notably, of American black culture both in the United States and around the world, as noted by Herbert Gans in his revised work on public taste, that bears comparison with Bourdieu's perspective and is a useful complement to it.[22] The influence of minority cultures provides evidence of the lessening prominence and, indeed, the masking of class-cultural relations with the further 'democratisation' of taste.

A further issue around conspicuous consumption, which did not interest Bourdieu, concerns the role of the celebrity in modern culture. The members of Veblen's leisure class were often famous and the object of gossip-columns, especially the younger ones and their sexual liaisons. During the twentieth century, another kind of pseudo-aristocracy emerged, pioneered by the Hollywood star system.[23] Stars became a major attraction for movie-goers and their luxurious and sometimes troubled lives were a matter of mass-popular attention. Such stars are typically *achieved* celebrities, in Chris Rojek's sense, rather than *ascribed* celebrities, that is, famous members of a hereditary aristocracy,[24] though some children of Hollywood and other stars, also born with silver spoons in their mouths and without having achieved much personally, have become celebrities too. Movie actors, singers, musicians and sports people have all typically achieved celebrity status through a combination of their own efforts and the aid of mass publicity. There is a third, latter-day category of *attributed* celebrity, people who are famous simply for being famous, usually fleetingly, such as reality TV participants.

All kinds of celebrity have been recruited to the endorsement of consumer products, bringing their special 'magic' to bear on sales to the public. Celebrities such as English footballer David Beckham, who has made as much money endorsing products as he has playing football. In his book, *Media Sports Stars*, Gary Whannel sums it up: 'In the cultural context of a fascination with style, fashion and décor, celebrities represent our fantasies of lifestyle, luxury, conspicuous consumption and display.'[25] Beckham's wife Victoria, known as 'Posh', the Spice Girls singer, has, since the decline of her own career, and in spite of occasional comebacks, been in the public eye principally as a leading footballer's WAG (wives and girlfriends of famous footballers), featuring regularly as a fashion icon in celebrity magazines like *Heat*, *Hello* and *OK!* In 2007, as David Beckham's football career faltered, he signed for a Los Angeles club and, with the anorexic Victoria, set off to join the Hollywood set. His football career was not over even then, however, as his later dalliance with AC Milan and return to the England fold demonstrated. His lingering attraction for football clubs, though, was as much to do with celebrity merchandising as fancy footwork.

Perhaps the most notable instance of sports-star endorsement is Michael Jordan's association with Nike at the height of his fame in the late 1980s and 1990s. A pair of sneakers, 'Air Jordans', was named after him in homage to his apparently superhuman power to leap. This was an exemplary case of the articulation of a life-enhancing sport (basketball), blackness and global – that is, American – consumer culture under the dominant sign of 'cool'. It is well known that Nike is a prime example of the postmodern consumer capitalism in which manufacturing is outsourced to cheap labour markets around the world, and where unscrupulous businessmen run sweatshops staffed by young women and under-age girls to supply material objects at very low cost to the high-definition brand company. Back in Oregon, Nike organises the whole process from design to marketing but only oversees, and from a considerable distance, working conditions at the actual point of production. In this regard, Nike has required considerable public-relations acumen to protect the brand from successive waves of criticism. Compounding the contradictions, Nike devotes enormous expenditure to sophisticatedly ironic and purportedly responsible advertising in a counter-cultural mode to sell their products, which are endorsed in particular by black celebrities with 'iconic' status such as Jordan and the golfer Tiger Woods. The business assumption is that the branded sign is more valuable than the thing itself, and so has to be cultivated and sustained in what can be an extremely volatile semiotic environment. Brand image is upheld by a kind of 'celebrity democracy', characteristic of the pervasive US ideology of competitive individualism, whereby anyone through their own efforts might achieve stardom.[26] 'Just do it', as the Nike slogan goes, and which has come to be invoked automatically by the tick of its logo, the swoosh (or, to put it facetiously, the swooshtika).

With campaigns such as P.L.A.Y. (Participate in the Lives of American Youth), involving Jordan and others, Nike claimed to be offering a solution to the problems of young blacks, especially by promoting sporting achievement as an alternative to crime. However, sensational stories in the American news media of young men killing people for their Nike sneakers competed with the firm's own claims to be issuing a positive message with a keen sense of social responsibility. Jordan himself became the object of criticism as well as veneration. As Walter La Feber comments:

> The sneaker crimes soon became only part of a larger set of charges leveled against Jordan. He was perhaps the most widely admired African-American in a world where one of every four African-American men was in prison, on parole or on probation. Nearly 40 percent of African men were found to be functionally illiterate. One of every three African-American children was growing up in poverty, even while living in the world's richest country. Jordan worked hard to be a role model but the odds of a 20- to 29-year-old African-American playing in the NBA [National Basketball Association leagues] was 135,800 to 1 (and for Hispanics 33,300,000 to 1).[27]

Jordan was attacked for representing an impossible dream of success that could only further deepen young black men's sense of failure and desperation. Yet he was also defended as representative of black pride and achievement; and, in Nike advertising, doing so in a cool manner that is attractive not only to young blacks but to all youth, sporting and otherwise, seeking personal identity by wearing mass-marketed signs of distinction.

In the 2005 movie, *Be Cool*, adapted from an Elmore Leonard novel,[28] the music producer/gangster, Sin Lesalle, reacts violently to a Russian gangster telling him to 'Be cool, nigger!' Before shooting him dead, Lesalle delivers the following speech:

> How is it you can disrespect a man's ethnicity when you know we've influenced every facet of white America, from our music to our style of dress, not to mention your basic imitation of our sense of cool? Walk, talk, dress, mannerisms, we enrich your very existence, all the while contributing to the gross national product with our achievements in corporate America. And, don't tell me to be cool. I am cool![29]

A long history of black people's oppression in the United States is magically erased in the present by association with a stylisation of success that combines capitalism with a rebellious attitude. In some ways, this process meets its apotheosis in the phenomenon of bling, defined in the Urbandictionary.com as follows:

> ***Bling* 1.** Jamaican slang that has been adopted by some African-American rappers and inserted into popular culture. The term 'bling bling' refers to the imaginary 'sound' that is produced from light reflected by a diamond. **2.** Synonym for expensive, often flashy jewelry sported mostly by African-American hip-hop artists and middle-class Caucasian adolescents. *v.* To 'bling-bling'; the act of sporting jewelry of a highly extravagant, gaudy nature. 'Damn Orlo, you sure be bling-blinging it tonight!' *n.* 'Man, I got tha bling-bling, yo.' **3.** A term for shiny accessories such as chrome wheels, diamonds, etc. *n.* 'You know you be lovin' my bling bling!'[30]

Zenga Longmore traces bling back to Nigeria's Yoruba culture, the source also for *itutu* (cool): 'Every Yoruba man and woman is a walking work of art.'[31] In black musical performance at the beginning of the twentieth century, Jelly Roll Morton's diamond-studded teeth constituted a precursor to Snoop Dogg's blinging style. As Minya Oh comments, 'From day one, hip hop has always been not just about how you rock the mic, but also how you look doing it.'[32]

Back in the 1970s, youth subculture theorists emphasised the appropriation of commodities, their combination with rebel music, demeanour and so on, in a process of *bricolage* that generated meanings resistant to the dominant culture, for instance, in punk.[33] More recently, Paul Willis has argued that the artefacts of commodity culture are all that most young people have and they use them creatively in order to produce their own meanings.[34] Should we then read bling as a romantic sign of subcultural resistance in the old sense or, rather, as a sign of the incorporation, and therefore neutralisation, of rebellion and disaffection into a dominant or mainstream culture? Is the black phenomenon of bling a parodic subversion of wealth and power or the expression of an aspiration to join the unequal scramble for fame and material success, if only through magical symbolisation rather than actuality in the experience of most would-be blingers of distinction? Situating bling in recent history, Tolliver and Osse observe:

> The influences shaping today's form of bling can be attributed to the edgy-slick marriage of two factors: (1) the birth and rise of hip-hop in American culture and (2) the values pumped constantly into the psyche of a young hip-hop nation during the era of Reaganomics. From the late 1970s to the mid-1980s, Hollywood provided a quick fix for a generation left disappointed by the broken promises of the civil rights era. We were fed a high-calorific diet of materialism in movies like *Scarface* (the blueprint for gangster rap), and in TV shows like *Dallas* (who can forget O.G.J.R. Ewing?), *Dynasty* (kindergarten for the likes of Lil' Kim, Trina, and Foxy Brown), *Miami Vice* with its smooth criminals and fly-ass cops; and finally, the sperm that birthed current lifestyle shows like *MTV Cribs – Lifestyles of the Rich and Famous*.[35]

This suggests that bling and hip-hop culture are associated with the decline of the civil-rights movement, disappointment at its accomplishments and a turn away from radical, egalitarian politics towards an embrace of resurgent capitalism since the crisis of the 1970s. Black cool, the cultural face of such a capitalist embrace, is nowhere more evident than in the music business.

In her satirical novel, simply entitled *Bling*, Erica Kennedy traces how the young singer, Marie-Jane Castiglione, renamed Mimi, is turned into a star by the black-music impresario, Lamont Jackson. Marie-Jane is of mixed race, with an Italian mother and an absentee black father. However, Lamont points out that her Italian heritage must be blanked out and her blackness accentuated, though her hair has to be dyed blonde. Lamont informs his protégée: 'White kids buy into coolness as defined by black artists. They want to be down.' Furthermore, he points out, 'Last week for the first time in history, all of the top ten singles on the Billboard chart were by black artists. Did you know that?'[36] The situation in the 2000s is very different from the 1950s when black music was still excluded from the mainstream and confined to a separate chart.

However, it would be mistaken to assume that the currently enormous success of the black culture industry in the US and around the world is entirely novel, since the complicity and incorporation of African-American music and style into white culture and economy has a long and complex history. Historically, Ellis Cashmore argues,

> black culture has been converted into a commodity, usually in the interests of white-owned corporations; ... blacks have been permitted to excel in entertainment only on condition that they conform to whites' images of blacks; and ... blacks themselves, when they rise to the top of the corporate entertainment ladder, have tended to act precisely as whites have in similar circumstances.[37]

Moreover, 'What we popularly accept to be black culture is, on close inspection, a product of blacks' and whites' collaborative effort.'[38] Cashmore calls into question the sign of 'authenticity' that is typically associated with black-inflected culture. Of course, American black music was born out of the suffering of slavery and has taken an acerbic stance towards the mainstream and white audiences, as was so with the decidedly 'cool' bebop maestros such as John Coltrane, Miles Davis and Charlie Parker in the 1940s and '50s. Yet, there is also a lengthy tradition of black entertainment fashioned specifically for the delectation of white audiences. For instance, the Sambo stereotype of buffoonery can be traced from the nineteenth century right up to aspects of Michael Jackson's public persona in recent times.

Cashmore also regards Tamla Motown as 'black music for white folks'. Time and time again, black musical forms – blues, soul, rap, etc. – have been incorporated into a voracious music business of giant corporations, mediated by entrepreneurs like Leonard Chess, Berry Gordy and Russell Simmons who have, in commodifying these sounds for a wider public, blunted their critical edge. Independent companies and labels in black and other music have functioned as research and development tools for the majors. The simple binary of 'sell out'/'authenticity', so frequently cited, does not make adequate sense of the dynamics of the black culture industry. For a start, it makes no sense of the late Michael Jackson, a product of Tamla Motown, with his plasticity and aspirant whiteness, not to mention his allegedly paedophile proclivities. In this and many comparable cases, there has been no real authenticity to sell out.

Rap might at one time have been regarded as a different case. Early on, its antagonistic discourse seemed too hostile for white audiences. We now know for sure that this was not so. The spectacular incorporation of rap represents the astonishing capacity of cool capitalism to repackage virtually anything for mass distribution. So even the most brutal, misogynistic and homophobic features of some strands of rap and hip-hop culture became another consumer item, to be tasted and discarded at will.

Yet the problem persists: how is it that black American culture – especially its music and style – is such a hugely successful source of entertainment on a global scale, actually increasing over the concluding years of the twentieth century and into the twenty-first, at the same time as all the evidence suggests that the material and social conditions of the largest segment of the black population in the United States had deteriorated badly? There is, to be sure, a significant and growing affluent segment of black America too, going through higher education and participating in the business world. Nevertheless, the conditions of existence for many blacks in the US remain those of dire local poverty, and of bleak nihilism associated with criminality and drug culture, only partly relieved in the imagination by ostentatious style, in the largest supposedly egalitarian democracy in the world. Is there some causal though paradoxical connection, then, between black cultural success and conspicuous consumption, on the one hand, and the enduring social subordination of most African-Americans on the other?

Mass Consumerism

During the period in which a 'cool' version of capitalism has risen to prominence, we have witnessed the remarkable revival of an old ideological figure, the sovereign consumer. However, as Russell Keat notes acutely, 'one is unlikely to find much explicit discussion of this concept in standard textbook accounts of a market economy'.[39] Nonetheless, it is the ideological lynchpin of the neo-classical or marginalist economics that matured in the late nineteenth century.[40] Although it never really went away, the figure of the sovereign consumer was reinstated spectacularly in its full glory from the 1970s. That this notion is not always stated clearly in technical economics is perhaps symptomatic of its taken-for-granted and totemic function in everyday commercial culture: the customer as king or queen. Still, in neoclassical economics, the sovereign consumer is a necessary fiction, a construction of an all-rational, calculating subject, forever seeking to maximise marginal utility in consumption choices. Rational consumer decisions, aggregated as demand, are said to trigger supply or, rather, result in success or failure on the supply side in the freely operating market. Nothing should be permitted to interfere with this magical process. The sovereign consumer tends to be invoked explicitly in rational-choice theory in order to back up the argument that taxes should be hypothecated, that is, demonstrably linked to specific expenditures so that citizen-consumers can decide whether the taxation is – or, more likely, is not – beneficial to marginal utility.[41]

There are two basic criticisms of the ideology of sovereign consumption that should be mentioned. First, sovereign consumption ideally depends upon perfect knowledge of what there is actually or potentially available to consume, since consumption is said to determine production. The counter-argument is that perfect knowledge of what could be consumed is impossible and that demand is not simply aggregated from the sum of rational choices made by consumers but is at least partly cultivated by suppliers through advertising and marketing. Thus, production has some determinacy over consumption and the consumer may not be very knowledgeable of how the process actually works in practice. This is an argument well understood by advertisers and marketers, who realise that a purely rational appeal to consumers is inadequate and that their irrational impulses need to be tapped.

The second criticism is similarly well known. It is that there is a false equalisation in the claim that we are all sovereign consumers. Some consumers are more sovereign than others. In effect, it is still a minority of people, according to any universal standard of comparison, who are in a privileged position, by sheer virtue of material advantage, to exercise their freedom of choice in consumption and to consume exactly what they want or even need. The ideological figure of the sovereign consumer is an isolated and utterly de-socialised individual. This was pointed out long ago by Karl Marx in his attempt to explain the social production of consumption.

Marx is generally considered to have privileged the determinacy of production over consumption. But this is only partly true since he sought to formulate a dialectical model of production, distribution, exchange and consumption in which each moment in the circuit has a measure of determinacy over the other moments. In his notebooks, prior to writing the first volume of *Capital*, Marx wrote on the determinacy of consumption:

> Without production, no consumption; but also, without consumption, no production; since production would then be purposeless. Consumption produces production in a double way, (1) because a product becomes a real product only by being consumed. For example, a garment becomes a real garment only in the act of being worn; a house where no one lives

is in fact not a real house; thus the product, unlike a mere natural object, proves itself to be, *becomes*, a product only through consumption. Only by decomposing the product does consumption give the product the finishing touch; for the product is production not as objectified activity, but rather only as object for the active subject; (2) because consumption creates the need for *new* production, that is it creates the ideal, internally impelling cause for production, which is its presupposition. Consumption creates the motive for production; it also creates the object which is active in production as its determinate aim.[42]

Read out of context, that statement might be construed as providing a Marxist warrant for an exclusive attention to consumption as the key moment in the circulation of commodities, a move indeed that has been quite common in contemporary studies of culture in 'the consumer society', with or without a Marxist rationale.[43] However, as Stuart Hall pointed out in his close reading of the 'Introduction' to Marx's *Grundrisse*, Marx, while noting how, in a sense, consumption produces production, at the same time, and unsurprisingly, emphasised how production produced consumption in three senses: 'First, production furnishes consumption with its "object". Second, production specifies the *mode* in which that object is consumed. But, third, production produces the need which its object satisfies.'[44] Surely, this is elementary and should not be forgotten when trying to make sense of consumption in a given historical period with all its admitted complexity taken into account.

To grasp how modern capitalism works as a dynamic system, it is necessary to examine how it is reproduced and how it deals with crises. In the twentieth century, there were two major moments of crisis that led to quite different resolutions: in the 1930s and in the 1970s. Mass consumerism had already developed prior to the first of these systemic crises. Following some hints from Gramsci's *Prison Notebooks*,[45] the Regulation School of political economy has addressed the emergence of Fordism as not just a system of mass production but as a principle of civilisation that inaugurated the modern phenomenon of mass consumerism, 'the formation of a *social consumption norm*', to quote Michel

Aglietta.[46] According to Aglietta, Fordism is an intensive regime of capital accumulation regulated by a particular mode of work and consumption appropriate to it. Inspired by Frederick Taylor's 'scientific management', Henry Ford pioneered the assembly-line in his Michigan motor-vehicle plant during the 1910s, putting into operation an extreme division of labour and precise calculation of working practices. This facilitated the manufacture of standardised motor vehicles at a fraction the cost of craft production. There was little point in manufacturing large numbers of units without being able to sell them. As Ford himself acknowledged, mass production called forth mass consumption. The first step towards creating a mass market for the Model T Ford was to pay Ford workers themselves an exorbitant – for the time – wage of five dollars a day. Other features of social regulation associated with Fordism included monitoring workers' form of life by sending 'sociologists' into their homes to check on the moral hygiene of their domestic arrangements.[47]

Fordism became systemic in the United States, throughout the advanced capitalist world and, also, in the Soviet bloc. It was associated with protected national markets but was susceptible to crises of over-production and falls in demand, which were offset up to a point in the US by credit arrangements to stimulate the rate of consumption. In the capitalist West, strong trade unionism and the welfare state developed with Fordism, particularly spurred on by Roosevelt's New Deal in the 1930s. The stock-market crash of 1929 and the Great Depression of the 1930s did not so much challenge Fordism as strengthen it, with the consequent move towards Keynesian demand-management economics and social-security provision that were characteristic of mature organised capitalism.

Fordism survived the crisis of the 1930s but not that of the 1970s. As Martyn Lee comments:

> The major crisis that was to beset Fordism towards the end of the 1960s and throughout the 1970s was not, as it has often been suggested, the product of some aberrant 'external' factor which destabilised an essentially healthy capitalist system. The crisis was not, for example, the result of the

trebling of the price of oil by the Arab cartel and the ensuing oil crisis of 1973. Nor was it caused by the exhaustion of natural resources. In truth, the major crisis of post-war capitalism was far more fundamental to the logic of capital itself.[48]

In Lee's opinion, 'the Achilles heel of Fordism was its inability to respond swiftly to changing economic circumstances'.[49] The shift into what has been called 'post-Fordism' is exemplified by the move from monolithic and classically bureaucratic companies, where everything is organised in-house, to a much looser network organisation, presaged by the break-up of classic Hollywood in the 1950s, when the major studios were obliged to sell off their first-run cinema chains and began commissioning independent producers.[50] The Hollywood majors survived and grew, however, by occupying the nodal position of power over distribution. Post-Fordism is characterised by a vertical disintegration of business structures, reduced inventories, 'just-in-time' supply and so forth,[51] followed by a reintegration of greater complexity,[52] which is probably more accurately identified as 'neo-Fordism'.

Robin Murray has pointed out that 'In Britain, the groundwork for the new system was laid not in manufacturing but in retailing.'[53] This is of general significance since post-Fordism tends to be most strongly connected to manifest changes in the landscape of consumption, facilitated by computerisation of inventory and delivery, product differentiation and an apparent cornucopia of choice. As Murray remarks, 'the emphasis has shifted from the manufacturer's economies of scale to the retailer's economies of scope'.[54] Greater emphasis is placed on design and the marketing rhetoric is of consumer empowerment: 'Instead of keeping up with the Joneses there has been a move to be different from the Joneses.'[55] All Model T Fords were black. The Ford Focus comes in many different colours and with stylistic and gadgetry variations for the customer to choose from. Yet, the Ford Focus is still a Ford Focus when all is said and done.

Although the economies of mass production necessitated an enormous expansion of mass consumption, this did not happen spontaneously. A great deal of effort was put into creating a consumerist mentality amongst the general public during the early part of the twentieth century, led by the development of what Andrew Wernick has called 'promotional culture as a total complex',[56] combining advertising, marketing and public relations. To trace the roots of that development in the US, Stuart Ewen has examined how 'captains of consciousness' articulated a business ideology that addressed ordinary people not so much as workers but as consumers, from the 1910s through the 1920s, until the rude interruption in this development that occurred with the crisis of the capitalist system in the 1930s.[57] Markets were developed both horizontally, that is, across the expanse of North America, and vertically, down the social hierarchy from the conspicuous consumption of elites to the routine consuming habits of the masses. Quite apart from anything else, this process involved an ideological battle in defence of capitalism against the threat of socialism and the growing appeal of communism in this period. In effect, consumerism was 'an aggressive device of corporate survival'[58] and 'a world view, a "philosophy of life"'.[59] At the beginning of the century advertising appealed to rationality by extolling the virtues of a product. However, in the 1920s, the approach turned from a rational appeal to messages that were intended to appeal to the irrational impulses of ordinary people. This was a particular feature of the early development of what became known as 'public relations'.

The ex-socialist and doyen of American journalism, Walter Lippmann, published his immensely influential book, *Public Opinion*, in 1922. Lippmann had come to believe that the rationality of ordinary people could not be trusted. Rather, their opinions needed to be cultivated in appropriate fashion by the media of mass communications and framed by respectable 'opinion leaders'. The public's consent to capitalist arrangements and the established institutions of representative democracy had to be, in Lippmann's term, 'manufactured'. In one sense, this was no more than an early recognition of the inevitably mediated character of information and knowledge in a large and complexly differentiated society. However, it was stated explicitly against what

Lippmann called 'the original dogma of democracy'[60] on behalf of the enlightened leadership of social and political elites.

Like Lippmann, Edward Bernays (Sigmund Freud's nephew and the man sometimes credited with inventing public relations as a profession as well as promoting his uncle's work in English translation in the United States[61]) was similarly elitist in his arguments and practice. He had been impressed by the Committee for Public Information led by George Creel,[62] in its campaign to turn a sceptical American public into becoming favourably disposed towards US intervention in the First World War, and had himself gone to the Versailles conference at the end of the war with President Woodrow Wilson. Bernays, who published his own book, *Crystallizing Public Opinion*, in 1923,[63] agreed with Lippmann's elite/mass view of society and the need to manipulate artfully the irrational impulses of ordinary people. He added the necessity for the public relations counsel to be au fait with all the channels of mediated communication, to draw upon sociological and psychological research, not only for knowledge but also for legitimising campaigns, and generally to be a student of the public psyche. Bernays's machinations, especially on behalf of American capitalism and its neo-imperialist foreign policies – such as the overthrow of the Guatemalan socialist government in 1954 – over his very long life (he died in 1995 aged 103), are too numerous to itemise here. Suffice to say, his principal aim was to combine commerce with politics, best illustrated by the 'torches of freedom' stunt he orchestrated in 1929. Working for American Tobacco, Bernays arranged for debutantes in the crowd at a women's rights demonstration in New York to light up Lucky Strikes to symbolise female emancipation. This stunt is credited with making cigarette smoking in public by women respectable. Previously, smoking cigarettes in public had been widely looked upon as unfeminine. Lucky Strike became the best-selling cigarette brand in America.

The progress of mass consumerism was rudely interrupted over the next few years with the advent of mass unemployment and serious doubt concerning the capacity of capitalism to survive in the face of an organised alternative – inspired by Marx and apparently under construction in the Soviet Union. Roosevelt's politics was perceived with some justification as being quasi-socialistic. The capacity of the capitalist system to steal the enemy's best tunes has been a key feature of its survival, adaptation and reproduction since that period, as was noted in Chapter 1 of this book. Suspicion of and opposition to capitalism also took the form of the emergence of consumer politics in the 1930s.[64] But whilst establishing standards for consumer products and protecting consumers from unscrupulous practices are undoubtedly progressive, they are by no means necessarily anti-capitalistic. Nor is the critique of advertising. Vance Packard's criticisms of dubious and downright crooked advertising practices from the 1950s, for instance, were not actually opposed to advertising as a persuasive tool of capitalist society.[65]

Corporate America was alarmed by Franklin D. Roosevelt and the upsurge of anti-capitalist sentiment in the 1930s, but it soon found a way to fight back and was aided by the fillip to American manufacturing and markets that resulted from the Second World War. Consumerism, American patriotism and citizenship were welded into a potent ideological mix. The National Association of Manufacturers (NAM), founded in 1895, became an important site for inter-corporate collaboration with the 'American Way' campaigns from 1936 onwards. As Ewen observes:

> To cure the middle class of its growing antagonism toward business, NAM's first general objective was to publicize the idea that there is a harmony of interests linking corporate America with the majority of ordinary Americans. An essential element here would be an attempt to use public relations techniques to provoke involuntary mental associations regarding the 'interrelation and inseparability' of the economic principle of 'free enterprise' and the political principle of 'democracy'. As recounted at a NAM Public Relations conference in 1939, the task was to 'link free enterprise in the public consciousness with free speech, free press and free religion as integral parts of democracy'.[66]

A profound manifestation of the capitalist comeback was the sophisticated corporate-sponsored propaganda about the future at the 1939 World's Fair in New York.

Now, we need to turn briefly to the history of advertising in tracing the emergence and transformation of mass consumerism over the twentieth century. In earlier editions of their comprehensive work, *Social Communication in Advertising*, William Leiss, Stephen Kline and Sut Jhally came up with a four-stage periodisation of the development of advertising strategy and typical modes of address:

> Stage One: The Product-Oriented Approach (1890–1925)
> Stage Two: Product Symbols (1925–1945)
> Stage Three: Personalization (1945–1965)
> Stage Four: Market Segmentation (1965–1985)[67]

The first stage concentrated on providing the potential customer with information about the product itself. In the second stage, 'Products are presented less and less on the basis of performance promise, and more on making them resonate with qualities desired by consumers – status, glamour, reduction of anxiety, happy families – as the social motivation for consumption.'[68] Television becomes very important at the next stage: ads placed the imaginary consumer within the advertisement or increasingly used celebrity endorsement. Already by the fourth stage, market differentiation features much larger than before, targeting products at particular 'lifestyle' segments of the public.

In the third edition of *Social Communication in Advertising*, the earlier four stages are modified as 'frames' and a fifth frame is added, as explained by Jacqueline Botterill: 'To play the game [of the fifth frame] it is necessary to be all-knowing about the practices of promotion, to seem to be uninterested in goods as such and impervious to social rivalry – in short, to be cool.'[69] The preceding four frames, all of which are still to some extent active, are usefully summarised:

> In a nutshell, a cultural frame is the representation of the relation between persons, products and images of well-being that is most characteristic of a specific epoch in marketing and advertising history. The first, called 'idolatory' (1890–1920), emphasizes above all the useful characteristics of the goods themselves; when images of persons appear, they are usually

highly stylized drawings. In the second cultural frame, 'iconology' (1920–1950), products and persons appear together in settings that are heavily determined by symbolic attributes, such as status and social authority. In the third, 'narcissism' (1950–1970), persons come to the fore in ads: products are personalized in terms of feelings such as romance, sensuality, and self-transformation. In the fourth, 'totemism' (1970–1990), the social grouping is the core representation, and products form the emblems of various group consumption practices.[70]

Cool Seduction

Concluding her seminal investigation into advertising and ideology, *Decoding Advertisements*, in which she produced a psychoanalytic critique of mode of address and subject-positioning in ads, Judith Williamson remarked:

> The advertising myth in our society is not a naive one, nor is it ideological brain-washing forced upon us from above. Ads are generally regarded as lies and 'rip-offs'. Whatever *effect* advertising has on people, it is true that their 'conscious' attitude to it will usually be sceptical. ...
>
> ... advertising can incorporate its mythic status (as a lie) into itself with very little trouble. Advertisements will always recuperate by using criticisms of themselves as frames of reference which will finally *enhance*, rather than destroy, their 'real' status. It is like their use of the 'liberated woman'...; 'even she' will go crazy about aftershave lotion adverts. Similarly ads which can incorporate criticisms of themselves have a much higher credibility than those which don't.[71]

In these words, written in the 1970s, Williamson spotted what has become the cornerstone of cool capitalism, namely the capacity to incorporate critique – apparently, any kind of critique – and turn it around to the advantage of capitalism itself. Empirical research on advertising over the past 30 years bears out the acuity of Williamson's observation.

As Jacqueline Botterill points out, a new cultural frame of advertising emerged towards the end of the twentieth century that absorbed 'cool' social mores and consumer attitudes.[72] If the periodic frame of 1880–1920 can be summed up as 'idolatry' (extolling the virtues of the product), the period 1920–1950 named 'iconology' (putting the consumer into the advertising image), 1950–1970 as the period of 'narcissism' (focusing on the self), with 1970–1990 as that of 'totemism' (emphasising group membership), then the current period, dating from the early 1990s, can be called that of '*mise-en-scène*' (featuring products as props for self-construction).[73] This latter-day frame is characterised by fluidity and restless movement in contrast to the static *tableaux vivants* of the preceding period of totemism.

The promotional complex targets notional 'lifestyle' segments in the population, rejecting the homogenising assumptions of mass-society thinking and appropriating a postmodern sense of 'difference'. Key focal groups in this respect are youth and urban professionals, the so-called 'culturati'. Consistent with the assumed scepticism of such groups, the advertising industry denies its own effectiveness, thereby seeking to undercut critical claims concerning its overwhelming influence. A game of reflexive knowingness is played out in the interaction between cool advertising and its most favoured subject groups: the hard-sell is frowned upon and everything is done in a tongue-in-cheek manner, not to be taken seriously. This subtle game is misrecognised by some rather gullible scholars of advertising as merely entertaining artfulness with no necessary economic significance rather than the commercial propaganda that it really is.[74] The disaffection of Douglas Coupland's 'generation X'[75] was a formative influence on present-day advertising rhetoric, though their successors, 'generation Y', are somewhat less sceptical of consumerism and rather more easily ensnared by cool capitalism.

Botterill's account draws upon many insights from the work of Jean Baudrillard, Daniel Bell, Colin Campbell, Thomas Frank and Naomi Klein concerning mass hedonism and the incorporation of counter-cultural themes and postures.[76] Her empirical research, including sample ads and interviews with young people viewing them, substantiates such insights and confirms the ubiquity of a process that I would term 'cool seduction':

> Contemporary young adults are sophisticated judges of promotional messages. They are able to comprehend and find pleasure in texts complicated by ironic, cynical, double meanings and intertextuality, and they expect advertising to be more than just 'typical ads'. Identification is closely related to resistance, and the characters in ads which are unable to resonate authenticity, credibility, and entertainment, and to ally with age demographics and personal sub-cultural tastes, were at best ignored, at worst heaped with scorn. The sample ads presented to subjects invoked heated emotional statements, and subjects quite freely expressed their opinions on matters of aesthetic judgement and character interpretation.[77]

It has even become a dictum of the promotional complex that the meaning of products does not so much emanate from designers and advertisers but rather from the customers themselves, revealed through a subtle process of insider market research and street-wise marketing. An old radical belief that cultural innovation comes from left-field, to use an American term with a much broader connotation than its basic denotation, is thereby incorporated into the reproduction of consumer capitalism. 'Coolhunting', and 'buzz', 'guerrilla', 'stealth' or 'viral' marketing are thus seen as the order of the day within the business, especially when it comes to selling to young people.[78] In his original 1997 *New Yorker* article on 'the art of the coolhunt',[79] Malcolm Gladwell traced the routines of two coolhunters in Boston and New York, Baysie Wightman and DeeDee Gordon, who knew how to talk with the kids, particularly the younger DeeDee. Even the 40-year-old though much younger-looking Baysie, working for Reebok, seemed cool. They were learning about trends in sneaker taste, especially at a brief moment of turning away from the more expensive trainers, inspired by the suicide of Kurt Cobain. These coolhunters were adherents of 'diffusion research', which distinguishes between 'innovators', 'early adopters', 'early majority' and 'late majority'. By the time the late majority have caught on, it is already time to move on to something different.

Typical of business literature, Gladwell recounts anecdotes of fortuitous encounters followed up by systematic market research and marketing campaigns. It is the initial insight that spurs the whole process: 'The key to coolhunting ... is to look for cool people first and cool things later ... Since cool things are always changing, you can't look for them, because the very fact they are cool means you have no idea what to look for.'[80] Joseph Heath and Andrew Potter helpfully summarise the 'three cardinal rules' of coolhunting discerned by Gladwell:

> First, the quicker the chase, the quicker the flight. That is, as soon as we think we have discovered cool, it slips away. Second, cool cannot be manufactured out of thin air. While companies may be able to intervene in the cycle of cool, they cannot initiate it themselves. When we add to these the last rule – that you have to be cool to know cool – cool becomes a closed loop, a hermetic circle in which not only is it impossible to either make or catch cool, but it is impossible to know what it is. Unless, that is, one is already cool, in which case you have no reason to look for it in the first place.[81]

An exemplary case of a cool marketing campaign was the launch of Diesel's Fifty-Five DSM range in England in 2002 by a company of self-styled guerrilla marketers called 'Freewheeling'.[82] It all began in East London with a fake 'pirate' radio station and parties in a local shop and club, creating the impression of demand rising spontaneously from the streets. Mystifying notions of 'not corporate' and 'cult' were built into the campaign, which included a music tour around the country. All the while, the marketing manager of Diesel in London kept a close eye on Freewheeling's activities, not entirely to his satisfaction. This illustrates the manipulative framing of cool marketing that performs a deception of which, in a sense, everyone involved in its unfolding is aware. It is meaningless to call such a complicated process 'coercion' as Douglas Rushkoff has done in his 'wake-up' book entitled *Coercion: Why We Listen to What 'They' Say*. He remarks upon how '"Cool Kids" respond to coercive techniques that acknowledge their ironic detachment'.[83] It is difficult to see quite how this is best named 'coercion' when it manifestly evokes 'consent'. In theories of power, consent is often contrasted with coercion in that the latter is backed up by force, including physical violence, whereas the former suggests ideological acquiescence acceded to more or less willingly. Perhaps it is better to describe the process as 'manipulation', but even that is a questionable or, at least, unfashionable idea in this context.

As Conrad Lodziak remarks quite rightly, 'the language of manipulation has virtually disappeared from explanations of consumerism'.[84] Earlier accounts of consumer society had critiqued the manipulation of needs by the dazzling effect of consumer culture.[85] However, a turn towards the concept of active consumption in scholarly research has severely undermined the force of such earlier critiques and, in effect, endorsed the defence of consumerism on the grounds of a pervasive sense of the popular empowerment that is promoted by consumer capitalism.[86] Lodziak does not seek to resuscitate a critique of the ideological manipulation of consumers. He believes instead that the sheer hegemony of consumer culture is much exaggerated by both business interests and uncritical scholars. Lodziak argues, however, that capitalism manipulates needs through its control of material resources and the alienation of labour. These manipulated needs permit 'a *limited autonomy*'[87] that is endlessly documented and celebrated by students of consumer choice. Crucial features of capitalism's manipulative power are how it controls people's time and offers only private solutions to public problems of meaninglessness and loss of identity. In effect, Lodziak proposes a do-it-yourself cultural solution whereby paid labour takes up less time and people are freed to produce for their own needs, an essentially anarchistic proposition, inspired by the thinking of André Gorz.[88]

While Lodziak may be correct in stressing the material conditions of life against the contrasting culturalist critique of ideological manipulation, on the one hand, and the equally culturalist defence of consumer empowerment on the other, he tends to underestimate the ideological and psychological aspects of consumer culture – how insatiable desires are inculcated but, by definition, must never be satisfied, so that ever more consumption is sought in order to keep the wheels of the system turning. Without delving here into the tortuous debates over basic needs and the social construction of needs, it is still necessary to consider how people are positioned and addressed as consumers under advanced capitalist conditions; and, indeed, how the process extends globally to frame the aspirations of 'developing' parts of the world, demonstrated most dramatically over the closing years of the twentieth century by communist China's turn onto the capitalist road both economically and culturally.[89]

Leslie Sklair talks of how

> The culture-ideology project of global capitalism is to persuade people to consume not simply to satisfy their biological and other modest needs but in response to artificially created desires in order to perpetuate the accumulation of capital for private profit, in other words, to ensure that the capitalist global system goes on forever.[90]

Further on, Sklair elaborates upon the culture-ideology of consumerism:

> The transformation of the culture-ideology of consumerism from a sectional preference of the rich to a globalizing phenomenon can be explained in terms of two central factors, factors that are historically unprecedented. First, capitalism entered a qualitatively new globalizing phase in the 1960s. As the electronic revolution got under way, the productivity of capitalist factories, systems of extraction and processing of raw materials, product design, marketing and distribution of goods and services began to be transformed in one sector after another. This golden age of capitalism began in the USA, but spread a little later to Japan and Western Europe and other parts of the First World, to the NICs [newly industrialising countries] and to some cities and enclaves in the Third World. Second, the technical and social relations that structured the mass media all over the world made it very easy for new consumerist lifestyles to become the dominant motif for these media.[91]

Sometimes it is said by critics that consumers are 'exploited' by the capitalist market. That, however, is stretching the concept of exploitation too far and weakening its force in the critique of labour exploitation, which remains one of the most important reasons for questioning capitalism, the other being ecological damage. It is perhaps better to talk of 'seduction'. Arguably, seduction might be seen as the counterpoint in the sphere of consumption to exploitation in the sphere of production in a mature and globalised capitalist system. After all, capitalism has many attractions, especially insofar as it promises to realise all people's desires in consumption, though offers rather less realisation in production. Several commentators have argued that self-identity has shifted from work into the sphere of consumption – that people realise themselves in what they consume, and, moreover, that this is experienced as freely chosen. The allure of capitalism in that sense is seductive and even erotically charged.

Baudrillard recognised the process in his own distinctive way with the McLuhanesque notion of 'cold seduction', connected to the eroticism of consumption and redolent of a simulated existence governed by capitalist imperatives of exchange. He linked this to the operations of media: 'the solicitation of advertisements and polls, all models of the media and politics, no longer claim credence, only credibility'[92] – a typically gnomic aphorism. He located cold seduction in 'the ludic realm' under 'the "narcissistic" spell of electronic and information systems, the cold attraction of the terminals and mediums that we have become, surrounded as we are by consoles, isolated and reduced by their manipulation'.[93]

From a more conventionally sociological point of view, Bauman is interested in the role of seduction in social control and the integration of a population into the capitalist way of life. He contrasts seduction with repression and says that outright repression is only marginally significant under conditions of mature capitalism. He points out that the consumer market's 'main attraction, perhaps, is that it offers freedom to people who in other areas of their life find only constraints, often experienced as oppression'.[94] It is essential that the seduced subject feels free to choose, even though the scope of choice may in fact be very limited, outmanoeuvred by the surreptitious machinations of capital. As Bauman argues:

> Seduction is the paramount tool of integration (of the reproduction of domination) in a consumer society. It is made possible once the

market succeeds in making the consumers dependent on itself. Market-dependency is achieved through the destruction of such skills (technical, social, psychological, existential) as do not entail the use of marketable commodities; the more complete their destruction, the more necessary become new skills which point organically to market-supplied implements. Market-dependency is guaranteed and self-perpetuating once men and women, now consumers, cannot proceed with the business of life without turning themselves to the logic of the market. Much debated 'needs creation' by the market means ultimately creation of the need of the market.[95]

Although Ewen, in his history of consumerism, saw consumer seduction as being largely focused on women positioned as 'housewives' and in need of beauty products,[96] Bauman's conception of the seduced consumer is not gendered. Nevertheless, today some of the fiercest kinds of cool seduction are focused upon females, especially young females, as documented by Alissa Quart in her research on 'the buying and selling of teenagers'. She examines how young girls are recruited to do unpaid viral marketing work in order to be 'cool'. As Quart says, the basic rule of marketing is to 'get 'em while they're young'.[97] This is successfully achieved today not only by involving young girls in selling cosmetics but in establishing a generalised consumer identification associated with 'cool' commodities across the genders so that nobody escapes the seductive lure of latter-day capitalism and its 'icons'. Neal Lawson comments on the role of cutting-edge products in this respect: 'An iPod and the right phone are now the essential trappings of youth – not just because they let you talk or listen to music at your convenience, but because of what they say about you.' The general message is that 'we are what we consume rather than what we produce'.[98] Before proceeding to consider that particularly prominent form of commodity fetishism today, it is necessary to pause for a moment on Bauman's category of failed or flawed consumers.[99]

Those who do not make it as successful consumers are marginalised and at least potentially troublesome. Because they are excluded from the lures of consumerism, an exclusion which is unlikely to be a free choice of their own, they must be kept an eye on, subjected to the discipline of Foucauldian panopticism.[100] They constitute an 'underclass', the 'collateral damage'[101] of cool capitalism, pregnant with criminality and the punishment it elicits, an ever-present warning to consumers to stay within the fold, and representing an ominous prospect of failure to the young apprentices of consumerism.

Commodity Fetishism and Mobile Privatisation

Karl Marx began his disquisition on capitalism with an analysis of the commodity. He particularly noted how exchange value distorted use value, evoking a curiously magical quality associated with the commodity, the kind of phenomenon that has since been thought about in terms of a Baudrillardian notion of sign value. That the price of a commodity should be more significant than its use was strange; that its symbolic value should become yet more important than even its price is peculiar indeed. As Marx remarked:

> A commodity appears at first sight an extremely obvious, trivial thing. But its analysis brings out that it is a very strange thing, abounding in metaphysical subtleties and theological niceties. So far as it is a use-value, there is nothing mysterious about it, whether we consider it from the point of view that by its properties it satisfies human needs, or that it first takes on these properties as the product of human labour. It is absolutely clear that, by his activity, man changes the forms of the materials of nature in such a way as to make them useful to him. The form of wood, for instance, is altered if a table is made out of it. Nevertheless the table continues to be wood, an ordinary, sensuous thing. But as soon as it emerges as a commodity, it changes into a thing that transcends sensuousness. It not only stands with its feet on the ground, but, in relation to all other commodities, it stands on its head, and evolves out of its wooden brain grotesque ideas, far more wonderful than if it were to begin dancing of its own free will.[102]

It is extraordinary how 'the definite social relation between men themselves ... assumes here, for them, the fantastic form of a relation between things'. Furthermore, 'fetishism ... attaches itself to the products of labour as soon as they are produced as commodities'.[103] The world under capitalism, in effect, appears as an 'immense collection of things'. These things loom much larger in consciousness than the reality of their production by human beings. The commodity contains within itself a process of concealment, a masking over, a profound distortion of the real conditions of existence. This is an ideological process at the very heart of capitalism. To say, however, that people tend to fetishise human-made things, specifically commodities for exchange, imbuing them with magical powers of a super-human kind, is a banal enough observation. Less commonplace are the deeply embedded frames of meaning that provoke such a banal observation. As we shall see in the next chapter, one such frame is the absolute necessity of market forces, functioning somewhat like the laws of physics. Here, however, we shall consider a related ideological frame – technological determinism, which denies human agency and reifies technology as the god of all things.

Today, the term 'technology' is often used to refer exclusively to information and communication technologies (ICTs). The most profound thesis on the social and cultural significance of such digital 'new media' is Manuel Castells's three-volume treatise, *The Information Age*,[104] in which he declared the advent of 'the network society', followed recently by his international collaborative work, *Mobile Communication and Society*.[105] Although compelling in many ways, Castells's thesis is especially vulnerable to the critique of technological determinism.[106] In his defence, Castells argues that the restructuring of capitalism and communism (in effect, its collapse) and the cultural and social movements from the 1960s and 1970s (including feminism) are of equal importance to 'the information technology revolution' in fashioning the world of the third Christian millennium. Yet, in spite of that caveat, Castells lavishes inordinate attention on ICTs and is probably usually read as the latest guru of technology's all-powerful determinacy.

There is no doubt that digitalisation and satellite communications have had enormous consequences, with regard, for instance, to various combinations of image and sound transmission, bringing about technological convergence and proliferating communicational services and gadgets such as the online mobile phone in hybrid combination with locational, musical and televisual features. Nevertheless, the processes by which such technologies come about and are used are much more complicated than the usual hype would suggest. Technological determinism assumes a linear process from scientific research and discovery to technical invention and implementation, with immensely consequential social and cultural impact, unfolding more or less smoothly over time. It is not just a simplistic model of socio-technical change but also a dominant ideological assumption, nowadays allied especially to free-market economics and politics.

By contrast, in his study of television Raymond Williams argued that technologies are developed and implemented in a complex set of determinations that are not only scientific and technical but also include economic, political and cultural factors.[107] Moreover, decisions about research funding, technical application and product development are deliberate, not always successfully so, but they are always made and sought intentionally. According to Brian Winston, there has to be a 'supervening social necessity' behind the combination of elements that typically result in a new medium of communication.[108] In the case of cinema, for instance, the formation of a mass entertainment market and the sociality of theatre in an urban-industrial society were at least as important determinants as, if not more so than, the inventiveness of 'great men' – the myth of orthodox cinematic history. As well as supervening social necessities accelerating the development of a medium at a particular moment in time, there is the brake on development that Winston calls 'the "law" of the suppression of radical potential'. In the case of the denigration of 16 mm film, its use thereby confined to 'amateurs' and 'subversives' for many years until taken up for news reporting, classic Hollywood's expensive 35 mm 'standard' was a means of controlling entry to the industry. There are accelerators, brakes and indefinite delays, then, in the development of communication technologies, no doubt most decisively for economic reasons but also as affected by cultural and political determinations. Technological innovation is quite definitely not an autonomous force in the invention of new products and the changing of society. Yet it is typically represented as such in expert and mass-popular discourses.

No kind of technological commodity is fetishised to a greater extent than the cluster of portable devices that now exist for computing, telephony and Internet-connectedness on the move, especially by young people. Here, 'cool' kicks in, sometimes with a vengeance. To quote from a few recent headlines: Steve Jobs, chief executive of Apple, like the gadgets his company produces, is 'The Coolest Player in Town';[109] yet, before long, 'the iPod is Losing its Cool';[110] Google is 'an insanely cool new search engine'[111] while 'Microsoft Struggles to Regain its Cool Amid the Upstarts'.[112] Attachment to these technologies is particularly associated with 'Generation Y' or what some have called 'the Google Generation'.[113] They are digital savvy, keener on the Internet than on television, and treat the mobile phone as a badge of identity and an essential tool of social life. Yet, they are also a generation facing economic difficulties with rising costs of higher education and housing plus the undermining of employment rights and pensions, due to the advances of neoliberalism, something which is hardly uppermost in the mind of a typical 20-year-old in otherwise privileged circumstances. Practiced in the sphere of consumption yet disadvantaged in the sphere of production, this is a generation of 'the affluent society'[114] quite possibly – indeed probably – facing an extremely stressful future, resulting in a 'generational crisis' that we will consider later in the book.

Ultimately, the technical development of communication technologies is not as interesting as their use and how they actually operate in relation to ways of life. It is a mistake, however, to fall into an ahistorical understanding of the present, impressed exclusively by the novelty of now, without exploring the unfolding of social and cultural processes over time. We need to situate recent developments around mobile communications in relation to the socio-technical transformations of modernity. That means, for example, recalling the historical role of television. To make sense of the sociality of television (in the first instance, but it was also of broader significance), Williams formulated the notion of mobile privatisation. For him, this referred to a relatively new patterning of everyday life associated with urban-industrial society in general as much as to the specific use of communication technologies. First, Williams notes 'two apparently paradoxical yet deeply connected tendencies of modern urban industrial living: on the one hand mobility, on the other hand the more apparently self-sufficient family home'. Developments in transport, especially the building of the railways and mass migration in steam ships, had increased the mobility of people and peoples. Yet at the same time the atomisation of modern societies had concentrated life outside paid work in the small family home. There had emerged 'an at once mobile and home-centred way of living: a form of *mobile privatisation*'.[115] Broadcasting fitted perfectly into this arrangement, not only with the radio and television replacing the hearth as the site of gathering together in the home, but also in giving access to events occurring at a distance.

The concept of mobile privatisation captures the contradictory role of television as a characteristic feature of modern life. Television facilitates a much expanded albeit imaginary mobility through the vast array of representations available to the ordinary viewer. Here, a distinction can be drawn between physical mobility – facilitated by modern transport – and the virtual mobility that is facilitated by telegraphy and broadcasting from the late nineteenth through to the mid twentieth century. Domesticity becomes the focus of expanded consumerism, labour-saving devices and the like; and indeed broadcasting's typical mode of address to the listener and viewer in the domestic setting with all that this entails. To some extent, broadcasting would come to schedule activities in the home: daytime programmes addressed to 'the housewife', children's programming when the kids get home from school, 'the toddler's truce', 'family viewing', adult viewing after 'the watershed' when children should be in bed. And with the advent of satellite communications from the 1960s it became possible, from the comfort of the home, to see events actually unfolding simultaneously on the other side of the world.

Returning to the concept of mobile privatisation several years after formulating it, Williams remarked: 'It is an ugly phrase for an unprecedented condition.' It was not just that people in urban-industrial societies were living in small family units (the nuclear family replacing the extended family) but that many were comparatively isolated and private individuals while 'at the same time there is a quite unprecedented mobility of such restricted privacies'.[116] Williams notes that in his novel *Second Generation*, published in the 1960s,[117] he had commented upon the sociality of motor car traffic:

> Looked at from right outside, the traffic flows and their regularities are clearly a social order of a determined kind, yet what is experienced inside them – in the conditioned atmosphere and internal music of the windowed shell – is movement, choice of direction, the pursuit of self-determined private purposes. All the other shells are moving in comparable ways but for their own different private ends. They are not so much other people, in any full sense, but other units which signal and are signalled to, so that private mobilities can proceed safely and relatively unhindered. And if all this is seen from outside as in deep ways determined, or in some sweeping glance as dehumanised, that is not at all how it feels like inside the shell, with people you want to be with, going where you want to go.[118]

So, mobile privatisation is not a social phenomenon confined to broadcasting in general and television in particular. It also includes driving a motorcar either by yourself or with a few significant others as passengers, separate from yet coordinated with, in some remote sense, strangers doing the same thing in their little, shell-like worlds. For Williams, these phenomena – watching television, driving a car – are synecdoche for a larger whole, 'a now dominant level of social relations'. He links this larger whole to the market system: 'The international market in every kind of commodity receives its deep assent from this system of mobile-privatised social relations.'[119] The shell, to return to our given examples, might be a house or a car, sites of private consumption and mobility.

It is not difficult to conjure up other examples appearing at a later date than Williams's preliminary ruminations on mobile privatisation: online desktop and laptop computing, portable telephonic and music-playing devices, being among the most obvious. An additional point to make, of course, has to do with screening – certainly in the convergence of computing and television, whereby everything is seen, literally, through a screen, mediated and packaged for consumption, sometimes quite active consumption.

Mobility is now such a hot topic that a new school of sociology has even been announced in its name.[120] During the 1990s the mobile phone became the coolest 'icon' of the age. In the 2000s its position has looked vulnerable to usurpation by the iPod/mp3 player. The most seductive victor, however, is a hybrid of the two: the all-purpose mobile communication device. The history of the mobile phone – or cell phone – is an exemplary one with regard to technological innovation and turnover, changing patterns of sociality and consumer seduction. The transition from first generation (1G) to second generation (2G) mobile phones – the shift from besuited business users, with their large and expensive bricks on display, to mass-popular use, particularly as a leisure medium for the young – was dramatic to say the least. Suddenly everyone seemed to have one and was using it incessantly. The transition to third generation (3G) and fourth generation (4G) devices (which enable online access to multiple services) has been much more stuttering, with an endlessly awaited and ever delayed 'tipping point' about to be reached.

Fortunes were made from the mass-marketisation of 2G, which eventually meant that phones themselves could be literally given away by the telecoms companies in order to sign up more and more customers to contracts. However, with such rapid success the market became saturated. The business dynamic then required the introduction of replacement devices and services at much greater cost to consumers (WAP, etc.). In the late 1990s, at the height of the dot.com boom, several countries, such as Britain and Germany, sold 3G franchises to the telecoms companies at astronomical figures in the billions, whether counted in dollars, euros or pounds. But very soon consumer reluctance to move on put revenue and future profits at risk. This can only be explained by the remarkably swift and embedded sociality that was fostered by actual 2G use. People were apparently satisfied with their 2G phones and were not much attracted by the extravagant promises of 3G.

Ethnographic research conducted in the late 1990s and early 2000s goes some way to explaining why this was so.[121] A great deal of attention is lavished in the trade press upon the practice of early adopters, those readily seduced by advertising claims and most enthusiastic about tooling up with whatever the market has to offer. However, these are not necessarily the most significant users. There are discernible patterns of mass use that are much more significant and, indeed, consequential for the take-up of new communication technologies. By the mid 1990s, mobile phones had become a striking feature of youth culture, seen as desirable objects in themselves and essential tools for the conduct of everyday social life. In fact, the typical compact design of mobile phones was especially amenable, and not accidentally so, to the young, with their tiny buttons and quick-finger facilities, including text messaging, the enormous success of which was never anticipated by the telecoms companies. For the young, however, it was cheap, easy and, equally important, mysterious to the grown-ups. Older people with failing eye sight and slower sensory-motor skills found it harder to use mobiles.

The mobile may at one time have been a luxury, but for some users it became a necessity. For keeping in touch with a circle of friends, arranging meetings and simply being in society, the mobile was seen widely as a must-have tool by the young, children and increasingly older people as well. This was accentuated by the fad of picture-messaging a few years ago. Research also shows that the mobile phone facilitated the routine conduct of work and domestic management for older groups. For example, working mothers found the mobile invaluable when arranging child care and keeping tabs on the kids. Mundane use of this kind became ubiquitous. The value of more expensive 3G mobile communications was not so obvious to such users.

At the same time, significant developments were occurring in mobile music-listening. The Sony Walkman was the pioneering device of the late 1970s and 1980s. It went through a typical process of diffusion, beginning with the young and eventually capturing the attention of older generations as well. It was designed and marketed deliberately in order to do so.[122] The

Walkman was originally a miniaturised cassette tape machine that played back but did not record. Thus, it took a device both of production and consumption and turned it into one solely of consumption. Cassettes had to be otherwise recorded or bought already recorded. Notionally, the earplugs allowed only the listener to hear, though others might be rather too well aware of a crackly noise nearby. The Walkman epitomised mobile privatisation in the 1980s. The individual could be cocooned in his or her own private audio-space separate from others in public space. It was objected to on similar grounds to the way the mobile was objected to later. There were health panics[123] and complaints about the breakdown of communication brought about, paradoxically, by a communication device.[124]

The Apple iPod and kindred mp3 devices slot neatly into the space carved out by the Sony Walkman. As the market leader in mobile devices for listening to music downloaded from the Internet, the iPod set the tone. Apple is one of the 'coolest' of business corporations, combining innovation, profitability and a rebellious style. Apple users have been encouraged to see themselves as 'outlaws', somehow distancing themselves from corporate capitalism while simultaneously contributing to the coffers of the same. 'Cool' is actually the dominant tone of capitalism today. Corporations have incorporated counter-cultural traditions and deployed signs of 'resistance' in order to market their wares. Where the original 'spirit of capitalism', often associated with puritanical Protestantism, emphasised deferred gratification and hard work, the 'new spirit of capitalism' is much more hedonistic and, indeed, 'cool'. Immediate gratification is sought and sold in the sphere of consumption. Consumers are, in effect, seduced by the delights of high-tech and 'cool' commodities, promising to satisfy their every desire, especially if they are 'different' and vaguely rebellious in tone. Great stress is placed on individual autonomy and the more complex notion of 'individualisation'.[125] The individual perpetually on the move, accompanied by a personal soundtrack and in constant touch, is the ideal figure of such a culture.[126]

In February 2006, the 3GSM World Congress was held in Barcelona.[127] This was an industry event, not something to trouble the mind of the ordinary punter. The key problem of the Congress, however, was to find ways of encouraging consumers to do more with their mobile communication devices. Executives at the conference will have been supplied with plenty of market research to tell them what consumers could reasonably be encouraged to want. It was still proving easy to sell new ringtones to consumers in large numbers but not much else. Picture-messaging had been a bit of a disaster, partly because of incompatibility between different systems, and because it was only a fad anyway. The reluctant customer was the industry's biggest problem. New services – such as email, music downloads, gaming and Internet access – were simply not selling in sufficient volume from the business point of view, despite all the hype in the trade press and on the specialist pages of the news press.

By this time, however, everyone knew what 'the killer application' (in the unfortunate term used by the industry in spite of occasional health scares over the effects of radiation) was, at least in broad terms: the hybrid device, most notably, combining telephony with music. Steve Jobs's announcement of the iPhone in January 2007 was greeted with great excitement, although other manufacturers had already produced such combinations. The 'cool' mystique of Apple, however, scored high, especially due to its elegance of design, led by Jonathan Ive.[128] Still, it was thought, though probably with little conviction, that more people could be persuaded to watch television on their mobile phones as well. The story has become very familiar over a number of years now. It is the story of successive false starts and re-launches, recurrent declarations that have all been heard before. If it were only about technology, all this would be incomprehensible. But, it is not. It is about sociality, cultural preference and economic contradictions too.

The mobile phone has been called an *Apparatgeist*.[129] Enthusiastic commentators on mobile communications tend to stress interactivity, and the opportunities for user/consumers to act as producers, though even such commentators are wary of overstating the case. For example, Gerard Goggin, in discussing how consumers are thus empowered, also notes a 'new myth' of the mobile phone in the celebration of the frequently remarked upon photographs taken and transmitted by 'citizen-reporters' from the London Underground trains that were bombed in July 2005.[130] It is doubtful, as Goggin recognises, to what extent such indistinct images actually informed public understanding of these events. Goggin also registers, in passing, the health fears reported upon by the Stewart Report of 2000.[131] Anxiety about the possible effects of radiation from the handsets themselves and from network towers periodically erupt and are usually dismissed as alarmist.[132] Use of mobile phones is a classic risk society issue, insofar as nobody at present really knows the extent of the risk.[133] It may take several years to really be sure about the safety or hazardousness of mobile communications.

Another crucial issue with regard to mobile communications and 'wi-fi' is their impact upon economic development in poorer parts of the world, most notably in Africa where landline infrastructure is poor and underdeveloped. Castells and his colleagues note the possibility that mobile communications may be leaping a stage of technological development.[134] This might well be true. Telecoms companies are producing cheaper mobile technology for use by the poor with the prospect of closing 'the digital divide' in an unequal world. However, the relation of mobile communications to the Third World and the development of underdeveloped regions has other aspects than simply that of a leap in technological stages. For a start, the telecoms companies have turned towards market diffusion in poorer parts of the world precisely because of the near total saturation of wealthier markets following the rapid take-up in the 1990s, and the difficulties of persuading users to move on to more expensive 3G and 4G handsets and services.

In their research on the mobile phone industry for SOMO, the Centre for Research on Multinational Corporations, Joseph Wilde and Esther de Haan observe: 'these days it is difficult to imagine conducting business or communicating with friends and family without a mobile phone'.[135] Seen entirely from the point of view of consumption, the story is about the social embedding and diverse uses of a set of marvellous new technologies. However, seen in a more complex framework that focuses upon the circuit of commodities and culture, including the actual production of such devices, a rather less positive picture emerges. Wilde and de Haan look at the structure of the industry, including original equipment manufacturers (OEMs), famous companies like Motorola and Nokia that design and produce mobile phones; and contract manufacturers (CMs), contracted by OEMs, that include electronic manufacturing services (EMSs) and original design manufacturers (ODMs). With regard to suppliers, there is an important distinction between first tier (direct) suppliers that produce handsets for an OEM and sub-tier suppliers that produce components for sale to manufacturers further up the supply chain. As the supply chain is traced from OEMs down to sub-tier suppliers the picture becomes increasingly murky.

Compared to the garment industry, outsourcing was until recently a much smaller part of the industry in mobile phone manufacture. In the 2000s, a dramatic change has been taking place, finally opening the industry up to the kind of critical scrutiny that has been applied to the garment industry not only since the 1990s, but going all the way back to Marx and Engels's enquiries into the working conditions, especially of women, in the textile industry in the mid nineteenth century.[136] Of course, since then, manufacturing has become much more global, with a general shift away from the original industrial states to newly industrialising countries (NICs). Such countries have established Export Processing Zones (EPZs) or Special Economic Zones (SEZs), where labour and environmental laws are relaxed in the interests of 'development'. In consequence, working conditions, hours of work, accommodation and rates of pay are shockingly poor by the standards of affluent parts of the world. By the mid 2000s Motorola had outsourced 30 per cent of its manufacturing to such places and Nokia 20 per cent. These companies have corporate social responsibility policies which they can always hide behind when criticisms are made of what actually happens on the ground where monitoring fails or has never been conducted seriously – in the SEZs of China for instance. Wilde and de

Haan comment on the economic importance of the latter, in a nominally 'communist' China going through a period of primitive capitalist accumulation:

> One reason for the incredible industrial development boom in southern China is the government's decision to create Special Economic Zones (SEZs) in southern cities like Shenzhen and Yuhai. When the Shenzen SEZ was first created in the early 1980s, Shenzen was a small fishing village that has since exploded into an export-manufacturing leviathan, producing 45% of the world's watches, one-third of the world's shoes and much of China's exportable electronic goods.[137]

For instance, Giant Wireless Technology, which has a large plant and extensive dormitory facilities in Shenzen, is a first-tier supplier to Motorola and several other mobile communication companies. Also in Shenzen, Hivech Startech Film Window produce lenses for Motorola phones. The SOMO report contains a case study of the health and safety conditions at Hivech Startech. There is insufficient ventilation, the air contains high concentrations of n-hexane, which causes damage to peripheral nerves, muscle waste, atrophy, dermatitis, nausea, jaundice, and may induce coma. It is banned in more developed countries. There is evidence of ill health issuing specifically from that plant, for which the company provides no compensation.

The examples from Shenzen are by no means isolated in China, and are also, for that matter, rife in countries like India and Thailand. In India, for example, it has been estimated that wages in mobile phone manufacturing constitute only 1–2 per cent of production costs. Excessive working hours, illegally low wages and unpaid overtime are widespread features of the industry in spite of leading companies' officially stated corporate social responsibility policies. Often they are not worth the paper they are written on. Unionisation is not allowed in SEZs, living conditions in dormitories are bad, women's rights ignored. These facts concerning extreme exploitation and other issues – for instance, the role of coltan in fuelling the Congolese civil war[138] – are discomforting, to say the least, for the taken-for-granted convenience of mobile communications in the everyday life of contemporary consumer culture.

4
MARKET VALUES

At this juncture, it is necessary to reiterate the historical scheme of capitalist development that was traced in Chapter 1. Broadly, three phases of capitalist development have been identified: liberal, organised and neoliberal. The liberal phase is that of classical capitalism when business and trade developed in a more or less unregulated manner in various national pockets. This was the phase of capitalism that Marx analysed in the nineteenth century, the origins of which Max Weber sought to explain in relation to religious belief. During the mid twentieth century, capitalism became 'organised' not only due to the growth of large corporations and monopolistic practices but very much in response to the socialist challenge represented by radical labour movements in the West and the formation of 'actually existing socialism' in the East. In the late twentieth century, with the collapse of communism and the retreat of social democracy, the phase of organised capitalism with its quasi-socialistic features, having already been called into question, approached complete dismantlement. In certain respects, there was a reversion to the liberal phase, qualified, however, by novel features, some of which are characterised in this book as 'cool capitalism'.

Much of what can be said of the new formation has to do with the hegemony of market values. Not even dyed-in-the-wool socialists would today deny the efficacy of a market mechanism in regulating supply and demand, and in setting prices. The failed history of Soviet central planning and the inefficient record of command economies generally have made this so. However, there are limits to the efficacy of the market mechanism that continue to incite political controversy. The market mechanism is most evidently in doubt with regard to what used to be called 'natural monopolies', where competition was considered less efficient and in many cases demonstrably inefficient, quite apart from being socially inequitable, compared to unitary public administration. The most prominent examples include, for instance, the supply of water, gas and electricity; healthcare and medicine; compulsory education; and certain kinds of transport such as railway systems. In these cases, the value of competitive supply and consumer choice is questionable, although the very same services are indeed subjected to 'market forces' around the world; and increasingly so with privatisation and globalisation during the currently neoliberal phase of capitalist development.

Recognising the efficacy of the market mechanism – particularly competition between small and medium-sized suppliers in, say, the clothing and food industries – is quite different from endorsing the total saturation of culture and society by market values. Moreover, it is not only socialists who object to exploitation of workers and unfair trading arrangements for suppliers across the globe in the routine operations of a market economy under neoliberal conditions. The value of the market mechanism, which is very much about communications, is not equivalent to an unquestioning adherence to market values whatever the human costs.

'Market values' is a vernacular term that is readily understood, but which is virtually synonymous in certain respects with the more technical meaning of 'business ideology'. As we saw in the last chapter, capitalist business has been very active ideologically when under threat, as it was during the 1930s. Typically, in the United States, this involved a direct appeal to 'the consumer', addressing citizens in effect as consumers. If the citizen is reduced rhetorically to the position of a consumer, then we are definitely on the terrain of market values in a pejorative sense.

The original use of 'ideology' was pejorative, but not all uses of the word are negative in meaning. Perhaps the most common use of 'ideology' now refers to political doctrine. So, for example, conservatism, liberalism and socialism are political doctrines that are often called 'ideologies', but with no necessarily pejorative connotation. Interestingly, the substance of such designation is not always generally agreed. Conventionally, conservatism means preserving and protecting what already exists, being resistant to change, maintaining established ways of doing things rather than supporting reform. Yet, 'Conservatives' such as Margaret Thatcher in Britain during the 1980s wanted to change things, and to a significant degree succeeded in doing so. Some commentators said that Thatcher was not actually a 'conservative' at all, but a 'Liberal', in the nineteenth-century sense, espousing the politics of *laissez-faire* and dynamic innovation against conservatism, at least with a small 'c'. Calling Thatcher a 'Liberal' would have been very confusing for many US citizens since 'liberal', in the lower case, roughly means 'left-wing' in the United States. Thatcher was not left-wing. She was, I think we can safely say, right-wing and, therefore, appropriately labelled a 'Conservative'. Her politics, however, certainly favoured liberal capitalist development. Or, should we say *neoliberal* capitalist development? Nomenclature in this respect becomes ever more confusing when you consider the fact that mainstream social democrats today – 'socialists', in a sense – are keen on 'market values'. Yet, socialism is supposed to be opposed to market values, at least according to Thatcher back in the 1980s and to other neoliberals now. Are such mainstream social democrats, then, neoliberals? Yes, actually, they are, yet they would claim to be beyond ideology, only interested in practical matters – the most ideological claim of the lot.

While use of the term 'ideology' to refer to political doctrine is unavoidable, there is a more analytically useful meaning, which is indeed pejorative, and which I will deploy here. This usage of ideology refers to distorted communications, where the distortion is motivated by unequal power relations. There is considerable dispute over the conceptual definition of ideology. Some positions dispense with a notion of distortion or misrepresentation entirely, thereby depriving the concept of its critical force. It seems to me that the principal value of the notion of ideology is as a critical concept. The critique has to do with how power relates to representation – that the powerful in society are in a strong position to represent their point of view as the only valid one; as, in some sense, being the truth. Corporate business is a powerful institution.

It is hardly surprising then that corporate business will seek to represent its interests ideologically, and, without doubt, it is in a privileged position to do so. This is no straightforward matter. The ideological framing of reality involves extremely complex institutional and discursive processes that will be considered in what follows in this chapter with respect to neoliberal discourse, the reduction of culture to 'enterprise culture', the inculcation of enterprising selfhood and the 'post-industrial' ideology of 'creative industry'. Still, however complex the issues involved, it is reasonable to argue that there is no more profound exemplar of ideological power today than the hegemony of market values in contemporary culture and society.[1]

Neoliberal Discourse

A straightforward but somewhat misleading characterisation of the shift from organised capitalism to neoliberal capitalism turns on a transfer of power from the state to the market, with 'state' and 'market' functioning as generic terms that conceal as much as they reveal. Organised capitalism was not only about state control over economy and society in the way that Soviet communism was; after all, it was essentially capitalistic. Moreover, the state has not been eliminated by marketisation, and nor has globalisation, which developed with the neoliberal turn, eliminated the nation state as such. Perhaps Lenin's notion of 'the commanding heights' helps to clarify the difference, as is argued by Daniel Yergin and Joseph Stanislaw, two leading chroniclers of neoliberalism.[2] Lenin coined the term in justification of his New Economic Policy (the NEP) in 1922. Critics had complained that the NEP, which permitted a limited resumption of local trading arrangements and private farming, amounted to a return to capitalism. Lenin, however, insisted that this modest scope for market activity did not entail relinquishing communist control over 'the commanding heights' of the economy, its major enterprise and financial arrangements. The post Second World War Labour government in Britain used the term to justify its 'nationalisation' of mining, railways and steel, which did not amount to a communist takeover of the whole economy. One feature of neoliberalism has, of course, been the 'privatisation' of such industries.

Yergin and Stanislaw tell the story of neoliberal reform since the 1970s as a matter of pragmatic change, as a move from failed instruments of political economy to more efficient means of achieving economic growth. The story is complex with multiple aspects, encompassing the partial withdrawal of state intervention from economic management across the capitalist world, accompanied by the literal collapse of communism in Russia and Eastern Europe and the effective retreat from communism in China, and the policies of international agencies like the International Monetary Fund (IMF), the World Bank and the World Trade Organisation (WTO). The official rationale, sometimes dubbed 'the Washington consensus', has been to open up markets, stimulate innovation and so enrich the world. Yergin and Stanislaw trace the formation of a global consensus in favour of neoliberalism. However, they also acknowledge that the turn towards neoliberalism, though quite possibly inevitable, did not happen without a 'battle of ideas'. The case had to be put by ideologues like the Austrian political economist Friedrich von Hayek and the American economist Milton Friedman; and a campaign had to be waged by politicians such as Keith Joseph and Margaret Thatcher in Britain.

As organised capitalism came into the ascendancy, Hayek met with Friedman and others at a Swiss Alpine resort in 1947 to form the Mont Pelerin Society, dedicated to turning back the advance of socialism and collectivism, and to the reinstatement of nineteenth-century liberal economics and politics. For many years, they were regarded as cranks, though Friedman's Chicago School of economics, which advocated tight control of the money supply (monetarism) to rein in the profligacy of governmental spending and reduce inflation, came to be recognised as the chief alternative to the Keynesian economics that prevailed until the crises of the 1970s. The Chicago School found a laboratory to try out its policies in Chile, after General Pinochet led a successful military coup against Salvador Allende's democratically elected socialist government in 1973. Hayek was the philosopher of the movement. His book, *The Road to Serfdom*, much derided at the time of its publication in 1944, was later to be widely regarded as a prophetic work.[3] It was of great inspiration to Joseph and Thatcher. Hayek was the darling of the right-wing think-tanks, most notably the Institute of Economic Affairs in Britain that became so influential in the 1970s and '80s.[4] *The Road to Serfdom* had been a dire warning about the worldwide drift into totalitarianism, which prompted Winston Churchill to claim at the 1945 general election that a vote for Labour was a vote for the Gestapo. Hayek's thinking was steeped in nineteenth-century liberal individualism and a visceral hatred of collectivism. His arguments concerning the role of the market mechanism as a means of communication essential to economic efficiency were, however, taken seriously even in the 1940s by his critics.[5]

David Harvey gives as good a definition of neoliberalism as I have come across:

> Neoliberalism is in the first instance a theory of political economic practices that proposes that human well-being can best be advanced by liberating human entrepreneurial freedoms and skills within an institutional framework characterized by strong private property rights, free markets, and free trade. The role of the state is to create and preserve an institutional framework appropriate to such practices. The state has to guarantee, for example, the quality and integrity of money. It must also set up those military, defence, police, and legal structures and functions required to secure private property rights and to guarantee by force, if need be, the proper functioning of markets. Furthermore, if markets do not exist (in such areas as land, water, education, health care, social security, or environmental pollution) then they must be created, by state action if necessary. But beyond these tasks the state should not venture. State intervention in markets (once created) must be kept to a bare minimum because, according to the theory, the state cannot possibly possess enough information to second-guess market signals (prices) and because powerful interest groups will inevitably distort and bias state interventions (particularly in democracies) for their own benefit.[6]

There is, in spite of the anti-government rhetoric, a role for the state in a neoliberal economy. As Harvey notes here, in addition to guaranteeing the integrity of money, maintaining social order and defending national security, the state has to create markets where markets did not previously exist. That involves the construction of artificial markets. This was the case in relation to the privatisation of public utilities by neoliberal governments over the closing decades of the twentieth century, but it also includes the insertion of market disciplines where full-scale privatisation was not actually implemented in such cases as the public provision of education and healthcare, so that there is, for instance, a competitive market in schooling and surgery. In practice, it has not been at all evident why market mechanisms and their attendant values should be introduced in these instances where they did not hitherto and spontaneously exist, not least because of the wasteful replication of effort. Here, then, it is especially clear why an ideological campaign had to be waged on behalf of neoliberal reform or, as it is sometimes called by ostensibly social-democratic parties, 'modernisation'.

In order to justify and legitimise neoliberal reform, language had to be changed. As Harvey remarks: 'Neoliberalism has, in short, become hegemonic as a mode of discourse. It has pervasive effects on ways of thought to the point where it has been incorporated into the common-sense way many of us interpret, live in, and understand the world.'[7] Neoliberalism is an exercise in 'creative destruction' in both the economy and discourse. In order to install the new discourse, the old discourse has to be discredited, in effect smashed ideologically. Socialist discourse that had claimed to represent the future was consigned to the dustbin of history. The old verities of market ideology that had at one time themselves been consigned to the dustbin of history were to be retrieved, dusted off and projected afresh, that is, re-presented as 'new'. To quote Harvey again:

> For any way of thought to become dominant, a conceptual apparatus has to be advanced that appeals to our intuitions and instincts, to our values and our desires, as well as to the possibilities inherent in the social world we inhabit. If successful, this conceptual apparatus becomes so embedded in common sense as to be taken for granted and not open to

question. The founding figures of neoliberal thought took political ideals of human dignity and individual freedom as fundamental, as 'the central values of civilization'. In so doing they chose wisely, for these are indeed compelling and seductive ideals. These values, they held, were threatened not only by fascism, dictatorship and communism, but by all forms of state intervention that substituted collective judgements for those of individuals free to choose.[8]

Harvey contrasts neoliberalism with the 'embedded liberalism' of welfare capitalism, the post Second World War compromise between capital and labour, with its 'web of social and political constraints and regulatory environment'.[9] As Yergin and Stanislaw point out, 'regulation' was an American idea designed to justify state control in the US that was short of European socialism and, therefore, acceptable for the time. Neoliberals are against 'regulation', at least rhetorically.

It is unsatisfactory to address neoliberalism only in the terms of technical economics and without recognising its ideological force and discursive purchase. Thatcher knew that. Harvey quotes her telling statement: 'Economics is the method but the object is to change the soul.'[10] The ideological project should not, however, be considered only as a matter of winning consent by capturing souls; it also distorts reality. Neoliberalism is riven with contradictions that are symptomatic of the distortion. As Harvey notes, these contradictions include: the assertion of individual freedom that is at odds with the actual authoritarianism of the regime; financial probity that is persistently undermined by dishonest operations, which occasionally erupt into scandal; the rhetoric of competition that is rendered implausible by the actual power of monopoly; and, how the commodification of everything distorts the humanity of ordinary social relations.[11]

Still, neoliberalism's mobilisation of popular consent has to be explained. Thomas Frank's concept of 'market populism' is illuminating in this respect. Writing about the United States in the 1990s, when the 'new economy' hysteria was at fever pitch, Frank commented upon the stock-market frenzy and culture surrounding it. He remarks: '"destroying the old" and making the world safe for billionaires has been as much a cultural and political operation as an economic one'.[12] Enthusiasm for the new high-tech economy, the Internet, and so on, brought together right-wing libertarians and left-wing academics. Management ideology with its 'revolutionary' rhetoric had cultivated a populist legitimacy for free-market capitalism. It now associated business with popular culture in opposition to any kind of elitism:

> From Deadheads to Nobel-laureate economists, from paleoconservatives to New Democrats, American leaders in the nineties came to believe that markets were a popular system, a far more democratic form of organization than (democratically elected) governments. This is the central premise of what I call 'market populism': That in addition to being mediums of exchange, markets were mediums of consent. Markets expressed the popular will more articulately and more meaningfully than did mere elections. Markets conferred democratic legitimacy; markets were a friend of the little guy; markets brought down the pompous and the snooty; markets gave us what we wanted; markets looked out for our interests.[13]

The legitimacy of market forces in any sphere of life, consumer sovereignty, widespread participation in capitalism through share ownership, anti-government rhetoric, 'cool' culture and the argot associated with it, all these elements emanate from the US but are now global in their reach, representing the popular appeal of neoliberalism around the world.

Towards the end of his life, Pierre Bourdieu, one of the leading public intellectuals in France, became a vociferous critic of what he called 'the scourge of neoliberalism'.[14] On receiving the Ernst Bloch Preis der Stadt Ludwigshafen in November 1997, he called for a 'reasoned utopianism' against the 'economic fatalism' that had overcome social-democratic politics in 'a period of neo-conservative reconstruction'. He was keen to point out that this revival of capitalist political economy in the raw was not backward-looking but was rather seeking to define the future.

> [T]his conservative revolution is taking an unprecedented form: there is no attempt, as there was in earlier times, to invoke an idealized past through the exaltation of earth and blood, the archaic themes of ancient

> agrarian mythologies. It is a new type of conservative revolution that claims connection with progress, reason and science – economics actually – to justify its own re-establishment, and by the same token tries to relate progressive thought and action to archaic status. It erects into defining standards for all practices, and thus into ideal rules, the regularities of the economic world abandoned to its own logic: the law of the market, the law of the strongest. It ratifies and glorifies the rule of what we call the financial markets, a return to a sort of radical capitalism answering to no law except that of maximum profit; and undisguised, unrestrained capitalism, but one that has been rationalized, turned to the limits of its economic efficiency through the introduction of modern forms of domination ('management') and manipulative techniques like market research, marketing and commercial advertising.[15]

Bourdieu does not use the term 'neoliberalism' here – he usually did – but that was indeed what he was referring to. Use of the term 'conservatism' might mistakenly be construed as referencing another significant current of the time, usually labelled 'neoconservatism', also emanating from the United States. Although both currents may in practice be intertwined, it is important to distinguish between them. Neoconservatism is much more impelled by a cultural critique of 'liberalism', in the American sense, and concerned with preserving a traditional notion of the American – or whatever other specifically national – 'way of life'. One of its targets, for instance, is 'multiculturalism'. Neoliberalism, on the other hand, is much more amenable to 'liberalism' in the American sense and is largely driven by an economic rather than cultural imperative. This is why and how neoliberalism – not neoconservatism – was readily inscribed into an ostensibly social-democratic politics by the likes of Clinton and Blair, and articulated with a 'cool' veneer.[16] However, it also has to be noted that neoliberalism, even in a social-democratic guise, is a threat to what is sometimes called 'the social state' or what Bourdieu often referred to as 'the left hand of the state'. He was alert to the fact that in France too, usually said to be one of the last bastions of welfare and organised capitalism, the right hand of the state was gaining the upper-hand, aided by the rightward turn of Mitterrand's Socialist government from the 1980s. In collaborative research, Bourdieu explored the miserable impact of a meltdown of the social state on France's working-class suburbs, *les banlieues*, during this period.[17]

Bourdieu recognised that the triumph of neoliberalism was not only political and economic but also discursive. With the aid of Loïc Wacquant, he interrogated 'NewLiberalSpeak', which he described as a 'new planetary vulgate':

> Within a matter of a few years, in all the advanced societies, employers, international officials, high-ranking civil servants, media intellectuals and high-flying journalists have started to voice a strange Newspeak. Its vocabulary, which seems to have sprung from nowhere, is now on everyone's lips: 'globalization' and 'flexibility', 'governance' and 'employability', 'underclass' and 'exclusion', 'new economy' and 'zero tolerance', 'communitarianism' and 'multiculturalism', not to mention their so-called postmodern cousins, 'minority', 'ethnicity', 'identity', 'fragmentation', and so on.[18]

Bourdieu and Wacquant regarded NewLiberalSpeak as a form of symbolic violence, which through the power of words defined what was sayable and unsayable, marking out the boundaries of the intelligible world, constructing 'a universal common sense'. The utterable and unutterable were demarcated by a set of binary oppositions:

state	→	[globalization] →	**market**
constraint			freedom
closed			open
rigid			flexible
immobile			dynamic, moving, self-transforming
past, outdated			future, novelty
stasis			growth
group, lobby, holism, collectivism			individual, individualism
uniformity			diversity, authenticity
autocratic ('totalitarian')			democratic[19]

There are two key ideological agents of NewLiberalSpeak: 'the *expert*' and 'the *communication consultant to the prince*'. Experts are lodged in governmental departments, company headquarters, and increasingly, instead of universities, think-tanks. They produce technical documents, particularly supported by statistics, in order to justify political decisions made on ideological rather than strictly technical grounds. The communication consultant to the prince may be 'a defector from the academic world entered into the service of the dominant, whose mission is to give an academic veneer to the political projects of the new state and business nobility'.[20] Bourdieu and Wacquant's exemplar of such an august type of intellectual is the British sociologist Anthony Giddens, proponent of 'the Third Way', in relation to Tony Blair and his New Labour government of the late 1990s.[21] They depict him as a latter-day Dr Pangloss, philosopher of 'the best of all possible worlds'.[22] Later ennobled by Blair, Lord Giddens's sociological integrity was seriously compromised by this fit of political engagement.

Enterprise Culture

Since the 1970s there has been a proliferation of discourse on 'culture', indicating an increased prominence for meaning in all spheres of life as though life had hitherto been comparatively meaningless.[23] In the European Romantic tradition, 'culture' had been counter-posed historically to 'commerce'. It was supposed to represent much finer values than those represented by money-grubbing, economic activity. Yet claims are now made repeatedly concerning the 'culturalisation' of 'economy' itself.[24] Management theorists write about 'managing culture' and 'culture change' in business, which often involves a shift away from older forms of bureaucratic hierarchy to flatter, apparently more democratic and participatory kinds of organisation.[25] Furthermore, social theorists have argued that all industry now approximates to the conditions of cultural industry in which design and style are fundamentally important in the fashioning of any commodity and vital to success in the consumer marketplace.[26] With regard to the transformation examined in this book, from organised and welfare capitalism to neoliberal and 'cool' capitalism, the notion of 'enterprise culture' figures large.

In Britain, late Thatcherism sought to replace the residues of socialism and state dependency with a revived culture of enterprise – with the values that had, in the Conservative memory, made Britain a 'Great' industrial and trading nation during the eighteenth and nineteenth centuries. The businessman and at one time Minister of Trade and Industry, Lord Young of Graffham, argued at the beginning of the 1990s: 'The two pillars of enterprise are openness of markets and the initiative of individuals.'[27] He insisted, following Adam Smith and Milton Friedman, on the superior efficiency of the market economy over state planning. Enterprising values amongst individuals, in his estimation, had not only been eroded by the growth of government control over the economy but also by the growth of bureaucracy in private business. To restore enterprise, it was necessary to set people free in order to take the initiative in the sphere of production and to make choices in the sphere of consumption. This was a particular national version of a political and business rhetoric that had long been a feature of US culture and society but which was given an immense boost in the 1980s during the presidency of Ronald Reagan.

American management gurus like Peter Drucker, Rosabeth Moss Kanter and Tom Peters were among the most celebrated ideologists of 'the new capitalism', their arguments aimed principally at professional and managerial workers.[28] They urged managers to be 'entrepreneurial' and 'innovative' rather than to play safe in their stewardship of the firm. 'Not to innovate is the single largest reason for the decline of organisations', said Drucker.[29] Kanter announced, in her potted history of recent American business: 'By 1983, the entrepreneur was the new culture hero.'[30] Amongst others, she cited Steve Jobs and Steve Wozniak for founding Apple Computer Inc., surely one of the 'coolest' of the newer corporations, following the blinkered and disappointing refusal of their daring ideas for desktop computing by Hewlett-Packard. Peters and his co-author, Robert Waterman, said that the relentless search for 'excellence' was the touchstone of successful enterprise.[31] 'Excellent' businesses were 'close to the customer'. They were 'obsessive' about serving the customer with 'quality'. In fact, for Peters, excellent management was an exercise in permanent revolution, to borrow Trotsky's phrase. In *The Tom Peters Seminar: Crazy Times Call for Crazy Organizations*, Peters ranted on: 'A constant state of disequilibrium is something all of us must get used to. Learning to love change (uh, revolution), thrive on chaos (uh, revolution), cherish change (uh, revolution) – that's the ticket.'[32]

At the same time, of course, policy changes were reducing regulation and governmental involvement in the economy. In countries with more developed state enterprise than the United States, privatisation was underway, amounting in Britain to the selling off of 'the family jewels', as an unreconstructed one-nation Tory, former Prime Minister Harold Macmillan, called it. In these countries and the US, government organisations were called upon to act like dynamic capitalist businesses. The key managerial text advocating such virtual capitalism within the public sector was David Osborne and Ted Gaebler's 1992 book, *Reinventing Government*, which influenced both American Democrat and British Labour Party circles, contributing to the mantra of 'the new public management'.[33] It situated itself as a response to the US tax revolts of the late 1970s when 'middle-class' Americans rebelled against their 'tax dollars' being wasted on the 'undeserving poor'. Of longer term historical significance, the authors located their work in the shift from the old 'smoke-stack' industrial and bureaucratic society to 'third-wave' post-industrialism, in the rhetoric popularised by Alvin Toffler. Typical of didactic managerial texts based on 'case studies', *Reinventing Government* identified ten lessons which 'entrepreneurial governments', local, regional and national, were already putting into practice and that others lagging behind them needed to learn in order to cope with the new conditions:

> Most entrepreneurial governments promote *competition* between service providers. They *empower* citizens by pushing control out of the bureaucracy,

into the community. They measure the performance of their agencies, focusing not on inputs but on *outcomes*. They are driven by their goals – their *missions* not by their rules and regulations. They define their clients as *customers* and offer them choices – between schools, between training programmes, between housing options. They *prevent* problems before they emerge, rather than simply offering services afterwards. They put their energies into *earning* money, not simply spending it. They *decentralize* authority, embracing participatory management. They prefer *market* mechanisms. And they focus not simply on providing services, but on *catalyzing* all sectors – public, private and voluntary – into action to solve their community's problems.³⁴

Critical researchers have examined the impact of such thinking on policy in Britain with regard to the public sector in general but also with special attention to venerable quasi-autonomous institutions of the state, most notably the British Broadcasting Corporation (BBC) and the National Health Service (NHS), where the entrepreneurial culture has vied with the principles of public service either to realise the latter more efficiently in practice – the official reason – or, as the evidence suggests, to undermine them fundamentally so that the rationale for public ownership and provision has been severely damaged by capitalistic managerialism – the actual effect.³⁵ In 2007, when Gordon Brown succeeded Tony Blair as Prime Minister of Britain, he renamed the Department of Trade and Industry as the Department of Business, Enterprise and Regulation, thereby indicating just how deeply the market values of enterprising business had become ingrained in European social democracy, with the caveat of 'regulation' to provide some kind of governmental guarantee for 'the public interest'.

The politically ambiguous 'governmentality' school of social and cultural analysis has traced the impact of such discourse particularly upon the self, encapsulated in the resonant title of one of Nikolas Rose's books, *Governing the Soul*.³⁶ In his later writings, Michel Foucault formulated the concept of governmentality as a much more general idea than the government of the state.³⁷ It is about 'the conduct of conduct' in the broadest sense. In fact, the very notion of governmentality obscures any distinction between government and market or state and capital. It is rather more concerned with the management of populations and the inculcation of self-regulation in relation to a concept of power that is less about domination than facilitation. It breaks with humanistic criticism of exploitation and oppression and refuses the conception of ideology as distortion in favour of a concern with the 'making up' of people and a diffuse notion of discourse. Rose argues that 'the forms of political reason that yearn for an enterprise culture accord a vital *political* value to a certain image of the self'.[38] He insists that this is not just a right-wing project but is consistent with contemporary mores. The emphasis is on rights and freedoms and not so much on duties and obligations. In Rose's estimation, 'enterprise links up a seductive ethics of the self, a powerful critique of contemporary institutional and political reality, and an apparently coherent design for the radical transformation of contemporary social arrangements'.[39] The problem with organisations, from this perspective, is that they lack 'enterprise'. The solution is to re-educate the self: 'The enterprising self is ... a calculating self, a self that calculates *about* itself and that works *upon* itself in order to better itself.'[40] In Foucauldian parlance, the enterprising self is a particular 'technology of the self' that inscribes an 'ethics of enterprise – competitiveness, strength, vigour, boldness, outwardness and the urge to succeed';[41] 'the individual is to become, as it were, an entrepreneur of itself'.[42] Such discourse is promoted by newer strands of organisational psychology and management theory seeking to transform working life. It is associated with a politics of the body that places great stress on healthiness and fitness. Rose points out quite rightly that this contradicts Daniel Bell's fears about the decline of the Protestant ethic being harmful to capitalism. Instead, asceticism is succeeded by a new kind of bio-politics (though not so new if the history of social Darwinism is taken into account[43]), which is about self-improvement, autonomy and enterprise training that also has a hedonistic aspect – offering, in effect, I would argue, not only a promising but an immediate reward structure.

In his research on retailing, Paul du Gay has sought to apply the governmentality perspective to the subjectivity of work and discovers what he claims is a blurring of the distinction between production and consumption. Writing in 1996, he sees these processes in relation to the British Conservative government's promotion of an 'enterprise culture' as a 'moral crusade' and to the American management discourse of 'excellence'. Du Gay remarks, 'Within the discourse of enterprise/excellence an active "enterprising consumer" is placed at the centre of the market-based universe.'[44] As was argued in the previous chapter of this book, the figure of 'the sovereign consumer' has been revived in neoliberal discourse. It clearly does connect up with the liberation theology of enterprise culture, particularly the idea of 'empowering' employees to take the initiative in business. Retail workers are indeed at the interface of commerce and consumption and are expected to empathise with the customer as a sales tactic. In clothes shops, for instance, sales personnel are given reductions on clothing so that they can dress in the appropriate way to do the job, which may be an elementary indication of du Gay's thesis that there is a blurring between production and consumption, though it is indeed very elementary. More generally, it might be argued that sales personnel are on the frontline of consumer culture's propaganda war or, in du Gay's more temperate words, 'a struggle for the *imagination of the consumer*'.[45] This is especially notable in the youth market.

Similarly to critical discourse analysts, Deborah Cameron has noted the linguistic aspect of the enterprise culture in the ordinary language that employees are accustomed to using when doing their jobs and, by extension, living their lives.[46] Retail work, for instance, is usually scripted by management, what might be called the 'have-a-nice-day' culture of customer interaction that will be examined in Chapter 5. Of broader significance, it may also be noted how the language of commerce functions in popular culture and might be said to colonise everyday life generally, with phrases like 'beyond its sell-by date' used to signify anything deemed behind the times. Natasha Walter, commenting upon Harvard Business School Professor Rachel Greenwald's marriage advice book, *The Programme: 15 Steps to Finding a Husband After Thirty*, mentions how female singletons are exhorted to adopt 'a strategic plan' and cultivate 'a personal brand' in order to situate themselves advantageously in the marketplace of coupling and to improve their terms of trade in making close relationships[47] – life and love as a marketplace.

To illustrate the popular appeal of enterprise culture and its role in articulating the ideological hegemony of cool capitalism, I shall here briefly outline my analysis of *The Apprentice*, a very successful and emblematic television programme of the 2000s, which is published in much greater detail elsewhere.[48] An American reality game show with several franchises around the world and a Chinese copy, *Winner*, *The Apprentice* presents an entertaining lesson in business to the television-viewing public. Fronted in the American prototype by the property tycoon, Donald Trump, *The Apprentice* is a series televised annually over several weeks in which a number of aspirant young entrepreneurs compete for a lucrative job as Trump's apprentice in the US or, in Britain, in Alan Sugar's employ, with the promise of becoming as rich as them. *The Apprentice* is educative in Antonio Gramsci's sense of offering a mundane political education not only for *cadres* but also for the masses, accomplished through sporting entertainment.[49] In the American version, Trump literally teaches a lesson each week with a catchy slogan – such as 'Respect Comes From Winning', 'Sell Your Ideas' and 'Let Nothing Get In Your Way' – in the manner of management advice books and training seminars. Each episode is designed to illustrate the truth of that week's lesson.

In the third series of the American version, transmitted in the US in 2005, the 18 contestants were divided into two teams, 'Book Smart' (university educated) and 'Street Smart' (no more than high-school educated), in order to test the respective merits of theoretical and practical knowledge (the series narrative, in effect, concluded that a combination of both was best). In the sixth episode the teams were given the task of producing a graffiti advertisement on a wall in 'the mean streets' of Harlem for Sony PlayStation's video game, Gran Turismo 4. For the Street Smarts, the project manager on this task was a young black woman, Tara, the only public-sector employee among that year's candidates for the apprenticeship. She saw the task as somehow connected to urban regeneration in Harlem and wanted to show respect to 'the community'. Although Tara appreciated that her target demographic was 'urban, hip, 18–34 males', in the eventual judgement of Trump, she allowed culture to overcome commerce in her management of the task. In Marcus Garvey Park, she hired the graffiti artist Ernie to 'execute our vision [of] the mean streets of New York'.

The project manager for the Book Smarts, Alex, was concerned that his highly educated team lacked street wisdom, so he conducted 'market research' with a bunch of young black men who were hanging around in order to make the artistic 'concept' of the project conform to 'the Sony message' and the customers' desire, which involved a 'bling, bling' picture of 'piles of cash raining down'. In this he was wise, since Trump's lesson that week was 'Shut Up and Listen'. Although the Street Smarts' graffiti billboard was judged to be better artistically, it was also considered less effective in selling the product. Alex won and Tara was fired. As Trump said to the loser: 'This was a marketing task and you didn't get it.' That particular example illustrates a general feature of cool capitalism. Signs of cultural difference and even rebellion are embraced by business but not to the detriment of business. The bottom line remains the bottom line, something that is easily missed by the social-scientific analysts of the 'culturalisation' of the capitalist market.

Every week in *The Apprentice* the winning team is instantly rewarded – no deferred gratification here. The winners of the graffiti ad episode were treated to a 'legendary' advertising photographer shooting their portraits in downtown Manhattan. Alex remarked that this 'taste of Mr Trump's lifestyle' had taken them from the mean streets of Harlem to 'the top of the world'. In a later episode, another victory for the Book Smarts, the winners were rewarded with a lavish, though healthy, breakfast in Trump's penthouse apartment, which they were astonished to discover was covered throughout in gold leaf. Trump as King Midas. Kendra, the eventual winner of the whole competition, enthused: 'Trump's pad was bling, bling. Trump must have been a rapper in a former life because I've never seen so much gold trim in my entire life.' In this episode, Trump spoke proudly of his extremely long gold-painted dining table, which went nicely with his quiff of bleached-blond hair. The table is so big that it had to be hoisted up the side of the skyscraper and passed into the apartment through an opened plate-glass window. 'We needed to erect a special crane to lift it up.' This was truly the high life in the eyes of that week's winners, dazzled by the ostentatious shine of it all.

The British version of *The Apprentice* is much less brash and rather more ironic in tone than the American prototype. This is a feature of global television and national franchising in that programme formats may have an international market but they must also be adapted to local conditions so as to factor in cultural difference. *The Apprentice* is a notable bearer of cool capitalist ideology in Britain as well as in the US. The mass-popular articulation of that ideological discourse by the show may be illustrated with reference to an episode transmitted in May 2007 on the BBC's largest audience television channel. In this episode the two competing teams, Eclipse and Stealth, had to design and market a new pair of trainers (sneakers in the US). The project manager for Eclipse, Muslim cockney Tre, immediately hit upon the winning formula for his team: 'All the street culture has been taken over by the big brands, yeh? So, what we're doing is we're reclaiming the streets. We're taking back to the streets. We're giving them a [sic] underground alternative to the mass-produced representation of their culture.' Members of the Eclipse team go out coolhunting on the street, talking with 'the crucial youth market'. They decide to name their trainer, 'Street'. It turns out that one of the team, expensively educated Simon, a Cambridge graduate from the select Hampstead Garden Suburb of London, can rap and break dance. The team decide to use his talents in their promotional video. Simon composes a rap and this white boy delivers it in a passably 'street' accent:

> Street is not about corporate branding, high-street fashions and rip-off pricing. It's not about country walks and village fêtes. Street is about giving back, revolutionising the system, taking back control. It's about knowing

yourself, knowing your style and representing your culture, representing the street. Reclaim the street!

Eclipse decides to donate 10 per cent from the £39.99 price of a pair of Street trainers to 'street youth centres'. Sugar points out to the team that this was a mistake:

> You're forcing the consumer to pay four pounds. They won't like that. I can promise you, they won't like that. What it should have been is that you are gonna give away some of your profits. That way the customer doesn't know what you're actually gonna give away but the sentiment is there.

Again, then, there are limits to cool capitalism set by the imperatives of marketing and profit. Still, Eclipse won and their reward was learning how to make cocktails at the Ritz. Simon went on to win the competition for that year's apprenticeship.

Creative Industries

Critics have often argued that the concentration of media ownership and control is crucial to the ideological reproduction of capitalist social relations, not only in legitimising the status quo but by inculcating appropriately submissive values and dispositions. The educative function of *The Apprentice* might be considered a case in point. In this respect, American and British network television, whether privately or publicly owned, could thus be described as an 'ideological state apparatus' in Althusser's term.[50] Such an example would illustrate the dominant ideology thesis or, with greater sophistication in Gramscian terms, instantiate a feature of the struggle for social leadership, that is, ideological hegemony in addition to economic and political power.[51] Hegemony theory offers a rather more nuanced account of ideological process than the simple functionalism of the dominant ideology thesis. It postulates a perpetual struggle for social leadership between contending forces, thereby stressing how media and cultural apparatuses are involved in winning consent for corporate capitalism and 'bourgeois' culture against various sources of resistance, and by countering actual and potential opposition.

The dominant ideology thesis has been reiterated comparatively recently in Herman and Chomsky's 'propaganda model' of the American news media,[52] and has been given considerable empirical substantiation by them and others, especially with regard to the representation of foreign policy and war, in particular influencing critical arguments and campaigning around coverage of the invasion and occupation of Iraq.[53] However, the equation of mainstream news with propaganda in a liberal democratic polity is extremely controversial, to say the least, and a matter of considerable dispute in scholarly circles.[54] A great deal of discussion in this field (and, indeed, of political agitation) turns on the question of the public sphere, the idea that there is and should be free and open debate of policy on important issues in a democracy; this encourages critical scrutiny into how such debate is in practice restricted and distorted by major economic and political interests.[55] Part of the analytical problem in producing a more complex view of ideological hegemony, however, concerns the limitations of an exclusive concentration on cognitive communications in media research, particularly the management of information and news. This perspective tends to underplay the role of affective – aesthetic and emotional – communications in culture and politics, in sum, the question of the *cultural* public sphere.[56] The problematic of the public sphere, then, not only raises questions of media policy but also of cultural policy in a much broader sense.[57] Some critical schools of thought and cultural politics place as much if not more emphasis on affective communications – from 'high' to 'mass-popular' culture – as on cognitive communications, that is, the circulation of information and news.

Towards the end of the twentieth century and into the twenty-first, well-established processes and structures of conglomeration, corporate concentration and hyper-commercialism were globalising intensively.[58] The leading media corporations are awesome in scale and transnational in reach, mainly though not at all exclusively headquartered in the US, such as AOL-Time Warner, Disney and Viacom. Take 'Hollywood', for example, just in terms of the movie business, and not to mention its complex forms of economic and cultural synergy.[59] As Toby Miller and his co-authors observe: 'Hollywood's proportion of the world market is double what it was in 1990, and the European film industry is one-tenth of its size in 1945.'[60] Such facts draw attention to issues of consumption, such as the prevalent experience of cinema spectatorship around the world being shaped by the sheer and in many cases overwhelming presence of the Hollywood product, defining the aesthetics of cinema, its typical images and narratives. Resistance has typically taken the form of public subsidy and protection for national cinemas and various kinds of alternative cinema movement. Both forms of resistance have been in decline for quite some time. Yet more typical today than counter-strategies are accommodative strategies for mimicking or achieving some kind of hybrid adaptation to Hollywood hegemony both culturally and economically.

The dominance of actual Hollywood is present not only at the point of consumption but massively at the point of production too. The authors of *Global Hollywood 2* make a significant addition to the New International Division of Labour (NIDL) thesis, which refers to the division of labour generally in a global economy; specifically, they have formulated the concept of a New International Division of *Cultural* Labour (NICL), referring to 'an emerging paradigm across music, cultural policy, sport and film'. They say: 'Any analysis of global Hollywood must take account of the politics, exploitation and stratification of labour.'[61] So:

> The NICL is designed to cover a variety of workers within the cultural industries, whatever their part in the commodity chain. So, it includes janitors, accountants, drivers and tourism commissioners as well as scriptwriters, best boys and radio announcers ... Cinema is now like the telephone-based systems of banking, marketing and ticketing ... in its twenty-four-hour 'follow the sun' use of regional hubs that service less-developed or highly developed nations. Advances in communications technology permit electronic off-line editing, synchronized special effects and musical scores across the world through digital networks.[62]

From a business point of view, it obviously makes sense to go where the labour is cheap and locations are convenient, which is controversial back in Los Angeles where there have been serious jobs losses. Cultural labour in the United States is the most expensive in the world. It is cheaper to employ creative workers and the multitude of supporting labour functions even in other rich countries like Australia and Britain. The production of Hollywood films in Britain, where there are sophisticated technical skills and facilities as well as lower wages, is an old story. Governments in countries rich and poor offer inducements for attracting American cultural production to their shores, with its perceived economic benefits – even if the beach has to be moved. This has been a policy priority for many cities and regions, from Liverpool to Queensland, not only in poor countries. Among poorer countries, Mexico is an ideal location, being not only cheap but nearby. Incidentally, it is not just that *Titanic* was made in Mexico; most of the television equipment upon which it is now viewed in the US was manufactured over the border 'down Mexico way'.[63] In effect, the NICL articulates embedded forms of neoliberal political economy geographically at the point of production. The audio-visual sector has been a major focus of WTO deliberations.[64] And the operations of GATS (General Agreement on Trade in Services) and TRIPS (Trade-Related Intellectual Property Rights) are of immense significance for cultural policy.

There is a problem, however, with exaggerating the role of cultural businesses in the world economy – a tempting characteristic of 'post-industrial' ideology in which symbolic power is supposedly greater than material power.[65] In this respect, size does matter. Four of the top ten largest corporations in the world are automobile manufacturers (General Motors, DaimlerCrysler, Toyota and Ford). Three of them – the second, third and fourth largest – are oil companies (BP, Exxon and Royal Dutch/Shell). The very largest is Wal-Mart, ten times the size of Disney. The largest cultural business, AOL-Time Warner, comes 100th. Microsoft is 127th.[66] These calculations of cultural business are strict in that they do not include equipment manufacture. Sony comes 47th if consumer electronics is included in the calculation.

Since the Second World War, a significant rhetorical shift has occurred from 'culture industry' through 'cultural industries' to 'creative industries' in theoretical and policy discourse, which is symptomatic of a widespread reduction of culture to economy in contemporary thought. This tendency towards economic reductionism runs counter to the scholarly tendency of cultural reductionism inspired by poststructuralist theory. In 1944, Theodor Adorno and Max Horkheimer, in *The Dialectic of Enlightenment*, replaced their earlier formulation of 'mass culture' with the new coinage of 'culture industry'.[67] These Frankfurt School theorists had come to believe that 'mass culture' was too positive a term and that putting the word 'culture' together with 'industry' was much more damning of the capitalist media and entertainment complex they had witnessed at close quarters during their exile in the United States as Jewish and left-wing intellectuals escaping from Nazi Germany. They distinguished between 'culture industry' – referring to the commodification of culture in general – and 'the cultural industry', which referred to particular branches of production in, for instance, the movie and popular music businesses.[68] Cultural commodities were characterised, for them, by repetitive formulae and pseudo-individualist ideology. The culture industry thesis was an influential feature of a switch from the privileging of political economy in classical Marxism to a much greater stress on culture and ideology in neo-Marxism. It also resonated with post Second World War cultural policy developments in Europe and the critique of a debased mass culture that was even more pronounced in the US. A widely shared assumption of the time was that 'authentic', 'high' and also 'folk' culture needed to be protected, maintained and where possible disseminated against an ever more dominant and meretricious mass culture or culture industry. In whatever particular manifestation – left-wing, right-wing or centrist – such thinking is now recalled and denounced routinely as elitist snobbery, conservative and hopelessly backward-looking.

From the 1970s, French sociologists questioned Adorno and Horkheimer's critique of culture industry and did the groundwork to establish a quite different way of thinking about 'cultural industries' which was to have an impact on social-democratic cultural policy. Bernard Miege made three important criticisms of the culture industry thesis. First, he argued that Adorno and Horkheimer's treatment of artistic creativity was indeed stuck in the past and failed to grasp how modern technologies of reproduction had irredeemably industrialised culture. Second, the singular notion of culture industry suggested that the field of cultural production and circulation was a much more unified and homogeneous totality than was actually the case. Third, this failure to appreciate the heterogeneity of the cultural *industries* distracted attention from the actual processes of cultural production and was, in fact, focused almost entirely on the market instead. So, Adorno and Horkheimer unwittingly allowed their own thinking to be framed, in effect, by the operation of market values. According to Miege the different cultural industries have different logics of production: the publishing logic, which deals with the problem of marketing and copyrighting ostensibly autonomous products such as novels; the flow logic, best exemplified by broadcasting, which has to supply a steady flow of serial product and maintain audience loyalty; the press logic, concerned with sustaining repeat purchase of a product that has routinely built-in and rapid obsolescence. Miege also distinguished between three different kinds of product: type one products, such as equipment and materials that do not constitute specifically cultural commodities at all, since they are not meaningful in themselves and are not made by creative workers; type two products that are cultural commodities proper, made by creative workers and infinitely reproducible, such as books and films; and type three products that are only semi-reproducible, such as live performances. Modern capitalisation of cultural production especially favours the second kind of commodity. For Miege, cultural industries are complex, internally contradictory and have particularly acute problems of valorisation in comparison with other industries where demand for commodities is rather more predictable.[69]

In 1985, Nicholas Garnham, with the aid of Joyce Epstein, wrote a seminal position paper, 'Cultural Industries, Consumption and Policy' for the Labour-controlled Greater London Council (GLC).[70] He pointed out that cultural industries are in competition with one another for limited consumer income, limited advertising revenue, limited consumption time and limited skilled labour. He also identified 'a contradiction at the heart of the cultural commodity', namely that, in comparison with other commodities, the cultural commodity is not typically used up in the process of consumption and, therefore, can be consumed several times; for instance, re-reading a book, listening to recorded music over and over. Hence, there is a marketing stress on an endless stream of novelty in order to persuade customers to consume new product. Also, the appeal of cultural commodities is very unpredictable; so hits have to pay for misses.[71] Because of the importance of cultural industries to the London economy and the difficulties of starting up and breaking into the market for smaller enterprises (most notably those representing alternatives to the mainstream in terms of meaning and participation), the Labour GLC developed a strategy for subsidising cultural industries that became very influential in Britain and elsewhere but was itself strangled at birth when this tier of regional government was abolished by Margaret Thatcher's Conservative central government in 1986. The GLC strategy inspired other local governments at city level where the Labour Party was in power around Britain, especially in de-industrialising cities like Sheffield and Glasgow. This soon transmogrified into something not at all distinctly socialist, somewhat differently from the intentions of the original GLC initiative.[72]

As Garnham has always acknowledged, the GLC strategy that he played a leading role in formulating challenged the elitist tradition of public arts patronage and was meant to be economically realistic. The orientation was stated bluntly by two colleagues at the GLC, Geoff Mulgan and Ken Worpole, in their book, *Saturday Night or Sunday Morning? From Arts to Industry: New Forms of Cultural Policy*:

> Who is doing most to shape British culture in the late 1980s? Next Shops, Virgin, WH Smith's, News International, Benetton, Channel 4, Saatchi and Saatchi, the Notting Hill Carnival and Virago, or the Wigmore Hall, Arts Council, National Theatre, Tate Gallery and Royal Opera House? Most people know the answer and live it every day in the clothes they wear, the newspapers they read, the music they listen to and the television they watch. The emergence and disappearance of new pursuits, technologies, techniques and styles – whether windsurfing, jogging, aerobics, Zen,

compact discs, angling, wine-making, CB radio, rambling, hip-hop, home computing, photography, or keeping diaries – represent changes that bear little relation to traditional notions of art and culture, and the subsidized institutions that embody them.[73]

From this moment in the emergence of an optimistically populist and economically savvy perspective on cultural policy, let us move on 20 years to a recent text, John Hartley's enthusiastic Introduction to his edited textbook, *The Creative Industries*. He begins by remarking upon

> the challenges posed in a world where creative innovation and risk are general necessities for both economic and cultural enterprise, where knowledge and ideas drive both wealth creation and social modernization, and where globalization and new technologies are the stage of economic life and experience.[74]

The first thing to note here is that the emphasis is no longer on cultural experience – the irrelevance of the 'traditional arts' to most people and the much greater appeal of popular and commercial culture – but rather on 'wealth creation', which in itself is not necessarily a problem. However, it is important to appreciate that a discourse once recognisably about culture is now about economics. This would not be surprising were it written by an economist or a management consultant but it is written, in fact, by an exponent of cultural studies, the author of *A Short History of Cultural Studies*, in which a practical orientation towards the creative industries is proposed as 'a new manifesto for cultural studies'.[75] That is, of course, a fairly minor academic matter, although not wholly insignificant.

A good example of the newer economic perspective on culture – that is, on the economics of the creative industries – is the thesis of 'the long tail', propounded by the editor-in-chief of *Wired* magazine, Chris Anderson. His book, *The Long Tail: How Endless Choice is Creating Unlimited Demand*, is symptomatic since it stresses the transformative function of information and communication technologies (ICTs) in 'the new economy'.[76] Anderson notes that inventories of cultural product in warehouses and shops have largely been made up of actual and probable hits; and have in consequence been limited. A great deal of cultural product has simply not reached the customer. However, online sales of, say, music and books, particularly books printed on request, eliminate the problem of storing stock. The virtualisation of such texts in digital code overcomes the cost of physical space. In consequence, inventories can be much larger than before and, in principle, without limit in scope and duration. This means that marginal products can be made more readily available to a consuming public, in effect making democratically accessible the kind of work that tended to be locked out by hit lists and dominant players in the market. Access for 'independents' is greatly enhanced, bringing about what the likes of Hartley call a 'win-win' situation whereby both cultural diversity and commerce are served equally, though not to the benefit of older cultural businesses that have restricted the market, most notably music majors and chains of bookshops. Such reasoning is in line with the argumentation of cultural industries scholars of the past, seeking to understand how the capitalist culture industry works instead of criticising it, and also exemplifies the latter-day discourse of the creative industries that draws a virtuous circle around culture and commerce, not only in business but, as we shall see, in government as well – that's cool.

Such reasoning is also consistent with Tyler Cowen's argument in *In Praise of Commercial Culture*, that, historically, we have the market to thank for cultural innovation and the flourishing of the arts, not public patronage.[77] The post Second World War development of public patronage of the arts in Europe was motivated and given an official rationale by 'market failure', the assumption that certain kinds of culture were in some sense valuable but were not commercially viable in a competitive marketplace, such as grand opera in Britain or even the national theatrical heritage that the National Theatre and the Royal Shakespeare Company are charged with maintaining at a cost to the taxpayer. According to Cowen, the historical record simply does not bear out the assumption that market failure necessitated state intervention. Moreover, public subsidy tends to invoke the kind of moralism and censoriousness of which the competitive market is utterly blameless. If Cowen is right, is there any justification, then, for public subsidy of culture? After all, 'subsidy' is anathema to neoliberalism. Anyway, it is not only neoliberal economists like Cowen who are hostile to the elitism and judgementalism associated with state intervention on grounds of cultural value and market failure. The policy discourse of creative industries solves the problem since it is motivated by the economics of wealth creation, not market failure, and has no particular cultural preference.

The term 'creative industries' first gained widespread attention – and soon became influential around the world – in a publication of the British New Labour Government's Department for Culture, Media and Sport (DCMS) in 1998, the *Creative Industries Mapping Document*. This reported the findings of a task force made up of members from various ministries – Environment and Trade as well as Culture – and from business, including such illustrious figures as Richard Branson (music, retail and transport entrepreneur), Alan McGee (record producer), Gail Rebuck (publishing executive), David Putnam (film producer) and Paul Smith (fashion designer). It listed 13 industries as creative industries, in the following order: advertising, architecture, arts and antique markets, crafts, design, design fashion, film, interactive leisure software, music, performing arts, publishing, software, television and radio. It is not just an alphabetical accident that advertising, which would not normally have appeared in such a text issuing from a ministry of culture, came first. However, in any event, the *Creative Industries Mapping Document* was not so much a text of cultural policy as of economic policy. The mapping document emphasised the sheer scale of the UK's creative industries sector, generating revenue of £60 billion a year at the time and employing 1.5 million people. Furthermore, it asserted: 'The value of the creative industries to the UK gross domestic product is ... greater than the contribution of any of the UK's manufacturing industry',[78] quite a declaration for the once proud 'workshop of the world'. This was all part of the short-lived rhetoric of 'cool Britannia', though of longer-term consequence.

A couple of years later, the mapping document was updated, and while the original definition of 'creative industries' was retained – 'those industries which have their origin in individual creativity, skill and talent and which have a potential for wealth and job creation through the generation and exploitation of intellectual property' – it now also stressed 'the close economic relationships with sectors such as tourism, hospitality, museums and galleries, heritage and sport'.[79]

More recently, the DCMS commissioned the Work Foundation to further develop 'the Creative Economy Programme'. The Work Foundation's report, *Staying Ahead*, published in 2007, observed that the UK had the largest creative industries sector in the European Union (EU) and was arguably the largest proportionately in relation to Gross Domestic Product (GDP) in the whole world; second only to the US in range, though much smaller in size. The creative industries account for 7.3 per cent of 'gross value added (GVA)', twice that of the tourist industry's contribution to the British economy and 2.7 per cent of total employment, though the percentage is higher if jobs linked but not directly involved in creative work are included, giving a grand yet vaguely computed total of 1.8 million.[80] In actual fact, such figures are not as impressive as the report makes out, though the calculated rate of growth at 14.9 per cent in the late 1990s, led particularly by software development, gives rather more convincing support to the claim that the creative industries are at the cutting edge of the economy as a whole. Still, a certain scepticism is called for, considering that the largest industrial sectors in Britain include armaments, finance and pharmaceuticals, which make up a much larger part of the economy than do the creative industries, and none of which were noticeably in decline until the beginning of the bank crisis in 2007–8.

In addition to establishing the quantifiable facts, the Work Foundation report is devoted to identifying the 'drivers' of 'the creative economy' – such as stimulating demand and providing education and skills – and what the government can do to help.

According to the report, 'Creativity and innovation are overlapping concepts.'[81] Also, the creative industries are integral to 'a paradigm shift' towards 'the knowledge economy' and the development of a 'new class of consumers'.[82] Typical of the Work Foundation's rhetoric is the following claim: 'Creative origination is sparked by challenges to existing routines, lifestyles, protocols and ways of doing things – and where societies want to experiment with the new.'[83] Moreover, 'expressive value' is said to be the fundamental source of material wealth in the world. The purpose of cultural industries and, more broadly, the creative industries, is to commercialise expressive value; hence the importance of exploiting intellectual property rights in order to 'grow' the business of a country: 'The business model of the creative industries depends significantly on their capacity to copyright expressive value.'[84]

Staying Ahead addresses the thorny problem of definition and why it is necessary to expand the notion of cultural industries into

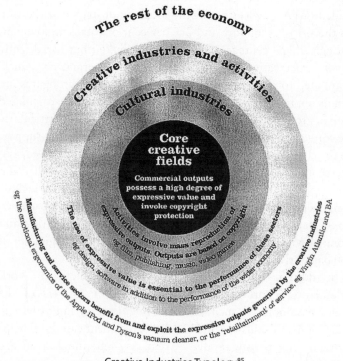

Creative Industries Typology[85]

the all-encompassing idea of creative industries in spite of the fact that advertising and art are not necessarily the same kind of thing. A diagram to illustrate what is at stake is helpfully provided.

At the centre, or 'core', of the diagram, copyrightable expressive value – the object of 'cultural industries' – is illustrated with a list of typical examples, including quite reasonably no doubt, video games. Circling further out are the 'creative industries', including design and software other than video games, that is, rather more 'functional' entities, and constituting 'an important bridge to the wider economy'.[86] This circle represents the mediation between 'cultural industries' and 'the rest of the economy', illustrated by 'the emotional ergonomics of the Apple iPod and Dyson's vacuum cleaner, or the "retailtainment" of service, eg Virgin Atlantic and BA'. Quite apart from the questionable examples and infelicitous language, as the modelling of an economy it is rather hard to take such an implausible scheme seriously. Are the creative industries – not to mention the cultural industries – being asked to do too much here? There is a pervasive blurring of categories going on and excessively fuzzy reasoning in the construction of this model. Another currently fashionable example of such confusion is the argument that 'creativity' in artistic practice and business management are roughly the same kind of thing.[87] Moreover, in 'the creative economy', economy seems to be swallowing up creativity whole rather like a Pac-Man on the loose, which is not quite the same observation as denying that the industrialism of culture exists, as some defenders of the artistic faith are inclined to do when presented with such economic reductionism.[88] It is tempting, however, to agree with Larry Elliott and Dan Atkinson's summary judgement on 'creative economy' rhetoric: 'Bullshit Britain reaches its apotheosis in the lionization of the cultural industries.'[89]

Creative economy rhetoric and the very notion of creative industries should be understood in relation to information society theory,[90] which originated with Daniel Bell's work on the so-called 'post-industrial society' (see Chapter 1) and was seized upon by Thatcherism to justify de-industrialisation – running down manufacturing and extractive industry in Britain – and is a feature much more generally of the transfer of such industry from rich countries, led by the United States, to 'developing' economies in the Third World where poorly protected labour is cheap and environmental degradation is allowed to let rip. In the 'creative/knowledge economy', informational and service jobs are supposed to replace jobs that have been lost in the older industrial nations, and they have indeed done so to a significant extent, resulting in reduced wages and poorer working conditions for a disorganised working class, and the dubious 'rise of the creative class'.[91] Garnham himself reads this trajectory in a similar way – 'we can only understand the use and policy impact of the "creative industries" within the wider context of information society policy'[92] – and asks some awkward questions about the cultivation of 'creative' work as an economic priority in what used to be a discourse of cultural policy:

> From a creative-industries economic perspective, quality and excellence are open to the market test of consumer preference. And access is by definition not a problem, since a successful creative industry has solved the access problem through the market. If it is successful, why does it need public support? If it is unsuccessful, why does it merit public support?[93]

The creative class thesis, formulated by Richard Florida, the American managerial theorist, has generated considerable excitement in cultural policy circles since it places culture at the heart of economic development, similarly to recent policy discourse in Britain. However, Florida is not primarily concerned with how governments seek to lever economic development and urban regeneration through public expenditure on 'flagship' projects and earnest schemes for training creative workers.[94] Instead, he is interested in explaining the rise of a new class – the so-called 'creative class' – and its spatial concentration in the labour markets of certain kinds of city that happens quite possibly irrespective of public cultural policy. He seeks to reveal the business secret of success in 'the creative economy'. His arguments are the very epitome of cool-capitalist thinking. While David Brooks had described the superstructure of the 'bobo' – bourgeois bohemian – lifestyle, Florida supplied a deeper account of the economic infrastructure giving rise to its formation. Brooks observed how the differences between business types and intellectual rebels had dissolved, so that each side of the divide was co-opting the other into its *modus operandi*, and he did note, in passing, that this is 'a cultural consequence of the information age',[95] but Florida went further.

Florida's 'rise of the creative class' is a new class thesis in succession to a series of such theses,[96] largely constructed according to a growth of informational and knowledge work in the older industrial states going through a process of restructuring associated with a 'technological revolution', and the devolution of older kinds of industrial work to newly industrialising countries (NICs). In formulating his thesis on the basis of US data, Florida is careful to point out that the Creative Class is one layer of a new class structure. He makes the startling claim that the Creative Class constitutes 38.3 million Americans and 30 per cent of the US workforce.[97] However, this is not quite so startling as it may appear, in that the Creative Class is divided into two segments: the Super Creative Class and Creative Professionals. The Super Creatives make up 15 per cent of Americans, representing 10 per cent of the workforce. Super Creatives range from artists, educators, librarians through scientists and engineers to computer and mathematical occupations.[98] The other segment – Creative Professionals – include lawyers, managers, technicians and 'high-end' sales personnel. The Creative Class is largely what would otherwise be called the professional-managerial class, including artistic occupations. Florida says that the 'distinguishing characteristic of the Creative Class is that its members engage in work whose function is to "create meaningful new forms"'.[99] It is reasonable to ask, exactly how many of those formally listed in the category would this actually apply to? The American working class consists of 33 million workers, according to Florida, whereas there are 55.2 million Service Class workers, 43 per cent of the workforce. As Florida says, the Service Class 'includes workers in low-wage, low-autonomy service occupations such as health care, food preparation, personal care, clerical work and other low-end office work'.[100]

What is the social character of this new Creative Class? Florida follows Brooks's typification of the bobos, which he calls 'the Big Morph' whereby there is 'a new resolution of the centuries-old tension between two value systems: the Protestant work ethic and the bohemian ethic'.[101] These people are on 'a passionate quest for experience' but they are not against working hard and making money.[102] Their creativity is, in fact, the driving force of wealth creation. Florida disputes Robert Putman's concern with social capital and lack of community.[103] For Florida, creative capital is more important than social capital. Creative people are individualistic and expressive. They like 'cool' scenes in which to hang out and where they can interact with similar go-getting bobos without necessarily reinventing the intimate communal ties of small-town America. The cultural characterisation of the Creative Class is at the crux of Florida's arguments concerning the success of certain kinds of city. Place matters in spite of the speed and convenience of remote communications across vast tracts of space facilitated by the Internet in a global world.

'Economic growth' derives from a combination of three factors, 'the three T's': Technology, Talent and Tolerance.[104] It is well established that high-tech is at the heart of post-industrial prosperity. However, this tends to be closely correlated with the attraction of talented people to particular places, Silicon Valley being an obvious example. For Florida, talent is defined by possession of a bachelor's degree, a rather crude calculator. Also crucial is tolerance, which tends to be found in cities like New York and Seattle. These are places that welcome diverse groups of people in terms of ethnic mix and lifestyle. Especially notable in this respect is that they are Gay-friendly places. Florida produces indexes that demonstrate the concentration of Technology, Talent and Tolerance in particular cities. For instance, he has a 'Bohemian Index ... a measure of the concentration of working artists, musicians, and the like in given areas'.[105] 'Seattle, New York, and Los Angeles top the list with more than 9 bohemians per thousand people.'[106] He even has a 'Coolness Index' that correlates with all the other factors that make for successful places: 'high-human capital individuals, particularly young ones, are drawn to places with vibrant music scenes, street-level culture, active nightlife, and other signifiers of "coolness"'.[107] In sum, 'ideas and intellectual capital have replaced natural resources and mechanical innovation as the raw material of economic growth [in] the age of creative capitalism.'[108]

Florida's thesis may seem like a complacent and self-congratulatory celebration of cool-capitalist America but he is rather more subtle than that, and registers a downside to the process, the '*externalities* of the creative age'.[109] For this reason, and for his general celebration of 'cool', it is understandable why Florida may be read in the US as a 'liberal'. Europeans are less likely to be taken in by such a slick management consultant. Unfortunately, not all researchers and advocates in the field of cultural policy research are sufficiently sceptical. Florida acknowledges that there is great inequality and uneven development in culture-led regeneration. However, he believes that everyone has the potential to be creative; nobody should be excluded. He claims to be alarmed by growing xenophobia in the US and restrictions on immigration.[110] The US has benefited greatly from the influx of talented foreigners, not least in the very recent period, he argues, but this is being undermined by anxiety over indigenous job losses and competition from China and elsewhere. Moreover, cities around the world are following the prescription for creative development, in Europe and countries like Australia and New Zealand. Unless the US remains open and tolerant – 'cool', in fact – Florida fears it may lose out in the future.

5
WORKING LIFE

> They no longer think in terms of the old ideas – socialism, trade unionism – because they are more attracted by glitter now.
>
> Mohan Lal[1]

Mohan Lal's no doubt old-fashioned exasperation at younger workers' attitudes at a Honda plant in India is a sad refrain. This chapter is concerned principally with the working lives of 'service' and 'creative' workers[2] in comparatively affluent societies – the groups that are perhaps most affected by the culture of cool capitalism – and not so much with those workers around the world whose lives are most savagely exploited and oppressed by the neoliberal political economy, the people to whom Mohan Lal is specifically referring, though it also applies to the workers addressed here. Part of the reason for concentrating on 'service' and 'creative' workers is that these class/occupational categories inhabit the socio-cultural space in which the values of consumption are said to have displaced the values of production, where people are supposed to identify themselves as consumers rather than as workers. I aim to show that this is at best a distortion of their lived experience and at worst an utter delusion. It is also important to consider the socialisation of such identities in contemporary youth culture, which is increasingly characterised by a debt-ridden hedonism.

In what follows the theories of Arlie Russell Hochschild on emotional labour and of Ulrich Beck and Elisabeth Beck-Gernsheim on individualisation are drawn upon to make sense of working lives framed by cool capitalism, lives that have also been addressed in the work of Barbara Ehrenreich and Richard Sennett. Ehrenreich, a journalist with an academic track record and a sociological imagination, has investigated both kinds of work – 'service' and 'creative' – by the anthropological ruse of 'going native'. For several months she gave up her professional-managerial status and its accoutrements, credit cards and the like, and moved away from home to make a living from a string of service jobs – at Wal-Mart, waiting on table, and cleaning – in another city. Ehrenreich found it extremely difficult to get by even with two jobs at the same time. Like other workers at various levels of the occupational hierarchy, she had to pay rent in advance yet was herself paid in arrears. The wages were low. Trying to make ends meet was extremely demanding and stressful – a not uncommon experience for many millions of low-paid workers in the United States, the richest country in the world. Ehrenreich's experiences at the lower echelons of the American labour market are recounted in her book, *Nickel and Dimed: Undercover in Low-wage USA*.[3]

In her next book of this kind, *Bait and Switch: The (Futile) Pursuit of the American Dream*, Ehrenreich explored the middle-class world of what, as we have seen, Richard Florida has somewhat unconvincingly called 'creative' work.[4] As a university graduate, prolific journalist and book writer, Ehrenreich calculated that it should not be too implausible to pass herself off as a public relations executive, 'journalism's evil twin',[5] though she did lack experience of corporate employment. This required a certain deception in rewriting what American's call a résumé and Europeans call a curriculum vitae. However, she did know, as a middle-aged woman, how insecure professional work had become for older people like herself. The American economy has experienced considerable 'downsizing' of managerial occupations and veneration of youth in employment, with the assumption that 'burn out' occurs around 40 to 50 or perhaps earlier in some professions like advertising and stock-trading. As it turned out, Ehrenreich was resoundingly unsuccessful during a year of trying to embark upon a career in PR. She learned a great deal more about the world of job-searching and career-coaching than she ever did about the PR business. Having mugged up on 'Core Competences and Skills ... Mobilizing Innovation, Managing People and Tasks,

Communicating, and Managing Self',[6] Ehrenreich put herself in the hands of career coaches and went through an endless round of job fairs, strenuous cyber-searching and networking, to no real avail.

In comparison with Ehrenreich, Sennett does not participate in unfamiliar worlds of work but instead interviews workers about their experiences and reflects upon the transition from post Second World War 'social capitalism' to the much harsher 'new culture of capitalism'. Having studied 'the hidden injuries of class' in the late 1960s and early 1970s,[7] Sennett returned to the topic of work in the 1990s with his *The Corrosion of Character: The Personal Consequences of Work in the New Capitalism*.[8] Like an old leftist, Sennett is concerned with the dignity of labour and working-class consciousness. He draws a family connection between Enrico, an Italian-American labourer and one of Sennett's respondents from *The Hidden Injuries of Class*, and his upwardly mobile son, Rico, a university graduate, new-economy executive and, by the time Sennett spoke with him, a business consultant – the very epitome of the American Dream. It turns out that Enrico, in the straitened circumstances of a poorer past, harboured an innocent hope for improvement in the future, whereas Rico is a much richer but cynical and dissatisfied survivor of the present. In effect, Sennett is chronicling the impact on 'character' of the transition from organised to neoliberal capitalism, and he displays a certain nostalgia for what he calls 'social capitalism'[9] – according to him, a rather more stable and humane time in the annals of history than now.

Emotional Labour

Arlie Russell Hochschild opened her classic book, *The Managed Heart: Commercialization of Human Feeling*, by citing Karl Marx's discussion from *Capital* of a blue-book deposition about a woman and her seven-year-old son who worked in a wallpaper factory.[10] The child laboured for 16 hours a day alongside his mother. This was a typical story of working life in mid-nineteenth-century Britain, concerning the fierce exploitation of women and children, poor pay and intolerable conditions of work, the kind of story that motivated campaigns for factory legislation and trade union representation. Similar stories are told today from factories around the world in poorer and 'developing' countries where a great deal of manufacturing industry has been transferred since the 1970s, especially to 'special economic zones' and 'export processing zones'. Back in the richer countries in which industrial capitalism originally developed there are few pockets of such beleaguered toil in what remains of indigenous manufacturing. Marx, however, wrote not only about long hours of poorly paid work, and the mistreatment of children and women as well as men in 'dark satanic mills' (Blake); he also wrote in his early work on the dehumanising *psychological* – that is, alienating – effects of exploited labour.[11] The worker was alienated from the product of labour, denied control in the workplace, and situated as a minor cog in a great mechanism of divided labour. In his later, 'mature' writings, most notably the first volume of *Capital*, Marx said little about alienation in a psychological sense and concentrated instead on the process of labour exploitation and the extraction of surplus value. Yet the theme of alienation with its humanistic features remained an enduring aspect of the critique of capitalism that engaged not only Marxist theorists and social scientists,[12] including research on the disjunction between conception and execution in the modern labour process,[13] but also non-Marxist and what is sometimes called today 'post-Marxist' sociology.[14]

The theme of alienation has, in effect, been restated in Hochschild's theory of emotional labour. In *The Managed Heart* she begins by comparing the working life of American flight attendants (air stewards), who at the time of her research in the late 1970s and early 1980s were still mainly female, with the female factory workers of nineteenth-century Britain.[15] This may at first sight appear to be an overstretched comparison. Surely, the working life of a modern flight attendant in the United States is nothing like so hard and debilitating as that of a Victorian factory worker. That, however, is not really the point. Hochschild is drawing an illuminating analogy between the emotional cost of an increasing number of jobs today and the physical cost of the most arduous kinds of manual work. She focuses upon what Americans call 'middle-class' work in the caring and service occupations, though arguably this is better understood as a facet of both working-class as well as some middle-class labour in comparatively affluent societies at the present time, especially evident in the enormous growth of 'service' work supposed to replace older forms of industrial work.

In formulating her sociology of the emotions in relation to work,[16] Hochschild drew upon a number of inspirational sources for theoretical insight. For instance, C. Wright Mills's observations on 'the great salesroom' of burgeoning 'white-collar' occupations in post Second World War America, which interrogated the sale of the self in the process of selling commodities.[17] In the 1950s too, Erving Goffman's 'dramaturgical' perspective focused upon the theatricality of self-presentation in everyday life.[18] Around the same time, the writings of David Riesman and others analysed 'the changing American character'.[19] And, of course, Sigmund Freud's work already had much to say about the emotional 'signal function' at the intersection of psychology and society.[20] Hochschild noted that *emotion work* and *emotion management* are general properties of ordinary sociality, facilitating routine interaction and the conduct of relationships; and that some people are more adept at it than others.[21] She believed that middle-class parents are better at the emotional socialisation of their children than working-class parents, a deeply questionable assumption that need not, however, detain us here. Something much more specific and problematic is occurring, in Hochschild's estimation, when employees are required to manage their emotions in an appropriately prescribed manner, according to 'feeling rules', for financial remuneration. This, then, becomes very specifically *emotional labour*, in Hochschild's precise sense, something that is done for a wage. She thus raises important questions of critical significance. How is emotional labour managed? And, what consequences does the management of emotion for a wage have on the self?

Much of *The Managed Heart* is organised around a comparison of the working lives of flight attendants and bill (debt) collectors.

These two occupations – flight attendants and bill collectors – represent 'the toe and heel of capitalism', service with a smile at one end of the foot and demands for payment with a grimace at the other end, quite a mixed bodily metaphor. The flight attendant, upon whom Hochschild mostly concentrates, is an exemplary figure for understanding the process of emotional labour, the manipulation of the self in order to manipulate the other. Statistics tell us that air travel is comparatively safe, yet it does not necessarily feel that way. Fear of flying is a common malady but not always a chronic one. Flight attendants seek to manage passenger anxiety by manipulating their own emotions. They smile reassuringly at the passenger and try to maintain a breezy demeanour in spite of turbulence. We all signal our emotions in social situations, by smiling and so on. When this is done at work – for a wage, to please the customer in the interests of smooth operations and ultimately company profits – how does it impact emotionally upon the person who is self-manipulating? Do we become the roles we play for pay? Is there an authentic self safe beneath the surface display of emotional labour? Is the acting done at work only on the surface or does it run deeper, transmuting our emotional selves into that which we pretend to be? By raising such questions, Hochschild extends Marx's critical analysis of commodification in capitalist manufacturing and marketing to the commodification of the self in present-day service work. Emotional labour turns the use value of emotion management into exchange value. She says:

> The transmutation of emotional life – the move from the *private* realm to the *public* realm, the trend toward standardization and commercialization of emotive offerings – already fans out across the whole class system. Commercial conventions of feeling are being recycled back into individual private lives; emotional life now appears under new management ... In the United States, this public culture is not simply public; it is commercial. Thus the relation between private emotion work and public emotional labor is a link between non-commercial and commercial spheres. The home is no longer a sanctuary from abuses of the profit motive. Yet the marketplace is not without images of home.[22]

In a later study, *The Time Bind*, Hochschild actually went on to explore how home has become more like work, ironically, for the growing numbers of wives and mothers who also go out to work, and how the workplace, for some of them, becomes more like home, a refuge from the stresses and strains of the domestic environment.[23] She had already coined the term, 'the second shift', inspired by a student's remark, to describe the domestic labour of working women.[24] Her research, then, is not only about the emotional costs of commodified and emotional labour but spans out to consider a whole series of socio-cultural features of what I call cool capitalism, including gender relations. However, Hochschild's ideas have also been extremely influential in research on paid service work in particular.

Hochschild's work has a huge range of applications, not only because of its fruitfulness for sociological research as such but because it is so relevant to many occupational experiences today. These include various kinds of retailing and shop work, serving in restaurants and hotels, the extraordinary resurgence of a once dying-out set of servant occupations that now support two-income couples in the professional-managerial class and not just the very rich, and much else besides. There is the comparatively new phenomenon of sales and services from telephone call and online centres that have been progressively outsourced to relatively cheap yet highly educated labour markets in places like India, offering jobs that require conversational skills and depersonalised formatting of websites lacking the intimate advantages of the face-to-face encounter with customers. Hochschild's sociology of the emotions at work has also had an enormous impact on medical sociology and the study of caring activities generally.[25]

In his research on Disney and the broader phenomenon he calls 'Disneyization', Alan Bryman has adapted Hochschild's ideas on emotional labour to study 'performative labour'.[26] In some ways the Disney theme-park host is the epitome of emotional manipulation through performance, creating a fantasy experience for the purposes of entertainment that brings the unctuousness of American consumer culture to a crescendo. The Disney host is trained in the 'have-a-nice-day' style of performativity that, in the early days of EuroDisney/Disneyland Paris, the French hosts were reluctant to mimic or were simply incapable of realising in performance. Like Disney hosts, workers in, say, shoe shops and telephone call centres are given scripts to learn and parrot to set the customer at ease in order to sell the product. The manifest inauthenticity of it all can, of course, have a quite unintended consequence in provoking a dismissive or downright hostile response from sceptical customers irritated by unwonted intrusion into their lives. Likewise in everyday conversation of all kinds, happy up-talk can either delight or annoy, rather like the endless mobile chatter of the social landscape today.

'Feeling capitalism'[27] has many ramifications, some of them grimly material, not just incitements to grumpiness. In an essay, 'Global Care Chains and Emotional Surplus Value', Hochschild examines how globalising capitalism affects care in the home.[28] She tells the story, borrowed from Rhacel Parreñas's research, of Vicky Diaz, a 35-year-old mother of five, college educated and a trained schoolteacher. Vicky works as a housekeeper on $400 a week in Beverly Hills, where she looks after a little boy called Tommy. Back home in the Philippines, she employs her own live-in domestic worker for $40 a week to look after her own house and children. What we see here is a link in a global care chain that is forged by the unequal wealth of the United States and the Philippines. In such cases it is quite common that the care worker at home is also a mother whose own children are being looked after by her mother. Such a story, one among many similar instances, illustrates and typifies a lived experience the construction of which might otherwise only be glimpsed at best – and possibly not all – as an obscure effect of remote structural relations. As Hochschild comments:

> Global capitalism affects whatever it touches, and it touches virtually everything including what I call global care chains – a series of personal links between people across the globe based on the paid and unpaid work of caring. Usually women make up these chains, though it's possible that some chains are made up of both women and men, or, in rare cases, made up of just men. Such care chains may be local, national, or global. Global

care chains – like Vicky Diaz's – usually start in a poor country and end in a rich one. But some such chains start in poor countries, and move from rural to urban areas within the same poor country. Or they start in one poor country and extend to another slightly less poor country and then link one place to another within the latter country. Chains also vary in the number of links – some have one, others two or three – and each link varies in its connective strength.[29]

Generally, studies of globalisation do not look at human relationships, so concerned are they with the abstractions of 'money, markets and labour flows'. They miss the 'global pattern' of 'displaced feeling'. Vicky Diaz is looking after somebody else's child rather than her own because of the unequal terms of trade in care, one of the features of capitalist inequality and the global scale of exploitation. Although the poor servicing the rich in this way is by no means new, since Marx's time exploitation has become ever more complex, now including the extensive exploitation of emotional labour at a distance. Hochschild asks, 'Is the Beverly Hills child getting "surplus love"?'[30] This is not just about the class expropriation of emotional labour power. It is also gendered and heavily racialised. The perspective Hochschild takes on the issue is that of a critical modernist:

> The critical modernist has a global sense of ethics. If she goes out to buy a pair of Nike shoes, she is concerned to learn how long the hours were for the Third World factory worker making them. She applies the same moral concern to care. So she cares about the welfare of the Filipino child back home. Thus, for the critical modernist, globalisation is a very mixed blessing. It brings with it new opportunities – and the nanny's access to good wages is an opportunity – but also new problems, including costs we have hardly begun to understand.[31]

Hochschild has edited a book with Ehrenreich, entitled *Global Woman: Nannies, Maids and Sex Workers in the New Economy*, which contains essays from around the world documenting in a series of case studies the complex networks exploiting women's labour of one kind or another internationally as the twenty-first century unfolds.[32]

Individualisation

While some socialists continue to put their faith in labour organisation and discern signs of resistance and renewed opposition to the machinations of capital,[33] others wish 'farewell to the working class'.[34] André Gorz has argued that the Marxist scenario of a potentially revolutionary proletariat, just about to move from a class-in-itself to a class-for-itself, was always fanciful and has become completely implausible with the transition to 'post-industrialism'. At one level, this is a reasonable observation regarding the changing composition of the workforce in the older industrial states. Heavy industry and manufacturing have declined, trade-union membership has reduced, and ostensibly socialist parties campaigning for election to government are no longer socialist. There has been a shift of employment towards the so-called service industries and the processing of information and knowledge instead of making things. Things are still made, however, but not necessarily in the same place as before. We do not, it has to be said, actually 'live on thin air', as some fashionable fly-by-night gurus put it.[35] Economic relations have indeed become more globalised, and there is a division of labour between intellectual and manual occupations often at a considerable distance from one another, yet they remain, for all that, *relations*. For instance, the wages of design in a 'post-industrial' country have to be realised and, therefore, supported by material production elsewhere, usually at a much lower wage.

As it happens, the disposition of labour and conditions of work in the older industrial states conforms much more closely to Ulrich Beck's thesis of 'Brazilianisation' than either right-wing or left-wing scenarios of 'post-industrialism':

> The unintended consequence of the neoliberal free-market utopia is a Brazilianization of the West. For trends already visible in world society – high unemployment in the countries of Europe, the so-called jobs miracle in the United States, the transition from a work society to a knowledge society – do not involve a change only in the content of work. Equally remarkable is the new similarity in how paid work itself is shaping up in the so-called

> first world and the so-called third world; the spread of temporary and insecure employment, discontinuity and loose informality into Western societies that have hitherto been the bastions of full employment. The social structure in the heartlands of the West is coming to resemble the patchwork quilt of the South, characterized by diversity, unclarity and insecurity in people's work and life.[36]

The conditions of work and, therefore, of life have become more precarious everywhere, giving rise to 'a political economy of insecurity' that does not, strangely enough, seem to call capitalism into question. There is undoubtedly a concomitant decline in working-class identity and loss of conviction in collective solutions to collective problems. That is why the notion of 'individualisation' appears so apt as a description of the present condition for most people in comparatively wealthy societies.

Beck's individualisation thesis is a corollary to his theory of 'risk society'[37] and needs to be seen in the context of that theory. In order to understand the risk society theory, it is necessary to appreciate the sharp distinction Beck makes between natural hazard and social or societal risk, a distinction that Anthony Giddens had trouble grasping although he has endorsed much of what Beck says.[38] The human encounter with nature has always been hazardous, not least because there are wild animals that will eat human beings given half a chance. Humans had to learn to run to save themselves and also to hunt. They had to learn how to swim in order not to drown. More generally, they have had to come to terms with hazardous nature so as to survive and flourish. Humans have been very successful in taming nature, keeping its dangers at bay and using its resources to their advantage. Even now, however, there are hazards of nature that humans can do little to control or prevent, such as the movement of tectonic plates on the Earth's crust that give rise to earthquakes and tsunamis. Such hazards are quite different, however, from socially produced risks. Human beings take risks deliberately in the hope that they can benefit from the results and can avoid or deal with any unintended consequences. The level of human risk-taking has risen exponentially since the advent of industrialism, which results in great wealth but also enormous environmental damage. Beck's risk society thesis most obviously relates to ecological politics. For instance, in his classic book, *Risk Society*, Beck discusses the dubious benefits and human-induced hazards of nuclear power with regard to the case of the Chernobyl power plant explosion and fall-out of 1986.

Human beings, of course, calculate the risks they take. That is what the insurance business is all about. The trouble is that risks are taken which are increasingly difficult to assess in terms of predicting probable and improbable outcomes. Advanced industrialism, especially impelled by the dynamic of capital accumulation, takes risks that are incalculable. For instance, products are released on to the market with precious little knowledge as to whether they are safe or not. In effect, massive real-life experiments are conducted routinely upon the public at large,[39] gambling with public safety and well-being in order to make a buck, as in the currently explosive use of wireless technology in telecommunications. Such arguments concerning modern risk could be seen as contributing to a critical analysis of capitalism, though Beck himself seldom says so. In fact, he is keen to leave behind what he regards as the outdated politics of Marxism.[40]

The rich try to protect themselves from the hazards of socially produced risk, and to a certain extent succeed in doing so; however, according to Beck, modern risks such as pollution are peculiarly democratic, since they affect everyone. This is such a significant feature of modern life that Beck goes so far as to argue that the risk society is superseding the industrial society. The really big issues of life, then, should be addressed in terms of risk, not only at societal and global levels but also at the day-to-day level of individual experience. Hence the concept of individualisation that Beck has devised and developed in a number of publications with his wife, Elisabeth Beck-Gernsheim. Beck-Gernsheim has been principally concerned with intimate life, gender relations, the position of women and changing family structures, child-rearing and social policy. In the book she wrote with Beck entitled *The Normal Chaos of Love*, they say:

> Individualization means that men and women are released from the gender roles prescribed by industrial society for life in the nuclear family. At the same time, and this aggravates the situation, they find themselves forced, under pain of material disadvantage, to build up a *life of their own* by way of the labour market, training and mobility, and if need be to pursue this life at the cost of their commitment to family, friends and relatives.[41]

Individualisation, then, puts people into a contradictory situation, having to choose between alternative commitments or to balance commitments that are difficult to reconcile with one another; for example, women negotiating the often countervailing demands of career and family. It is as though the ethical dilemmas of existentialism have become normalised for everyone, all are now free – indeed, condemned – to choose agonistically. So, individualisation is not necessarily a negative phenomenon but is in many ways a liberating condition, particularly for those whose choices had hitherto been limited. The difficulty is that there are no guarantees underwriting comparatively free choice. Individualisation 'covers a complex, manifold, ambiguous phenomenon, or more precisely a social transformation ... Time-honoured norms are fading and losing their power to determine behaviour.'[42] People become the directors of their own lives but with no certainty or permanence to the directions taken. In *Risk Society*, Beck had already expanded the point with regard to the self-fashioning of biography:

> Individualization of life situations and processes thus means that biographies become *self-reflexive*; socially prescribed biography is transformed into biography that is self-produced and continues to be produced. Decisions on education, profession, job, place of residence, spouse, number of children and so forth, with all the secondary decisions implied, no longer can be, they must be made. Even where the word 'decisions' is too grandiose, because neither consciousness or alternatives are present, the individual will have to 'pay for' the consequences of decisions not taken.[43]

In another co-authored book, *Individualization: Institutionalized Individualism and its Social and Political Consequences*, in a chapter written by Beck himself, entitled 'A Life of One's Own in a Runaway World – Individualization, Globalization and Politics', a 15 point typology of individualisation is given.[44] It is worth reflecting on each of these points in turn in order to consider their accumulative meaning.

First, a 'compulsion to lead a life of one's own' emerges only 'when a society is highly differentiated'. This derives from the fine divisions of labour and social spheres that developed with industrialism and continue in a modern 'post-industrial' society where people work in many different occupations and live in a whole range of different social enclaves.

Second, a 'life of one's own is not peculiar to oneself'. This repeats the contradictory make-up of individualism as such in so far as great numbers of people are required to live highly individualised lives by the very institutional structures of society, giving rise to 'the paradox of "institutional individualism"'. It is not surprising, then, that many of these individualisms are really quite similar to one another. Still, individuals are required to take command of their own lives.

The third point virtually repeats the second: a 'life of one's own is ... completely dependent on institutions'. Beck explains that this point has to do with de-traditionalisation, the fact that lives are no longer circumscribed by the rules, conventions and guidelines of tradition. Still, there is compulsion in the sense that there are sanctions on not living a life of one's own.

Fourth: 'Living a life of one's own therefore means that standard biographies become elective biographies, "do-it-yourself-biographies", risk biographies, broken or broke-down biographies.' Individuals become the authors of their own biographies. Biographies are no longer written for people, as it were, by fate and tradition. However, 'freedom' comes at a price. Such individualised biographies can go catastrophically wrong. Here Beck acknowledges an explicit connection to neoliberalism, which is otherwise denied in his and Beck-Gernsheim's account of individualisation: 'The neoliberal market ideology enforces atomization with all its political will.'

Fifth: 'In spite or because of the institutional guidelines and the often incalculable insecurity, the life of one's own is condemned to activity.' That can be put more strongly. Under the disposition of individualisation, individuals are obliged to indulge in frenetic activity. Not to do so is to lead a failed life – that of, say, abject poverty, hopeless unemployment, addiction and even illness, all of which the individual is held personally responsible for.

Hence, the sixth point: 'Your own life – your own failure'. In these conditions, do not try to blame social forces and structures for your plight. Society is no longer held to blame. You are to blame; guilty, quite possibly having never found out what the crime was that you are supposed to have committed, like Kafka's Josef K.

Seventh, the circumstances in which you live are peculiarly incomprehensible: 'People struggle to live their own lives in a world that increasingly and more evidently escapes their grasp, one that is irrevocably and globally networked.' Moreover, 'In the global age, one's own life is no longer sedentary or tied to a particular place.'

The eighth point repeats an earlier point, now in relation to the wider picture of globalisation: 'The other side of globalization is detraditionalization.' People will, however, traditionalise. Traditions may be discarded but newer ones – often repeating older ones – are then invented.

Ninth, summing other points up and indicating their interrelatedness: 'If globalization, detraditionalization and individualization are analyzed together, it becomes clear that the life of one's own is an experimental life.'

Tenth: 'the life of one's own is a reflexive life'. It is constantly under scrutiny, discussion and negotiation. 'Active management', Beck remarks, seems an appropriate description here.

Eleventh: 'Living a life of one's own is, in this sense, a late-modern form which enjoys high esteem.' I would add that there are plenty of role models too. Celebrities are heroes and heroines of individualisation.

On the twelfth point, Beck gets a little philosophical: 'The life of one's own, seen in this way, is a radically non-identical life.' This has something to do with the value of 'equal but different'.

Things have started to look up by the thirteenth point: 'Living your own life therefore can mean living under the conditions for radical democracy.' So, the excessively self-examined society of individuals is apparently conducive to greater democracy. Everything is potentially a matter for democratic participation, debate and deliberation, which presumably would not be so if we were not all let loose to fend for ourselves.

Things are really looking up by the fourteenth point, especially with regard to ecological politics: 'The decline of values which cultural pessimists are fond of decrying is in fact opening up the possibility of escape from the creed of "bigger, more, better", in a period that is living beyond its means ecologically and economically.' There are prospects, then, for 'creating something like a co-operative or altruistic individualism'.

This all leads on to the fifteenth and final point: 'The dominance of the life of one's own thus leads to an opening and a sub-politicization of society, but also a depoliticization of national politics.' So in Beck's scheme of things there is an affinity between individualisation and sub-politics, which is a politics of single-issue campaigns that can capture the attention of publics jaded by the machinations of official politics, established parties and national government.

In spite of Beck's positive remarks about sub-politics and the *frisson* of existential freedom conjured up by the idea of individualisation, it is understandable why some might interpret it as being strikingly consistent with the everyday life associated with neoliberal capitalism and even, perhaps, with cool culture. It also has a certain affinity with Fredric Jameson's observations concerning the disorientation of postmodernism and the construction of subjectivities attuned to living in what have become very peculiar circumstances.[45] Also, in the context of a theory of transformed modernity – what Beck calls 'second' or 'reflexive' modernity, following the cataclysm of the 1970s – individualisation and neoliberalism would seem to go together. After all, neoliberalism is a reaction to the post Second World War Keynesian command management of national economies; the social wage guaranteed by the welfare state; public protection for the individual from dire poverty, unemployment, and the sufferings of ill health from 'the cradle to the grave'; and such measures as 'equality of opportunity' in educational provision. The shift from Fordist organisation and job security to flexible labour markets and complex networks in a global economy are characteristic of the neoliberal restructuring that has been so consequential over the past 30 to 40 years. There has been at least a partial reversion to nineteenth-century principles of *laissez-faire*, including economic internationalism, minimal state intervention, the immiseration of the weak and enrichment of the strong.

Beck and Beck-Gernsheim, however, explicitly deny any affinity between individualisation and free market individualism, saying that it is a misunderstanding common in English-speaking countries.[46] This is partly justified by a refusal of reductionism and a claim that individualisation has several aspects not all of which are functional to neoliberalism – such as sub-politics, presumably. However, it is hard not to see some affinity between individualisation and the alienating and stressful conditions of working life generally and particularly in service and creative occupations today. The creative industries are notable sites of individualisation at work under neoliberal conditions. Especially pertinent to the matters in hand are Alison Beale's observations on culture and policy in Canada, a country very much on the frontline of the confrontation between organised capitalism and neoliberalism due to its close proximity to the United States and its participation from the mid 1990s in the North American Free Trade Agreement (NAFTA). Beale is particularly concerned with the situation of women at work in creative industries that are undergoing neoliberal restructuring. It is important to appreciate that a legacy of British colonialism in Canada means there is greater state intervention in the interests of public service and social provision, such as public-sector childcare facilities, than is characteristic of the US free market tradition. Also, and similarly to France, Canadian politicians were keen to assert a 'cultural exemption' in the face of unrestricted marketisation and the ideological sway of 'the consumer model' in which the autonomy of producers is undermined by an alleged consumer sovereignty of 'choice'. Tensions and consequences of a changing policy context have had a general impact in every sector, but acutely so with regard to the choices of women employed in, for instance, the so-called creative industries where apparent advances in position have coincided with deleterious effects in working life. Beale remarks:

> The work patterns associated with 'feminized' labour are common among a significant portion of female workers in the cultural sector. Assembly piece work, word processing and telephone work in the home, and part-time and contract work in the workplace are typical of cultural and communications industries in the NAFTA nations. Work in these areas is subject to the insecurity linked to the right of companies (under NAFTA) to seek out cheaper labour in other countries. The representation of women, minorities and the disabled is higher in public sector and regulated cultural industries in Canada than in private non-regulated businesses such as newspapers ... so that the loss of public-sector jobs and the deregulation of the workplace associated with globalization may have a negative impact for women and others in this area.[47]

Talk of 'deregulation' is misleading in tracing the effects of 'reprivatisation'. In point of fact, the notion of 'deregulation' is something of a misnomer in failing to register that privatised and marketised conditions themselves constitute a regulatory regime, and are probably more accurately named 'reregulation', by which I mean the pressure market forces and bottom lines come to have on every decision and action taken. Beale herself acknowledges the point while stressing the gendering of such reregulation in the implications of this 'lopsided approach' for women:

> Changes in the way cultural production and distribution are funded – the greater assumption of risk, and cost, by workers and consumers, the discouragement of collective forms of work and the privileging of cultural industries with foreign sales potential – build on existing gender inequities in cultural funding. The underpaid and volunteer labour of women, and their patronage of the arts and cultural industries, has played a very significant role in sustaining cultural production in Canada (as elsewhere), but it is primarily women's consumption that has been recognized by the state in its 1990s obsession with identifying audiences and consumers. This lopsided

approach favours the cultural consumption of women with more disposable income, and underplays women's subsidy of culture in other forms, mainly unpaid or underpaid work.[48]

Moreover, although very nearly half the labour force in the cultural sector is female, women are mainly near the bottom of hierarchies with comparatively few in positions of power and control. Neoliberalisation does nothing to ameliorate this situation, in spite of much trumpeted anti-sexism policies, and instead exacerbates it, particularly because it is so difficult for women to bear and care for children in careers that are so insecure, time-consuming and stressful.

The transition from organised to neoliberal capitalism in the mode of cultural production and circulation is especially marked in the transformation of British broadcasting and television since the 1970s. Public service broadcasting was effectively invented in Britain during the 1920s and pioneered by the internationally renowned BBC, which was the sole broadcasting organisation in Britain until the 1950s when commercial television was introduced. Although publicly owned and financed by a compulsory licence fee, the BBC had a greater relative autonomy from government than other state-owned bodies of its kind. And when advertising-funded television was set up in Britain the commercial companies were also required by law to observe public service principles of balanced broadcasting and universal provision. This dual system of public service broadcasting persisted successfully until the 1980s when the proliferation of channels delivered by various technologies was underway, accompanied by the entrance of leaner start-up companies, intensified competition and increased marketisation generally in the British industry. Under the public service arrangements that pertained until the 1980s and persisted to an extent into the 1990s, there was a clearly delineated division of labour before 'multitasking' set in, and many jobs, particularly at the BBC, were for life. The system came under criticism for being static and too consensual, which partly changed in the 1980s with developments in 'independent' production facilitated by Channel 4, the new 'publishing channel', from 1982. In one sense this was a progressive development in opening up television to a wider range of voices and representations, both cultural and political. However, the growth of independent production companies, outside the BBC and the established companies with regional franchises, was also a feature of neoliberal marketisation with all its negative entailments.[49]

Although television, like other cultural and media industries, is an exceptionally risky business, it is in many respects strangely risk averse. In addition to synergistic multiple exploitation of intellectual property, and the 'recombinant culture' that is often seen as a feature of postmodernism,[50] there are two principal means of devolving risk in a post-Fordist or neo-Fordist regime of accumulation and mode of regulation as applied to the television business. First, the reduction of in-house production and the practice of outsourcing product from a network of smaller companies devolves risks to 'independents', as Hollywood had discovered as long ago as the 1950s.[51] The major corporations retain control, however, over distribution, which is where the locus of power lies in the cultural and media industries, augmented by the editorial function. Production is largely done by cost-cutting 'indies', as is 'research and development'. The second principal means of devolving risk is, to put it bluntly, to lay it on the workers. Work in British broadcasting and television, similarly to elsewhere in the world, has become increasingly temporary, casualised and insecure since the Thatcherite reforms of the 1980s and 1990s.

Thatcherism attacked 'restrictive practices' in broadcasting, where strong unions had in the old days protected their members and campaigned for relatively high wages for permanent staff. Since the 1980s union power has been much weakened in radio and television, as it has in other industries. The 'job for life' has largely become an anachronism. With the partial exception of 'core' managerial functions, 'flexible' labour and contractual insecurity became commonplace for most new entrants to the broadcasting industry, particularly among 'creatives'.

For some older broadcasting workers it became harder to sustain their careers past early middle age, though some of them, especially those with well-established track records, benefited from new small-business opportunities that arose from forced 'independence' and intense market competition in a 'disorganised' broadcasting industry. It became much more difficult to build a career for successive age cohorts entering the business.[52] A sharp divide opened up between the comparative securities of higher management – accountants, MBA holders and the like – and the insecurities of 'creative' personnel, who have to manage themselves guilefully through various projects and recruitment avenues. Many are now obliged to move perpetually from one short-term contract to another, relying on whatever reputations they have cultivated, or being prepared to work for very little – or both.

Broadcasting in Britain was thus transformed from a bureaucratic and cumbersome Fordist framework into the looser, network structures and career trajectories of post-Fordism, or, rather, neo-Fordism. Costs were driven down in the highly competitive independent sector – now supplying innumerable cable and satellite channels as well as the terrestrial channels – where wages have shrunk and working conditions have become extremely fraught and stressful. Poor pay and overwork have all grown apace.[53] It is extremely difficult for women to sustain a broadcasting career past the age of 40, when many of them go missing from the business. It is also hard for younger people to make their way in the early years of a broadcasting career. Stories abound of extreme exploitation of the young with many of them working for barely subsistence wages in the often forlorn hope that they will eventually pass on to something better. As James Silver has reported:

> It is television's dirty little secret. The eager young faces that flit about on every production set, making sure that scripts are photocopied and the coffees are made and the taxis are booked. Always among the first to arrive in the morning and the last to leave at night, desperate to make and secure the all-important step on the first slippery rung of the industry ladder. Many are so determined to forge a career in the glamorous world of television that they are prepared to work for little or nothing to achieve it.[54]

Angela McRobbie has analysed the youth labour market in London's 'creative industries' in general. She had already produced detailed research on the training and prospects of young fashion designers.[55] Fashion, according to McRobbie, is a tough business. Britain is well regarded internationally for its fashion and design education. Yet McRobbie uncovers a fatal flaw in the curriculum. Young fashion designers are taught fine-art values – tempered these days by cool, street-wise aesthetics – rather than the craft skills of cutting and sewing. Moreover, students do not typically learn much about the exploitative economy of manufacturing garments, the sweatshops at home and abroad. Some of them, the better ones, swan off on graduation to the great fashion houses of continental Europe, where they may be and usually are themselves badly exploited. On returning to Britain, they typically set up in business – imbued as they are with the individualising values of 'making it' – designing, marketing and sometimes even making prototypes of their wares. Very often this amounts to back-breaking work and self-exploitation. Most briefly successful designers do not make much money and many of them go broke. Freelancing for big firms, or simply giving up the ghost by, for instance, entering sales in department stores, are common outcomes for this particular career trajectory. It makes a mockery of the rhetoric of 'creative Britain'.

More generally, McRobbie remarks: 'Requiring risk-taking activity and high degrees of mobility of its workforce, cultural work also relies on disembedded and highly individualized personnel.'[56] Cultural workers are required to work upon themselves, to fashion a useful self and to project their selves through strenuous self-activity; to be, in effect, self-reliant whether self-employed or temporarily employed. The social obligation of representing a capable and individualised self is especially pronounced for young workers in the meritocracy of 'creativity' promoted by New Labour in Britain. In many ways, this imaginary recalls the figure of the romantic artist, a lonely individual with special insight and abnormal capacities. Now that typification, exemplified by celebrity publicity, is a model of success for 'creative' youngsters from conventionally 'artistic' occupations all the way through to cooking and hairdressing. McRobbie draws a connection between the values of youthful – indeed, 'cool' – clubbers and such imagery of creative work, which is so much at odds with the realities of mundane labour in an exceptionally insecure labour market. The glamour of it all masks over the poor prospects and inevitable though not widely publicised pitfalls: 'more and more young people opt for the insecurity of careers in media, culture or art in the hope of success'.[57]

Youth culture itself is an integral element in the mix of individualised life and work. Speed is also of the essence; exemplified by the creative industries. This is a volatile, rapidly changing world in which you have to be fit in order to survive. No longer are creativity and artistry at odds with business; they are instead one and the same. For McRobbie, all this is linked to 'the pervasive success of neo-liberal values'.[58] And while at work you may cultivate a modishly eccentric persona, that does not mean you can actually be a rebel, 'It's not cool to be "difficult"'.[59] Individualised work in the creative industries demands 'creative compromise' that is appropriate to a relentlessly 'upbeat business',[60] and furious networking by ambitious young people.

To put it summarily, the developments traced here concerning individualisation amount to a thoroughgoing Americanisation of the self in a neoliberal world and cool culture.

Generation Crisis

Individualisation and extreme exploitation of young people in the cultural and media industries point up a generational issue in working life, the way in which conditions have become more insecure under neoliberalism among comparatively affluent populations in wealthier parts of the world. However, even now 'the problem of youth' is seldom discussed as an economic matter as such. It is generally framed by moral considerations, that changes in morality are alarming for older generations, signalling either a decline of values or, alternatively, liberation from worn-out codes and ways of experiencing life whether at work or in leisure. In fact, leisure is often seen as the principal site of the youth problem.

Young people, certainly in late-modern circumstances, are said to rebel routinely against their parents either for good or ill. There is a longstanding tradition of anxiety about juvenile delinquency and the persistent sense of an apparent crisis in the maturation process. There is also a tendency, countering such misgiving, to romanticise youth, to see, for example, spectacular subcultures as representing some kind of 'resistance through rituals'.[61] Resistance to what exactly, however, has always been somewhat unclear. Sentimental young Marxists of the 1970s discerned resistance to capitalism in youthful mores. However implausible that imaginary was at the time, it is now so completely unbelievable to the extent that not even they who once espoused it and those whom they influenced believe it. According to some insouciant sociologists, we have entered a 'time of the tribes' when young people's self-identity and collective association have seemingly taken on a pre-modern cast.[62] This even less plausible imaginary is uncomfortably close – or perhaps, on the contrary, conveniently close – to marketing ideology and its rhetoric of finely differentiated lifestyles. In fact, that may be closer to the nub of the matter in so far as a great many young people have gone through a rigorous, indeed Olympian training in the strenuous business of consumerism, for which 'the world of work' is very much a secondary consideration.

There is a recurrent impression of an unbridgeable gulf opening up between generations, in which there are mutually incomprehensible ways of relating to life and little continuity between the generations. It has recently been characterised by a perceived 'disconnectedness' of younger people (in a book with the subtitle: 'Why Our Kids are Turning Their Backs on Everything We Thought We Knew'[63]). Exasperation at youthful conduct, and also the discovery that kids ain't so bad after all, are not so new. The perpetual recurrence of 'the generation gap' has to do with the drama acted out every generation over the acquisition of autonomy, which is as good a definition of growing up as any. The younger generation have to achieve autonomy and it is hardly unforeseeable that this should take the typical form of a rebellion against, and distancing from, the older generation, fortified by the not unreasonable assumption that old people are past it and the young are the inheritors of the future.

What is perhaps the distinguishing characteristic of present-day youth culture in capitalist society is formed very early these days, in childhood. As Madeleine Bunting has remarked: 'Cool is of the ultimate symbolic importance, and what is cool is usually anti-adult, oppositional, rebellious.'[64] Juliet Schor identifies the source of cool in the United States:

> Cool has been around for decades. Back in the fifties, there were cool cats and hipsters. In the sixties, hippies and the Beatles were cool. But in those days, cool was one of many acceptable personal styles. Now it's revered as a universal quality – something every product tries to be and every kid needs to have. Marketers have defined cool as the key to social success, as what matters for determining who belongs, who's popular, and who gets accepted by peers. While there is no doubt that the desire for social acceptance is a central theme of growing up, marketers have elevated it to the sine qua non of children's psyches. The promotion of cool is a good example of how the practices of marketing to teens, for whom social acceptance is even more important, have filtered down to the children's sphere.[65]

These are not just the crazed imaginings of disgruntled elders and social critics. Books have been written by experts that explain exactly how to do cool marketing to kids.[66] Schor points out quite rightly that the genius of cool is its versatility, that it speaks meaningfully to both 'dorks' and 'jocks'. Still, there are consistent themes in cool discourse; for instance, that expensiveness promises social exclusivity. The rhetoric may derive from black street culture but it has a widespread appeal in white mainstream culture. It is also consistent with an orientation to active consumption, learning from consumers themselves and flattering their apparently spontaneous tastes. Crucially important, of course, is that 'kids are cool and adults are not'.[67] Moreover, 'The world of children's marketing is filled with variants of the us-versus-them message.'[68] 'Anti-adultism' is accompanied by a process of 'age compression', whereby consumers are cultivated at younger and younger ages, including most notably the sexualisation of pre-pubescent girls, also commented upon by the critic of youthful 'viral marketing', Alissa Quart.[69]

The US is in the vanguard of youthful cool, consumer culture; but, interestingly and perhaps surprisingly, a recent survey by the National Consumer Council (NCC) in Britain notes that 'British children are more consumer-oriented than their American counterparts. Children in Britain are more brand aware and less satisfied than US children with what they have to spend.'[70] The New Labour think-tank, the Institute for Public Policy Research (IPPR), endorses the NCC's observation and, like Schor in the US, advocates civil society and governmental action to control marketing to children and young people. In its report, *Freedom's Orphans*, the IPPR also notes that cool consumerism is most acutely experienced among relatively deprived and disadvantaged youth, and, in effect, exacerbates social inequality. However, the IPPR makes a quite astonishing and dubious – not to say pseudo-social-scientific – assertion as well: 'in just over a decade personal and social skills became 33 times more important in determining relative life chances'.[71] Such argumentation exemplifies neoliberalism's distortion of social-democratic politics in the recent period. The problems of working-class youth are defined in terms of a lack of middle-class graces. Hence the IPPR recommends a 'capabilities approach' to reforming the socially inept young. They need training in social skills in order to achieve adult responsibility and compete in the world of work, it is argued, as though that is a solution to the McDonaldisation[72] of work for many young people in comparatively affluent societies today. The lower end of the labour market is poorly paid and de-unionised. Junk jobs are done with little commitment or pride in the work, hardly surprisingly. Nor is it surprising that the cool culture of consumerism is treated as much more meaningful in everyday life.

In Britain, the Financial Services Authority (FSA) is similarly concerned about youthful incapacity for dealing with the material aspects of life but proposes, less fancifully than social-skills training, a rather more practical approach to financial education for the young in order to avoid serious debt and maintain solvency in straitened economic circumstances that are worsened and mystified by the sway of cool consumer culture.[73] The FSA found 18- to 24-year-old young people to be lacking in knowledge and actually indifferent to basic issues of personal finance. With the aid of research from Bristol University, the FSA also concluded that older generations were not much better informed about matters of personal finance.[74] Public ignorance in this respect is particularly grave considering the rising and indeed critical levels of personal indebtedness due to easily obtained credit not only in Britain but also in the US, where such enthralment was pioneered and, in the later years of the twentieth century, enormously expanded.

Another problem which hits the young particularly hard is the rising cost of housing, both rented and 'owned'. This is especially problematic in Britain where the 'property-owning democracy' entails owning your own house, usually the largest part of most people's wealth among the working and middle classes, and where the housing stock is relatively low per capita. Thirty years ago the sale price of a modest house or flat was about the same as an average annual income, whereas now it is normally at least five times, and in some places rising to as much as ten times, an average income.[75] It has been much easier in recent years to get a mortgage than, say, 30 years ago, but the repayment costs on such expensive housing are, of course, much higher. This trend was interrupted suddenly by the 'credit crunch' of 2007–8 – either temporarily or for the foreseeable future, it is too soon to tell. Occasionally, as we have also seen over recent years, when house prices dip some homeowners find themselves in 'negative equity'. These factors are basic facts of economic life, as are interest rate changes, and are of material significance for everyone but acutely so for the young, whose hedonistic consumerism puts them at a serious generational disadvantage in coping with such problems. These are not the only factors contributing to a material crisis for the younger generation. The costs of education, and the diminishing rewards they face in the future for a lifetime's work, are further exacerbations of their plight.

The youth problem is economic and not just an issue of cultural difference. Young American, Anya Kamenetz, has described her own generation as 'a broke generation'.[76] For her, the 68 million

Americans aged between 18 and 34 make up 'generation debt', the title of her book on the topic. The problem of youth is one of money. As a recent college graduate herself, Kamenetz is only too aware of the burden of debt resulting from higher education, with its exaggerated promise of greater lifetime earnings. She connects the problem to the transition from organised to neoliberal capitalism; the local effect in this respect is to push more of the costs of study onto students and their families. From the 1960s, public grants for students in the United States were more extensive than Europeans often realise. State funding in Europe has indeed been more universally available for higher education, but here also, as in the US and with Britain in the lead, all of that has been cut back, and growing numbers of students, making up the enlarged participation rate, are increasingly dependent on loans to educate their individualised selves. Students also typically fall into credit card debt in order to supplement their inadequate loans, and they represent a reserve army of the McDonaldised labour force as well, doing casual work in fast-food joints, supermarkets and so forth in order to get by. There is no guarantee of a good, lucrative career at the end of their studies either.

Kamenetz also notes: 'We twenty-somethings have grown up marinated in the most aggressive advertising and marketing environment ever known.'[77] And 'compulsive shopping is only one symptom of an underlying imbalance between what young people have and what they dream about'.[78] Life for the young is exceptionally risky. They are relatively healthy yet they too need what for many is unaffordable medical insurance. In these circumstances, the very idea of saving for retirement is a joke, and not only because it has always been so for the young. The topic of pensions does not constitute a compelling subject for young people, who are of course immortal. In *Banking on Death*, his monumental study of 'the boring world of pension provision', Robin Blackburn opens with the following observation: 'Damien Hirst's pickled shark is entitled "The Impossibility of Death in the Mind of the Living". Perhaps a butterfly case could represent another thought: "The Impossibility of Old Age in the Mind of the Young (and not so Young)".'[79] In an uncertain world, however, there are some things that we can be sure about. If you do not die young, you will grow old. And then die.

To be sure, pensions do not interest young people – but they should. Their pensions are already being stolen in affluent countries like Britain and the United States. Historically, only the very privileged have been comfortably off in old age. Officers and some gentlemen may have had pensions from the state. Most people, few of whom lived to be old by current standards, could not even think of retirement. And, if they were too old to work, they became dependent on their children or on the mean pittance of charity. Bismarck inaugurated the change with the introduction of the first generalised public pension scheme in the late nineteenth century. Lloyd George followed suit in Britain a century ago. And in the mid twentieth century modern pension schemes as we know them now were developed. This is a very recent history. In capitalist societies, state pensions were a feature of the organised capitalist response to the challenge of socialism. Under neoliberalism, as the challenge of socialism has subsided, they are no longer strictly necessary to the survival of the system. What then is the solution for the elderly? Well, the market of course.

Public provision has not exactly been withdrawn but rather gradually eroded. And even occupational and market-based schemes are becoming less advantageous for retirees. Part of the reason has to do with the way schemes were set up when social democracy was hegemonic, including Roosevelt's New Deal as well as European welfarism. 'Pay-as-you-go' meant that, in the early days, as people retired they became pension beneficiaries without having made a lifetime's contribution. In effect, current pensions are paid for by those who are still working. To a large extent, they still are. Demographic change, with ageing populations growing in proportion to younger generations, puts enormous pension pressure on public finance – a fact which is emphasised by the 'realists' who advocate reduced benefits, especially in continental Europe where public/occupational pensions were particularly generous (reaching in France at one time as much as 80 per cent of final salary, though more typically 66 per cent).

Basic state pensions, even at the best of times, have always been meagre and were supplemented for the professional-managerial class by occupational, corporate and marketplace pensions. Older schemes of this kind were 'defined-benefit' schemes whereby pensions were calculated as a proportion of final salary times years of employment within the scheme. Final salaries are usually the highest of a working life for members of the professional-managerial class. One way of reducing pension pay-outs, then, is to shift from final salary to average salary calculated across years of employment. This is happening in pension schemes within public employment, a fact that is little recognised or appreciated among younger employees. Occupational and corporate schemes in the private sector have shifted from 'defined benefit' to 'defined contribution' schemes so that the costs to the employee are fixed but the benefits are determined by stock-market values that fluctuate unpredictably. So, while basic state pensions have been reduced in real terms, occupational schemes, beginning in the private sector but developing in the public sector too, are having their benefits reduced as well. Retirement age is also being extended due to increased longevity. Not long ago, retirees would not typically have been drawing pensions for very long, so they could be allowed to retire younger than retirees today and in the future who are likely to live longer.

None of these developments tend to be of compelling interest for younger people, though many of them are becoming aware that the post Second World War 'baby boom' generation now entering retirement are peculiarly privileged. Indeed, it has to be said, they will probably turn out to be the most privileged generation in history, whether past or future. Occasionally I imagine that over the next few years there will be an outbreak of drive-by shootings of old people by young people who believe they are being ripped off by them. But that, of course, is an understanding of the situation cultivated by the New Right in the US, keen to push everyone onto their own – or, rather, market-based – resources. It is vital however to resist too exaggerated a sense of discontinuity between generations, and to recover a greater appreciation of their interdependence, that is, some sense of mutuality between young and old.[80]

Admittedly, this is a story of doom and gloom told by an older person in the hope of stimulating greater awareness in younger people. What has been going on reminds me of the recipe for boiling a live frog. If you throw the frog into boiling water it will jump out, but if you put it into cold water and boil it slowly it won't notice until it is dead. No doubt that is overstating the case. Still, it is true that younger workers face longer working lives and less generous pensions than in the 'golden age' that immediately preceded the eruption of neoliberalism. Add to that historical point a consideration of the more immediate issue of generation debt and youthful hyperconsumerism, and it becomes reasonable to suggest that cool young people are the ragged trousered philanthropists of today.[81]

6
ANTI-CAPITALISM REVISITED

This book is a work of critical social science, not of practical politics. It is critical of capitalism whilst also recognising how capitalism has become curiously immune to criticism. It seems that capitalism, as a matter of fact, is unsurpassable. For better or worse, capitalism is apparently here to stay, having survived any conceivable challenge to its reason to be. That is a judgement held not only by supporters of capitalism but also by many of its critics. We have seen the implosion of communism with the collapse of the Soviet Union and the neoliberal transformation of Eastern Europe. Even an ostensibly communist power, the People's Republic of China, has taken the capitalist road, admittedly with feudalistic features and while retaining the authoritarian characteristics of communism in the sense of what used to be called 'actually existing socialism'. The manifest failures of Marxism-Leninism and Maoism have rendered the very idea of communism ludicrous.

None of this has been good news either for social democracy in capitalist society, which to a significant extent owed its success to the threat of communism. Although at least partly resulting from considerable struggle, social gains were conceded under capitalism in order to ward off something worse at times of crisis in the past. That threat to capitalism has passed and social democracy has been hollowed out by largely accepting the rule of 'the market'. What could socialism possibly mean today, other than a sentimental attachment to a lost ideal and nostalgia for more propitious times? Yet socialism has not evacuated the field entirely. It has had a resurgence in South America, the original laboratory for neoliberal transformation. South Americans learnt the hard way – and early – what the rule of the market meant. This has been fertile ground for a socialist rebirth – however fragile it may be, faced with the hostility of the United States – supported by its allies and network of international agencies.

Rather like the hasty obituary for Mark Twain, the announcement that socialism is dead was somewhat premature. At the 2005 World Social Forum Hugo Chávez talked of 'twenty-first century socialism', and theorists in the heartlands of capitalism try to figure out what that might mean. They place particular emphasis on 'the social' and do not equate socialism with state domination of civil society. And while socialists may no longer talk of the complete overthrow of capitalism, they are inevitably critical of exploitation, the core principle of capitalism. Erik Olin Wright argues that a renewal of the socialist project involves thought about what is *desirable*, what is *viable* and what is *achievable*, none of which is an all-or-nothing matter.[1] Articulating what is desirable is a proper task of social philosophy and important in ideological struggle, but, of course, from a practical point of view, it is not enough. Nothing is certain, neither the once-and-for-all triumph of capitalism nor the inevitability of socialism. There are no guarantees either way. In addition to desirability, Wright gives due consideration to questions of viability and achievability that exceed the terms of reference of this book. More directly relevant here is the argument that capitalism's profit-driven and market-expansion dynamics need to be checked, not only because of the social harm they cause, according to socialist critics, but also, and yet more consequentially, because of the costs to the environment that derive from 'a consumption-oriented society and the creation of artificial consumer "needs"'.[2] The limits to capitalism are not, as classical Marxists would have it, necessarily *sui generis*, essentially integral to capital itself; they are rather and to a significant extent external, that is, they concern ecological balance and natural survival, confronting the limits of nature, as will be argued later in this chapter.

In conclusion, I wish to comment on two kinds of contemporary enslavement, in a metaphorical sense: the attachment to cool brands and the poorly kept secret of sweated labour around the world. The latter has been a particular flashpoint in the revival of anti-capitalism and the emergence of a global justice movement. Finally, it will be necessary to comment upon the ecological limits to capitalism, not as a deterministic fact but as an existential problem.

Cool Brands and Sweated Labour

The most prominent feature of cultural and public space today in 'the West', and increasingly across the rest of the world as well, is that of a logoscape, festooned with signifiers of arches, shells and checks or ticks, signs of signs, signs upon signs. Such signs overwhelm non-commercial signs, endlessly suggesting that the great benefactor of all that is desirable, indeed of all that is needed, is corporate capital. Other signs, especially anything to do with the public as opposed to the private sector, are dull and colourless in comparison. Incessant propaganda on behalf of the commodity, however, is at one step removed from commercial products themselves. There is a meta-sign framing the message, that of the almighty brand. The sell is duplicitously soft – that is, insinuated – not hard in the old-fashioned way. It has something to do with wish-fulfilment, identity and pleasure.

Brands are cool. In Britain, there is an organisation called Superbrands, which issues an annual list of 'cool brands'. Brands may be cool by definition, but 'cool' itself is almost impossible to define. It is somehow ineffable. To try to say exactly what it is, is uncool.[3] The allure of the brand, then, is a kind of psychological magic, hard to explain, yet effective. Nevertheless, brand culture is not universally accepted; brands are controversial, not least of all due to Naomi Klein's influential book, *No Logo: Taking Aim at the Brand Bullies*, published right at the beginning of the third Christian millennium. Klein's book analyses the marketing of branded goods, their manufacture, and the practices that project the brand as the focal point of anti-corporate politics. She notes how, since the 1980s, major corporations have shifted from preoccupation with the product to promoting the brand as a lucrative object in its own right. Brand identities are of course much older, but they were never of such importance as they became both economically and culturally in the closing years of the twentieth century. And, as Klein remarks: 'Cool, alternative, young, hip – whatever you want to call it – was the perfect identity for product-driven companies looking to become transcendent image-based brands.'[4] She also mentions how black culture has been mined to add value to brands. Even the most widely recognised brand on Earth, Coca Cola, was represented as 'underground' in order to enhance its appeal to 'trend-setting cool kids'.[5] This was a notable feature of how far 'the mass marketing of rebellion'[6] went for corporate capitalism.

In truth, cool brands are the bearers of cultural homogeneity, effectively marketing sameness all around the world. This fact has to be masked over by the brand corporations: hence the coalescence of identity politics with its ultimate value of 'difference' and the 'lifestyle' rhetoric of cool marketing. It is an extraordinary ideological trick to advertise products to millions and millions of people with the message that association with the brand – branding your self – delivers individuality, the mark of difference, the paradoxical myth of non-conformist conformity. In making this argument, Klein was simply reiterating a truism half a century after Adorno and Horkheimer had put the case forcefully, but hardly originally even then. It is not, however, the most important aspect of Klein's thesis, which centred on an older observation concerning the mystified relation between apparently innocent consumption and exploitative production. Her immediate detractors could hardly answer that claim with credibility, so, in Britain at least, they concentrated on a common-sensical defence of brand culture instead. As *The Economist*, in an issue seeking to refute Klein, declared on its cover, 'brands are good for you'.[7] On the leader page, it was asserted that brands offer protection, not exploitation. They provide 'a guarantee of reliability and quality',[8] which may have been truer in the nineteenth century than in the twenty-first. Steve Hilton, a Conservative Party publicist, added to that defence in the left-liberal *Guardian*:

Brands make it worthwhile for companies to invest in new technology, new products and services that make our lives easier and more pleasurable. Why would Ford bother inventing a car that doesn't pollute if no one knows that Ford has done it?

Brands enable consumers to make informed choices, quickly. Imagine going shopping in a world without brands. You may occasionally dream of the rustic idyll that anti-capitalists promote: a world where local needs are met by local farmers and artisans. Fine – you can have that if you want, as long as you're also prepared to take the higher infant mortality, lower life expectancy, lack of education and absence of social welfare provision that is the inevitable consequence of a world without capitalism generating the money to pay for public services and social progress.[9]

Hilton was on stronger ground in making the point that brands help the confused shopper to make choices than he was when arguing that health and welfare are only provided by capitalism. There is a two-word answer to that fallacious argument: socialist Cuba, where infant mortality is lower, longevity greater, and education and healthcare superior to any other Third World – 'developing' – country. Moreover, there are no sweatshops manufacturing cool brands for consumer capitalism in Cuba – that is, at the time of writing – though Fidel Castro may possibly once have been tempted by them in the past, in his desire to reintegrate Cuba into 'the global economy'.

The effacement of 'the public' as a separate entity from 'the private' is especially marked in the corporate takeover of public space, most obviously in the privately owned shopping mall where business interests prevail in serving the customer. Agrarian capitalists enclosed common land in the early phase of capitalism; now corporate capital encloses the commons of every kind, actual and virtual. At the same time, corporations no longer bother to own the means of production, as did capitalists of old. They transcend place, closing down factories where labour is expensive and outsourcing production to suppliers where labour is cheap, and political authority gives no protection to local workers. Instead, the locals are offered up as factory fodder to the global machine of value extraction.

Klein visited Cavite, the largest 'free-trade zone' in the Philippines.[10] There she saw the shanty towns and dormitories for young, mainly female workers. It is a work camp enclosed by a 'wall of fear',[11] where the profits are virtually free of taxation, labour rights are suspended, working hours are long, and the $6 a day minimum wage is often waived for hard-pressed contractors.[12] For Klein, Cavite typifies the 'industrialization in brackets' where multinational brand products, such as clothing and electronic gadgets, are actually made. It is not exceptional. There are worse places in China. Although the stories of sweated labour from the 'developing' world are particularly shocking, Klein notes a correspondence with some working conditions nearer home: 'zone workers in many parts of Asia, the Caribbean and Central America have more in common with office-temp workers in North America and Europe than they do with factory workers in those Northern countries'.[13] Actually, they also have something in common with a few factory workers in North America and Europe too.

Back in North America, 1996 was 'the year of the sweatshop'. Labour unions, like UNITE for garment workers, political activists and students combined to combat the nexus of cool brands and sweated labour. As Andrew Ross, editor of a collection of campaigning essays, remarked, 'matters of style are not disconnected from labor issues'.[14] His edited volume compiled data on sweatshop conditions in not only the 'developing' world but also in the US, and made the connection with past struggle in the early twentieth century within that very country, where historical amnesia is so endemic. Personal stories – like that of a migrant worker from Ecuador, Lina Rodriguez Meza, who labours in a New York garment sweatshop on a pittance – convey something of a Third World experience in Manhattan itself.[15] Such experiential cases are important for making the connection between anti-brand campaigns on, say, university campuses and the need to organise resistance, which is palpably relevant in the US. It is also relevant elsewhere, at a distance, but this is more difficult since liberal-democratic niceties do not apply where worker representation is often prohibited and resistance is put down violently.

The garment industry is particularly prone to sweatshop manufacturing methods even in the old industrial heartlands because of the emphasis on fashion in which capitalisation can be very low, and, in the early stage of the fashion cycle, short production runs are called for at high speed.[16] Because of the showcasing of fashion, its sheer cultural prominence, especially for the young, the garment industry became a flashpoint and favoured focus for campaigns during the 1990s. Such campaigns, however, are apt to go quickly out of fashion in a culture with a very short memory span. 'It's so old hat to complain about Gap and Nike and all the rest of it. What's this year's issue?' That attitude is an especially pernicious one and thoroughly symptomatic of the culture of cool capitalism. To some extent it merely reflects the cycle of news, in that stories typically emerge, are hammered to death and then forgotten about, irrespective of whether the issues have been resolved. Like many environmental issues, sweatshop scandals and the moments of protest intermittently visible in the news agenda are only the tip of the iceberg – perhaps an unfortunate metaphor at a time of possibly chronic global warming. For instance, as recently as September 2007 in Britain, a *Guardian* inquiry revealed that high-street brands like Mothercare, Gap, Matalan and H&M were selling clothes made in India for 13p an hour,[17] a story that soon dropped off the public agenda to become yesterday's news yet again.

Klein not only analyses the nexus of cool brands and sweatshop labour in *No Logo*, she also reflects on the emergence of resistance to brand culture in North America and Europe. In fact, *No Logo* was widely received on publication as the manifesto of anti-capitalist or anti-corporate politics. The world had just been stunned by the successful protest against the World Trade Organisation's meeting in Seattle at the end of 1999.[18] *No Logo* came out within weeks of that inaugural event. In it, Klein had already reviewed the activities of such networking organisations as Adbusters and Corporate Watch in Canada and the US, and Reclaim the Streets in Britain. And in the *New Statesman* in January 2000, she asked: 'What are we to make of the extraordinary scenes in Seattle that brought the twentieth century to a close?'[19] The beginnings of 'a movement of movements' had been discernible at Seattle with the involvement of the Longshore Workers Union and the steelworkers, ecological activists and socialists, as well as young anarchists targeting the brands. Klein was in touch with these various currents of opposition, though it was the anti-brand campaign that she focused upon in her book and about which she had both supportive and critical arguments to make.

Adbusters pioneered the practice of 'culture jamming', inspired by the French Situationists of the 1960s.[20] Klein describes culture jamming as 'parodying advertisements and hijacking billboards in order to drastically alter their messages' as part of 'a climate of semiotic Robin Hoodism'.[21] Therein lies its strength and its weakness. Significantly, Kalle Lasn, the leading figure in Adbusters, subtitled his book on culture jamming, 'The Uncooling of America™'. He begins by itemising the faults of American culture:

> America is no longer a country. It's a trillion dollar brand...
> American culture is no longer created by the people...
> A free, authentic life is no longer possible in America today...
> Our mass media dispense a kind of Huxleyan 'soma'.
> American cool is a global pandemic.
> The Earth can no longer support the lifestyle of the cool-hunting American-style consumer.[22]

According to Lasn, what America needs is 'a rebranding strategy'; easier said than done. Uncooling America would take something more than a few 'subvertisements' and occasional outbreaks of carnivalesque protest, which is not to deny the agitational role of 'semiological guerrilla warfare', in Umberto Eco's phrase,[23] merely to note its limits, along with those of all exclusively *cultural* politics (as Klein herself does). At the time of *No Logo*, culture jamming was a flourishing subculture on the Internet and it still survives, not only on the Net but also in the glossy *Adbusters* magazine.[24] Klein notes the paradox whereby such symbolic contestation takes on the very character of what it opposes and how easily absorbed it is into what I have been calling cool capitalism. Still, anti-brand campaigning may produce a boomerang effect whereby the very exposure of the brand makes it vulnerable to hostile publicity, serving in effect as 'the corporate Achilles heel'.[25] Brands like Levi Strauss and McDonald's, however, may have been wounded but they have hardly been slain. Brands do fail – and there are some spectacular cases[26] – but that is just part of capitalism's ruthlessly competitive process of creative destruction.

Towards the end of *No Logo*, Klein makes an especially interesting remark: 'for the system to function smoothly, workers must know little of the marketed lives of the products they produce and consumers must remain sheltered from the production lives of the brands they buy'.[27] You would think so ... but, in today's system of instantaneous global communications supplemented by the worldwide distribution of commercial messages and Hollywood movies and television shows, it is impossible to conceal the markup on the commodities that sweatshop workers labour over for scandalously poor reward. Moreover, there has been plenty of exposure of 'globalization's dirty little secret'[28] to shake consumers out of their ignorance and complacency. And yet indifference or, worse, facile realism persist, even with such awareness.

Quite possibly of greater consequence than the refusal to think or care about the real costs of global brand culture – or, for that matter, about the growing inequality in the world, instead of the 'trickle-down' beneficence of economic growth touted by apologists for neoliberalism – is the cluster of issues remarked upon by Klein earlier in *No Logo*:

> Despite the widening gulf between rich and poor consistently reported by the UN and despite the much-discussed disappearance of the middle class in the West, the attack on jobs and income levels is probably not the most serious corporate offense we face as global citizens: it is, in theory, not irreversible. Far worse, in the long term, are the crimes committed by corporations against the natural environment, the food supply and indigenous peoples and cultures.[29]

One No and Many Yeses

Around the turn of the millennium a phenomenon erupted that was variously named 'anti-capitalism', 'anti-corporatism', 'anti-globalisation' and 'the movement for social justice' or 'the global justice movement'. Not all currents of what was also known as 'a movement of movements' were necessarily anti-capitalist. Some may have been opposed to the excesses of neoliberalism but not to capitalism as such. Others might not even have thought that capitalism was the problem and may have evinced opposition exclusively to, say, the environmentally damaging industrialism that was rife under twentieth-century communism as well as capitalism. 'Anti-corporatism' had a distinctly American and populist flavour in opposing 'big business', especially multinational and transnational corporations rather than capitalist business per se. As a defining term, moreover, it was confusing in a European context where 'corporatism' had been a feature of the organised capitalism – characterised by state direction of business organisations – which preceded the advent of neoliberalism that, in turn, was supposed to turn back the state. Although some strands of the movement of movements were hostile to any kind of 'globalisation' and were inclined to defend the local or the national against all its incursions, great tracts of the movement were keenly internationalist and, in this sense, were by no means opposed to globalisation in principle. In contrast to the other labels, 'social justice' was a positive designation, open and universalising, though so general that it might mean virtually anything. In a more technical sense, it was unclear to what extent the movement was 'anti-systemic',[30] in so far as it targeted a system rather than a random and atomised series of, shall we say, abuses to be redressed.

Paul Kingsnorth entitled his survey of what he called 'the global resistance movement', *One No, Many Yeses*. What was the 'no' that signified the object to be resisted? The 'no' is to 'neoliberalism, with all its power and all its machinery of death'.[31] If there is any unity at all to the multiple 'yeses', for Kingsnorth it is summed up by the Zapatista slogan '*Ya Basta!*', that is, 'enough is enough'. Apparently, this novel phenomenon is postmodern: 'If the Zapatista uprising was the first post-modern revolution, Seattle was the first post-modern street protest.'[32] Such a claim is typical of the discourse surrounding the movement of movements, suggesting that it was not the revival of an older phenomenon – revolutionary socialism, for instance – but the articulation of something completely different, perhaps not even real in any modernist sense. The Zapatistas were not interested in seizing power or in overthrowing the capitalist state. In fact, they were trying to defend something old, namely the traditional peasant economy and way of life of Chiapas in Mexico against the dispossession resulting from implementation of the North American Free Trade Agreement (NAFTA) that was to turn into the Free Trade Area for the Americas (FTAA). Likewise, the Seattle protest was about stopping something happening – the latest round of neoliberal reform of the global system. In a curious way, then, the movement of movements was conservative, seeking to conserve something rather than create something new.

Kingsnorth's survey zigzags from San Cristobal de las Casas, the original site of the Zapatista uprising in 1994, the massive Genoa protest in July 2001, resistance to the neoliberal turn of the African National Congress (ANC) in places like Soweto, the Reverend Billy's Church of Stop Shopping in New York, tribal resistance in West Papua, the second World Social Forum gathering at Porto Alegre in January 2002, the *Movimento dos Trabalhadores Rurais Sem Terra* (the Landless Rural Workers' Movement) in rural Brazil, to Democracy Unlimited in Humboldt County, California, which campaigns against corporate America, especially the oil business.[33]

The eruption of the anti-capitalist movement of movements in the early 2000s was greatly facilitated by the mobilisation of groups through the Internet and the use of mobile phones in coordinating action. In effect, it not only became a significant presence on new media but, crucially, broke into old media as well. This was exceptionally important in garnering popular support for the Zapatistas, and effectively protecting them against what might and probably would have been brutal military repression, halting it in its tracks. The Zapatistas used the Internet to publicise their cause to the outside world; and in doing so attracted the attention of mainstream news media, especially television.[34] On a broader front, the spectacular presence of anti-capitalist protest in worldwide media was greatly enhanced by its theatricality, with the entertaining antics of the White Bloc and Pink Fairies representing a much more playful face of the movement than violent tendencies like the Black Bloc.[35] This moment in the history of the movement exemplified the operations of Jürgen Habermas's latter-day 'sluicegate' model of the public sphere, whereby public protest by social movements forces issues onto the agenda of the official public sphere that would not otherwise be placed there by big business and big government – indeed, that would normally be closed off to widespread public attention by such powerful systemic institutions.[36]

Yet the tactics of the movement, like that of many previous and similar forms of opposition during and since the 1960s, were arguably much more successful, albeit briefly, in the cultural politics of the public sphere – that of symbolic contestation – than in what some would regard as politics proper, effecting actual shifts in power relations with material consequence.[37] And, of course, behind the communicative brilliance and spectacular media presence, there were significant political differences within the movement itself, representing not only its strengths but also its weaknesses. Simon Tormey has sought to clarify these differences and the difficult problems the movement faced in its development. He refers to 'the essentially kaleidoscopic nature of anti-capitalism'[38] and offers a typology of the main cleavages of position within the movement.[39] This involves two sets of contrary positions cross-hatched with one another: 'Ideological affirmative' in contrast to 'Post/non-ideological negative'; and 'Radical/revolutionary' in contrast to 'Reformist'. This produces four broad clusters of a plethora of different tendencies. For instance, revolutionary socialist positions, very familiar from the history of the Left, combining ideological affirmation and the perspective of revolution, contrasted with, say, supposedly non-ideological and reformist social democracy, which was not at all prominent in the movement. In fact, more characteristic of the movement and strongly defining its temper were autonomist and 'single-issue' positions, which were often revolutionary in rhetoric yet typically reformist in practice.

Several commentators and supporters applaud the sheer variety and lack of centralised organisation or shared focus in the movement, contrasting it favourably with a failed left-wing politics of the past and its authoritarian tendencies. Others pined for some commonality, some coherent focus, or at least a minimally agreed programme. As it happened, the movement was overcome by a particular focus derived from the reaction to 9/11 and the Bush dynasty's desire to have another crack at Saddam Hussein. The so-called 'war on terror' raised martial tension in the world culminating in the invasion and occupation of Iraq in 2003. All around the world there were mass peace protests, featuring, for instance, the largest demonstration ever on British soil in February 2003 when between one and two million people marched in London against the war just about to be launched by 'the Alliance'. The anti-war movement emerged as a shared focus for the movement of movements, drawing in many more sympathisers, while simultaneously eclipsing it, at least in popular consciousness, for the time being.

A talking shop for the nascent movement of movements, the World Social Forum (WSF) was convened at the beginning of 2001 in Porto Alegre at the instigation of the Brazilian Workers Party and ATTAC, the French organisation that has campaigned in favour of the Tobin tax[40] on financial transactions in the global stocks and shares market. In comparison with other parts of the movement these were unusually respectable exponents of opposition to the neoliberal excesses of capitalism – a political party that captured the presidency of Brazil, and the creation of *Le Monde diplomatique*, wishing to tax capitalism rather than abolish it. The Workers Party had built a base in the government of Porto Alegre where it pioneered the people's budget, but it would subsequently disappoint many supporters and sympathisers under President Lula's 'third way' policy for national government. The World Social Forum was meant to be a counter-point to the World Economic Forum, in which representatives from the transnational ruling class meet annually at Davos in Switzerland to discuss the problems of running capitalism. The WSF also meets annually, sometimes in Porto Alegre and sometimes elsewhere

– for instance, in Mumbai in 2004. There are regional fora as well, such as the European Social Forum.

The WSF and its offshoots seek to combine a diversity of perspectives and strategies, which occasionally results in considerable dissensus and, indeed, acrimony, as happened in Nairobi, Kenya in January 2007. Alex Callinicos, of the British Socialist Workers Party, active within the anti-capitalist movement and one of its leading chroniclers,[41] has tried to make sense of the movement's difficulties since mobilisation against the Iraq War. Taking the Kenyan WSF as his starting point, Callinicos notes how this may have been an unwise venue to choose because of the sheer distances and costs of travel in a very poor continent. The Nairobi WSF attracted 46,000 delegates, half from Kenya itself and a quarter from the rest of Africa. It was sponsored by a mobile phone manufacturer, entrance and catering were expensive, and conduct of the forum was criticised for elitism and lack of democracy. The problem was not, however, just to do with the African setting and organisational failings. Callinicos also notes a sense of crisis too in the European movement,[42] particularly concerning the decline of ATTAC and differences over the centrality or distraction of the Iraq War as a focus for the movement.

For Callinicos, however, the main problem was not to do with mobilisation around the Iraq War, the failure of the anti-war campaign and its dispiriting aftermath, but rather with 'The ideology of autonomous social movements' as 'a growing obstacle to the further development of the movement'.[43] This has led to 'the increasingly dysfunctional way in which the anti-capitalist movement organises itself'.[44] It frustrates the formation of a common programme, however minimal. In this respect, then, Callinicos represents a more 'traditional' view of politics in which something like a party is probably necessary – however unfashionable that may be when diversity has become a cult – in order to bring together disparate grievances and pursue a coherent strategy once differences have been aired and a workable consensus has been hammered out that may result in the disciplined action of a 'united front'.[45]

At a rather abstruse intellectual level, it could be said that the differences within the anti-capitalist movement and other sections of what can still be called 'the Left' divide, broadly speaking, along modernist and postmodernist lines. Typically, postmodernists believe that there has been a fundamental break with the condition of modernity in which capitalism framed the culture and indeed set the terms for its counter-culture, whereas modernists believe that we are currently experiencing a working out of the conditions of modernity in an intense, extensive and discombobulating way.[46] On the one hand, Michael Hardt and Antonio Negri's works, *Empire* and *Multitude*,[47] are influential examples of the postmodernist position. On the other hand, James Petras and Henry Veltmeyer's stinging critique of Hardt and Negri, *Empire with Imperialism*, may be taken to represent an enduringly modernist position. A consideration of these positions is directly relevant to the issues in hand. As Petras and Veltmeyer say, 'Single-issue anti-imperialist mobilizations, like the anti-globalization movement, erupt, extend and then become routine and decline, as they fail to connect with popular mass struggles to challenge for power.'[48]

Hardt and Negri's *Empire* is especially questionable in arguing that imperialism is no longer connected to nation states but is today a supranational phenomenon, colonising the whole of life, more or less coterminous with global capitalism itself. This was an extraordinary claim to make at a time of such violent neo-imperialist action by the United States, especially its assault on the Middle East. From the Hardt and Negri position, as with much of the Left, it could be argued that the Iraq War was less about freedom and democracy than about oil, that is, it was a military conflict undertaken on behalf of global capital. Nevertheless, the capitalist interests thus furthered were specifically *American* capitalist interests. Petras and Veltmeyer are at pains to point out the actual relations between multinational corporations (MNCs) and nation states, especially the US, and how states represent the interests of such corporations, not least of all, for instance, in WTO negotiations.

The headquarters of 227 of the top 500 MNCs in the world are in the US. Western Europe has 141 and Asia 92. In effect, 'Almost three-quarters (73%) of big corporate institutions are located in the Euro-US sphere of power'; and, 'Of the top ten MNCs, 80 percent are American and 20 percent European.'[49] Petras and Veltmeyer insist that 'What is called "globalization" is in reality the extreme concentration and extension of a US empire, or at least a Euro-US empire, which is complicated by the gradual emergence of Asian MNCs.'[50] It is difficult not to agree with them that 'The imperial policies adopted by Washington are in direct response to the power and centrality of the biggest MNCs in the US economy.'[51]

The comparative vagueness on these matters in Hardt and Negri's work is not only postmodernist but also idealist in a very old sense. 'Empire' is presented as a virtually extra-terrestrial category, a *zeitgeist*, instead of a material reality grounded in actual interests and struggles. However, as Petras and Veltmeyer acknowledge, the category of 'multitude', while similarly generalised, is less problematic. Insofar as it clusters together the variously exploited and oppressed of the world, 'multitude' may well refer to a common though multiply segmented condition, providing some grounds for a minimal programme cognisant of many different kinds of grievance. Hardt and Negri, of course, are keen to escape from a classical Marxist imaginary of the proletariat conventionally defined as the agent of revolution. Marxists have always had difficulties writing the peasantry into the narrative when, in practice, peasants have often been key players in actual revolution. Hardt and Negri are also rightly concerned to include 'immaterial labour' in the narrative of actual or potential revolt, in recognition of dramatic changes in the composition of the labour force in older industrial states and the impact of the information technology revolution.

Hardt and Negri are followers of Gilles Deleuze and Félix Guattari, yet in their discussion of multitude they do not spell out explicitly the French theorists' concept of the rhizome,[52] which is especially useful for making sense of the appearance of opposition to the system and is relevant to an understanding of not only al Qaida,[53] but also the various eruptions of anti-capitalism over time. The rhizome is the kind of plant that gardeners hate, such as the Japanese knotweed. It does not have a single root and is, therefore, difficult to root out. Its network structure proliferates underground, popping up almost anywhere. Just as it is cut down here, it grows there. Not all rhizomes are bad from a horticultural point of view. The potato plant is a rhizome. Deleuze and Guattari sum up: 'the principle characteristic of a rhizome: unlike trees or their roots, the rhizome connects any point to any other point, and its traits are not necessarily linked to traits of the same nature; it brings into play very different regimes of signs and even nonsign states'.[54] The rhizome is further characterised by 'transversal movement'.[55] Like the rhizome, then, just when it seems to have been cut out, anti-capitalism pops up again, possibly in unexpected places.

It was perhaps surprising that the most significant experiment in radical socialism around the turn of the millennium should have emerged from the Latin American military.[56] As Richard Gott has documented in his biography of the Venezuelan president, Hugo Rafael Chávez, he owes his charismatic authority not only to military strength but just as importantly to a longstanding commitment to the poor and a thoroughly democratic and common touch.[57] He came from a lower-middle-class background with no wealth to speak of and worked his way up through the military ranks, educating himself in left-wing thought and the political history of national liberation in South America, making connections with radical forces in Venezuela along the way. Chávez came to prominence in 1992 when he led a failed *coup d'état*. His admission of defeat on television and hint that he would be back brought him considerable popularity. Dignified in defeat, Chávez spent only two years in prison, plotting while he was there to build a movement that would eventually take power through electoral politics. It is the combination of electoral legitimacy and participatory democracy that makes Chávez and his movement so formidable.

As leader of the Revolutionary Bolivarian Movement (MBR-200), Chávez articulated his politics to the Latin American tradition of anti-imperial struggle and national liberation led by the Venezuelan Simón Bolívar in the nineteenth century. This allowed him to distance his project from the record of conventional left-wing politics, whether communist or social-democratic. It also recalled a continental perspective similarly evinced by Che Guevara, the Argentinean who engaged in revolutionary action in both Cuba and Bolivia during the 1960s. To observers, Chávez's position was somewhat ambiguous and difficult to pigeonhole. Yet his hostility to US imperialism was never in doubt. He won the 1998 presidential election in Venezuela with 56 per cent of the vote. His immediate policy was to halt neoliberal privatisation, not necessarily to nationalise the economy as Fidel Castro had done in Cuba. However, Chávez wanted immediate constitutional change, which was put successfully to the vote in 1999 with 72 per cent approval. This involved renaming the country, *República Bolivariana de Venezuela*. Presidential powers were increased, though the presidency was restricted to two full terms in office, something that Chávez was later to regret (he lost a 2007 referendum to reverse this restriction by just 1 per cent, though his two-terms rule was eventually rescinded by popular vote in 2009). The legislature became unicameral and a transparent set of arrangements for public law and administration were established in principle. Chávez sought re-election in 2000 and won with 60 per cent of the vote. His manifest electoral legitimacy, however, did not protect him from exceptional measures to unseat him – a failed coup in 2002, soon followed by a strike-lockout. There was a further failed attempt to unseat Chávez in the 2004 recall referendum, another provision introduced by his own constitutional reform.

The attempts to overthrow Chávez were supported not only by bourgeois and imperialist interests, tacitly approved by the United States, but also by the leading trade union body. He had annoyed the *Confederación des Trabajadores de Venezuela* (CTV), which was aligned with the *Acción Democrática* party, by introducing state-monitored elections in unions, a measure that was criticised by the International Labour Organisation (ILO). During the strike-lockout in 2002, the CTV effectively halted oil production and exports, which amounted to an economic coup. The *Union National des Trabajadores* (UNT) was set up as an alternative, pro-Chávez organisation and drew support from unions previously affiliated to the CTV.

The participation of trade unionists in trying to overthrow Chávez illustrates the degree of institutionalised hostility to the Chávez revolution, which includes much of the state apparatus itself. The Bolivarians have sought to circumvent such obstruction particularly through setting up missions to enact progressive reform and by functioning according to principles of participatory democracy in such areas as education and health – with, for instance, literacy programmes, expanded opportunity for higher education, and free medical care. This strategy also exemplifies Chávez's commitment to the poor and dispossessed, including indigenous people, among whom he is very popular. Yet he has met with enormous media hostility both at home and abroad. He has permitted large sections of the press and broadcasting to pour scorn on his every move. Admittedly, the licence for RCTV was not renewed in 2007, which has been judged a fatal error, seriously undermining his popularity.[58] However, its endless flow of soap operas can still be viewed on cable and satellite services. Chávez himself has a penchant for broadcasting lengthy speeches on television *à la* Castro, and has a talk show, *Alo Presidente*, on the state-owned *Venezolana de Televisión* (VTV). For these reasons and others, he is reported very unfavourably abroad, even in 'left-of-centre' publications like the *Guardian* and *New Statesman* in Britain. This is remarkable considering the tolerance he has shown to illegitimate opposition in Venezuela. Television stations promoting the violent overthrow of a democratically elected president or prime minister in the US or Britain would have been immediately shut down and the ringleaders incarcerated.

Chávez's great advantage is oil. It fuels redistributive growth in Venezuela, with serious taxes on private business and revenue from increased public ownership. It also enables deals and alliances with sympathisers abroad, such as the Castro brothers in Cuba and Ken Livingstone in London. It is also seriously problematic since the price of petrol in Venezuela is even cheaper than in the

US. Any attempt to reduce subsidy and raise the price would be perilously unpopular.[59] Chávez's 'endogenous growth' programme is founded on oil riches, though his policies, including agrarian reform, are designed not only to end injustice but also to diversify the economy. Yet Chávez's Bolivarian revolution, in spite of winning yet another election and facing street demonstrations by right-wing students and persistent subversion from the Right, remains, at the time of writing, extremely controversial on the Left as well as the Right. Petras and Veltmeyer, for instance, contrast Chávez's Venezuela extremely unfavourably with Castro's Cuba, and they virtually accuse him of being complicit with neoliberalism rather than being one of its finest adversaries.[60] Others are much more positively disposed to Chávez, bordering on hagiography in their praise.[61] It is important not to see Chávez in isolation, though undoubtedly his project is rather special and quite possibly exceptional. There has been a resurgence of socialism in South America, including that of Evo Morales's presidency in Bolivia,[62] as well as developments in Argentina, Brazil and elsewhere.[63] At present, South America is undoubtedly in the vanguard of anti-capitalism, which is a reasonable thing to say in spite of the unpopularity of vanguardism in left-wing politics today.[64]

Limits to Capitalism

Is capitalism eternal or historical? Has capitalism finally resolved the riddle of history, thereby transcending time itself and setting the limits of the possible for ever more? Today, it is generally assumed that this is so, which at the very least is a belief of breathtaking hubris. Hubris has always been a fatal weakness of the powerful, the very stuff of tragedy, signalling the inevitable fall after ascent to the giddy heights. Long before such hubris took hold, Karl Marx and Friedrich Engels had, with youthful bravado, declared the bourgeoisie to be their own gravediggers. Early capitalism was socialising the economic process and in so doing created the conditions for proletarian emancipation. This was said in the context of issuing a call to action. If the capitalists were their own gravediggers, then surely all the workers had to do was stand around and wait for them to do it. Yet at the same time, Marx and Engels were calling for communist-led workers to bring about 'the forcible overthrow of all existing social conditions'.[65] Inscribed here is a classic tension between determinism and voluntarism, not only in politics but also social theory. However, there is no necessary irresolution between determinate conditions and the conditions for action. Time and circumstance have to be conducive to effective action; and action changes the conditions.

Still, it is comforting for critics to learn that the enemy's options are limited and may eventually run out. Marxists believe that there are indeed limits to capitalism. It is well known that capitalism is prone to crisis, that every now and again it looks as though it might fall apart and collapse. It looked that way in 1929, and in 1973 some observers thought the same. But the capitalist system has demonstrated extraordinary resilience, an impressive capacity to solve the periodic problems that inevitably crop up, and to come out of a crisis apparently stronger than ever. That happened in the post Second World War period and it has happened again since the trouble of the 1970s. Organised capitalism was the solution to the crises of the mid twentieth century and neoliberal capitalism was the solution to the crises of the late twentieth century. In both cases, the legitimacy of capitalism was sorely tried yet on both occasions legitimacy was restored, each time by producing a cultural complex that seemed to have transcended bad old capitalism – in the first instance, it looked as though something like socialism had been achieved; in the second, it looked as though both capitalism and socialism had been surpassed by a post-ideological condition, a cool way of life.

In the Introduction to the revised 2006 edition of his classic, *The Limits to Capital*, originally published in 1982, David Harvey continued to insist that 'the internal contradictions of capitalism' are at 'the crux of our problem', not 'the environmental crisis'.[66] He went on to argue that 'we have to recognize that almost all our environmental, political, social and cultural distresses are the product of a system that seeks out surplus value in order to produce more surplus value that then requires profitable absorption'.[67]

He was not denying the gravity of the environmental crisis but was instead claiming that it is incomprehensible and irresolvable without acknowledging the damaging effects of capitalism's dynamic force. By implication, the environmental crisis will not be solved by capitalist solutions.

What, then, are the limits to capital that make it incapable of ultimately solving economic – and environmental – crises? Capitalism must accumulate in order to accumulate yet more. From the perspective of capitalism, there are no imaginable limits to capital accumulation. There is no rest for the wicked. This ineluctable force of capital accumulation is, however, always likely to generate crisis, a likelihood borne out on several occasions during the history of capitalism. Crises result from a tendency within the system for the general rate of profit to fall. Commenting on this tendency at the time of the 1970s crisis, Andrew Gamble and Paul Walton remarked:

> In Volumes I and III of *Capital*, applying the labour theory of value, Marx demonstrated that there is an inherent tendency for the capitalist system to stagnate and fall into crisis as a result of the falling rate of profit. This prediction, which is stated as a tendency rather than some iron law, may be countered by forces which prevent its occurrence during particular historical periods. The uncovering of this long-term tendency was regarded by Marx as one of his major achievements.[68]

In passing, they complimented Andrew Glyn and Bob Sutcliffe's empirical demonstration of the tendency in Britain during the late 1960s and early 1970s.[69] Profits may decline for a number of different though sometimes interconnected reasons: the changing organic composition of capital (replacing the source of value in labour power with machinery), pressure of rising wages, downward pressure on prices resulting from increased competition, and so forth. Harvey describes the thesis of a declining rate of profit as the 'first cut' of a Marxist theory of crisis.[70] Harvey himself places particular emphasis on the over-accumulation of capital blocked by insufficient investment opportunity; and, 'since capitalists will be capitalists, overaccumulation is bound to arise'.[71] A developed theory of the solutions sought to crisis focuses upon 'fixes' for realising bottled-up capital, most notably 'the historical fix' of finance capital – 'the second cut' – and 'the spatial fix' that led to a dramatic phase of globalisation in the late twentieth century – 'the third cut'.[72] Harvey's thinking is pertinent to making sense of the significant growth of East-Asian capitalism and especially China's economic 'boom': 'The insatiable thirst of capitalism for fresh supplies of labour accounts for the vigour with which it has pursued primitive accumulation, destroying, transforming and absorbing pre-capitalist populations wherever it finds them.'[73]

It is conventional wisdom that capitalism has won out and proven itself master of the universe since the 1970s. Yet there are considerable doubts concerning the health of capitalism today. Robert Brenner, for instance, argues that capitalism has experienced a long downturn in its fortunes since 1973, represented by a comparatively poor profit rate, occasionally relieved by minibooms that soon peter out, such as the 'new economy' bubble of the mid to late 1990s that suddenly burst around the turn of the millennium,[74] and, of course, 'the credit crunch' brought about by the hyper-virtualisation of finance capitalism in the late 2000s. Brenner contests the neoliberal argument, which is widely accepted on the Left as well as the Right of politics, that the original post Second World War downturn was caused by wage militancy in the 1960s and the costs to the state in the older industrialised economies of North America and Europe of the 'social wage', governmental spending on welfare and the like. Compared to the 1950s and '60s the dynamic of capitalism has been weak since the 1970s, the aggregate rate of profit for G7 countries having fallen by as much as 40 per cent in this period. Brenner explains the crisis that has bedevilled US capital in particular as resulting from German and Japanese competition in the earlier phase, exacerbated by further East-Asian competition in the later phase. In the decades immediately following the Second World War, wages in the reviving German and Japanese economies were much lower than in the United States. Since then, low wages in the East and throughout the newly developing industrial nations have enabled fierce price competition that has hardly been solved by the shift from manufacturing to service work in North America and much of Western Europe, even though profitability in non-manufacturing sectors of the West has been much higher than in manufacturing. None of this is to deny that the rule of capital and market values have been massively dominant over the past 30 to 40 years, or to claim that socialism has shown much sign of recovery as a viable alternative system. It is true that capitalism has been rampant and its propaganda extremely confident.

The latest phase of expansionary capitalism has again been led by the US. We have entered a phase of heightened martial tension in the world, supplemented by a series of catastrophic events resulting from hazards of nature that are greatly exacerbated by industrial capitalism's damaging impact on the natural environment. In this regard, Naomi Klein's book *The Shock Doctrine* proposes a thesis on the rise of what she calls 'disaster capitalism'. The situations in which it operates have on a number of occasions actually been brought about by the machinations of over-accumulated capital, recalling old arguments concerning capitalism's devotion to war and the development of a kind of military Keynesianism, which though driven by neoliberalism belies one of its most cherished assumptions. As Harvey has remarked, 'Marxists, ever since Luxemburg first wrote on the subject, have long been attracted to the idea of military expenditures as a convenient means to absorb surpluses of capital and labour power.'[75] Klein draws a parallel between shock therapy experimentation conducted by Ewen Cameron at McGill University in the 1950s and recent theatres of disaster capitalism, from policies imposed on poorer countries indebted to the IMF and World Bank to war zones, most notably post 'Shock and Awe' Iraq. Electric shock treatment was used, unsuccessfully it must be said, to destroy the psyche of patients in order to recreate their mental health – a form of 'creative destruction'. Similarly, destruction is a prelude to creating a social order congenial to global capital and its culture of consumerist democracy. Cameron's research was of interest to the CIA and received CIA funds because it was deemed of use to the agents of US national security. So the parallel drawn by Klein between violent psychotherapy and violent geopolitics is not too fanciful.

In *The Shock Doctrine*, Klein examines 'the interaction between superprofits and megadisasters', and claims that 'In scale, the disaster capitalism complex is on a par with the "emerging market" and information technology boom of the 1990s.'[76] She describes how it works as follows: 'the original disaster – the coup, the terrorist attack, the market meltdown, the war, the tsunami, the hurricane – puts the entire population in a state of shock'.[77] It is not difficult to itemise the occasions: the overthrow of Allende in 1973 that created the opportunity to experiment with the Chicago School's economic shock therapy (the original laboratory for neoliberalism); 9/11 and its domestic and international policy consequences; marketisation in Argentina after 1976; Russia after 1991; Iraq after 2003; the Indian Ocean coastland after 2004; New Orleans after 2005; and to add, necessarily, the 'credit crunch' of 2007–8. George W. Bush's 'War on Terror' unleashed great opportunities for 'disaster capitalism': 'Although the stated goal was fighting terrorism, the effect was the creation of the disaster capitalism complex – a fully-fledged new economy in homeland security, privatized war and disaster reconstruction tasked with nothing less than building and running a privatized security state, both at home and abroad.'[78] And 'Through all its various name changes – the War on Terror, the war on radical Islam, the war against Islamofascism, the Third World War, the long war, the generational war – the basic shape of the conflict has remained unchanged.'[79] Klein resists the temptation of conspiracy theory to account for the enthusiasm of business for the money to be made out of reconstructing disaster zones, the latest fix for capital. As she says:

> The truth is at once less sinister and more dangerous. An economic system that requires constant growth, while bucking almost all serious attempts at environmental regulation, generates a steady stream of disasters all on its own, whether military, ecological or financial. The appetite for easy, short-term profits, offered by purely speculative investment, has turned the stock, currency and real estate markets into crisis-creation machines, as the Asian financial crisis, the Mexican peso crisis and dot.com collapse all demonstrate. Our common addiction to dirty, non-renewable energy

sources keeps other kinds of emergencies coming; natural disasters (up 430 percent since 1975) and wars waged for control over scarce resources (not just Iraq and Afghanistan but low intensity conflicts such as those that rage in Nigeria, Colombia and Sudan), which in turn create terrorist blowback (a 2007 study calculated that the number of terrorist attacks since the start of the Iraq war had increased sevenfold).[80]

She concluded by arguing that the disaster complex will obviously exploit the effects of global warming that are delivered by 'the market's invisible hand'.[81] The only serious attempt to halt the process would be a concerted effort to reduce global warming and bring about peace in the world. This raises the question of 'growth', which is connected to the endless search for capital accumulation that has put nature and life on Earth at such great risk. Recognition of the impending and grandest of all likely crises/disasters is a challenge not only to neoliberalism and cool capitalism but also to their critics and active opponents. As the late Andrew Glyn pointed out shortly before his death: 'A reorientation of priorities away from growth would require a major shift for most of the left.'[82]

The problem of capitalism and the ecological problem of environmental sustainability come together around the theme of 'the limits to growth'. Back in the 1970s, the Club of Rome – a gathering of business people, politicians and scientists – commissioned a group of American researchers to examine the evidence for the natural limitations to economic growth. They issued a dire warning about environmental degradation and, although their calculations have often been called into question, in the mid 2000s they affirmed their gloomy prognostications should urgent action not be taken on a genuinely comprehensive basis.[83] Yet still, the cardinal value of all mainstream economic discourse is growth. Assessment of a national economy's health is normally made with emphatic reference to its rate of growth; and, of course, China's 10 per cent annual growth rate has been persistently viewed with awe, especially in a faltering US economy. In a sense, 'economic growth' is the vernacular expression for what Marxists have called 'capital accumulation'. Both 'bourgeois' and Marxist economists tend to agree that the strength and persistence of capitalism is measured according to the rate of accumulative growth.

As we have seen, limitless capital accumulation, founded for good or ill on the exploitation of human capacities as well as natural resources, is always likely to undermine itself. Limitless exploitation of nature, moreover, is more than likely to destroy the very conditions for survival on this planet. These problems are related to one another. Towards the end of the last millennium and into the present one, that relation was sharply focused by the issue of global warming and climate change more generally, which passed through the sluice gate of the public sphere from the left field of ecological politics into mass-popular consciousness on a global scale. Carbon emissions, derived from the human exploitation of nature driven by the unrelenting pursuit of economic growth, have given rise to much heated debate. It would be inappropriate at the conclusion of a book on the cultural face of capitalism to go into ecological questions in any depth – that would require another book – but it is nonetheless necessary to remark upon these extremely complex matters, however briefly, since cool capitalism, to put it bluntly, is a profound distraction from the truth of capitalism and its damaging effects on the planet.

Oversimplifying the debate in order to clarify what is at stake, we find on one side the hot heads prophesying doom and disaster unless something is done drastically to halt the perilous trends that threaten to engulf us all, and, on the other side, the cool dudes who dismiss the doom-mongers and call more or less complacently for business as usual. That simple bifurcation of contrary positions is not quite fair, to be sure, and it does not do justice to the genuine aporias thrown up by the present condition. It really is difficult to decide who exactly is right and, in consequence, what to think and how to act. On the side of the hot heads there are figures like George Monbiot, for instance, whose book *Heat* sets out the seriousness of the problem alarmingly, and carefully sifts through various means of slowing down and reversing global warming.[84] On the other side is an equally sophisticated figure, Bjorn Lomborg, the self-styled 'skeptical environmentalist'.[85] The title of Lomborg's book, *Cool It,* perfectly sums up his stance on the matters in hand.[86] Monbiot himself is a sceptic with regard to many of the ostensible 'solutions' to 'the problem'. He is extremely hostile to the replacement of oil with bio-fuels since this would severely undermine food production in order to make up for diminishing oil reserves. Still, reducing global warming, he maintains, will require a massive reduction of carbon dioxide emissions over the next 20 years (as much as 90 per cent for rich countries), largely through rationing and turning towards alternative energy sources of a mixed kind, including wind power and hydrogen. Electrification of railways and road transport, since electricity does not emit carbon dioxide, is a vital matter. Although Monbiot favours individual action with governmental backing, such as building heat-efficient housing, he does not believe that individual action will have much effect by itself. Restriction on air travel is a great deal more important than, for example, choosing not to use plastic bags, which is trivial by comparison. Effective solutions must be collective and a matter of state and inter-state regulation. Monbiot is, as it happens, somewhat agnostic on the role of capitalism in addressing the ecological question, though he is very critical of corporate capital and neoliberal economics.

Although hitherto sympathetic to arguments for carbon capture and storage (CCS) – which when properly developed would permit even the burning of coal, the dirtiest of fuel sources, to generate energy – Monbiot seemed to switch position in August 2008 by dismissing the CCS solution, to the extent that he was prepared to countenance nuclear power as the safer and more immediately effective option: 'I have now reached the point at which I no longer care whether or not the answer is nuclear.'[87] This was occasioned by his support for the campaign to stop a new coal-fired power plant being built at Kingsnorth in Kent on the English south-east coast. Although that coal plant was supposed to be 'CCS ready', it was unclear what 'readiness' actually meant in this case. Moreover, the House of Commons Environmental Audit Committee had recently cited the UK Energy Research Centre and Climate Change Capital's estimation that CCS technology was prohibitively expensive. Thus, Monbiot appeared to throw in his lot with James Lovelock's long-held and much disputed contention that nuclear is a necessary solution if the planet is to be saved from catastrophic global warming. Monbiot's apparent U-turn was met with consternation from many ecological analysts and activists. Ulrich Beck had already remarked that panic over global warming in addition to the long-term depletion of fossil fuels was, in effect, re-legitimising the domestic use of nuclear power and reducing anxiety over the storage of nuclear waste with its very lengthy and perilous after-life.[88] In response to Monbiot, the former National Union of Mineworkers' leader, Arthur Scargill, insisted, unsurprisingly, that coal was not 'the climate enemy' so long as CCS was properly implemented, and he also pointed out Britain's evident advantages in this respect in spite of the Thatcher government's decimation of the indigenous industry.[89] To go further, the question of coal use is obviously crucial on a global scale, especially when China's coal reserves and rate of use are taken into account. Moreover, it is important to factor in how the costs of technology tend to drop dramatically from developing prototypes to widespread deployment, which is not to deny the urgency of producing measures to reduce climate change.

Monbiot is especially relentless in attacking what he calls 'the denial industry', though even the US presidency no longer denies the seriousness of the impact of global warming on the environment. In spite of Monbiot's claim that scientific opinion is hardly divided at all on the issue, a claim which is justified by the pronouncements of the Intergovernmental Panel on Climate Change, there are indeed gainsayers whose arguments are not entirely meretricious,[90] such as Lomborg. According to Lomborg, the global warming crisis is much exaggerated in the kind of arguments made by the likes of Monbiot. Lomborg fixes on the issue of polar bears to make his point in such a way that attracts journalistic attention.[91] In his film, *An Inconvenient Truth*,[92] Al Gore had in passing commented upon the incidence of polar bears drowning in the Arctic when ice flows break up. Lomborg points out that a great many more polar bears are shot each year in Canada than the relatively small number who drown when the ice melts in the North routinely during summer months. And, in fact, the population of polar bears in the world has increased over recent decades. Lomborg also argues that polar bears would adapt in any case to changing weather conditions should the world warm up significantly. Lomborg does not, however, deny that global warming is happening. Instead, he argues that it is not as serious a problem as the critics suggest. Moreover, there are more serious problems in the world, such as poverty and AIDs, that need to be addressed, and could be for far less money than the drastic measures advocated to reduce global warming. In fact, Lomborg presents himself as an economic realist applying cost-benefit analysis to the alleviation of various problems, establishing priorities and trusting in free market economics. Monbiot attacks exactly this mode of reasoning: 'is it possible to put an economic price on human life?'[93] Lomborg replies blithely: 'Cost-benefit analyses show that only very moderate CO_2 reduction is warranted, simply because cutting CO_2 is expensive and will do little good, a long time from now.'[94]

Another variant of neoliberal reasoning is applied to the ecological problem in the British government's 2006 *Stern Review on the Economics of Climate Change*.[95] Differently from Lomborg, Sir Nicholas Stern's report did not downplay the seriousness of the problem at all. It acknowledged the need for governmental and inter-governmental action and, indeed, regulation. The Stern report also stressed that the first of a series of international frameworks for tackling the problem should be a coordinated system of emissions *trading*:

> Expanding and linking the growing number of emissions trading schemes around the world is a powerful way to promote cost-effective reductions in emissions and to bring forward action in developing countries: strong targets in rich countries could drive flows amounting to tens of billions of dollars each year to support the transition to low-carbon development paths.[96]

An obvious inference to make here is that the richer, most heavily polluting nations, of which the United States is the leading such nation, might to a certain extent see their way out of the problem by buying up emissions quotas from poorer, low-polluting nations, thereby funding those nations to develop green technological solutions for themselves, that is, not to industrialise to the same extent as, say, the US. Yet again, an ostensibly 'free trade' arrangement works to the benefit of the rich rather than the poor.

Then we have Jonathon Porritt's *Capitalism as if the World Matters*, in which he puts the case for a capitalist solution to the ecological problem. Many environmentalists believe that the problem does lie with capitalism and that some kind of socialist solution is necessary, though they do not typically propose the immediate overthrow of capitalism to realise that end. Others – and not only the professional deniers paid to represent the interests of big corporations – believe like Porritt that capitalism can solve the problem. But Porritt does not believe the solution lies with the bad old capitalism that we all either love or hate but with a nice new, fluffy sort of capitalism that, should it ever come to pass, we may all grow to love. He dismisses socialist solutions on the grounds that 'actually existing socialism', by which is usually meant the communist states that were toppled towards the end of the twentieth century, had a terrible environmental record. Porritt's argument for a capitalist solution is not, however, symmetrical, since he himself acknowledges that actually existing capitalism also has a very bad environmental record. It is difficult to see, according to this mode of reasoning, how a different kind of capitalism, some imaginary capitalism, is any more likely than a putatively different socialism, an imagined socialism, to solve the problem, especially since actually existing capitalism is currently in charge of a worsening condition.

Porritt's argument for a capitalist solution deploys a five-part distinction between different kinds of capital: 'natural capital', 'human capital', 'social capital', 'manufactured capital' and 'financial capital'. While it might be readily accepted that manufactured and finance capital are forms of capital, it is much more questionable whether natural, human and social resources should be defined as 'capital' at all. Moreover, Porritt readily acknowledges that a notion like 'corporate social responsibility', the very kind of notion that must be necessary for capitalism to become nice, is a delusory – indeed, ideological – idea, restricted to the phantasm of 'stakeholder dialogue'.[97] Porritt even quotes Joel Bakan on the psychopathic qualities of 'the corporate person'.[98] As Bakan pointed out in his book and film, *The Corporation*,[99] business corporations are legally obliged to privilege, in George W. Bush's mantra, 'shareholder value' above all else. Whatever they say, profit always comes before the social good,[100] or, for that matter, the environment, which is not to say that capitalism can actually afford to destroy the environment, though it may do so.

Critics of capitalism today are quite prepared to concede that capitalism can survive almost anything.[101] Environmental crisis is not only a problem but also an opportunity for new kinds of capital accumulation, as is quite evident already in the rise of green capitalism. Some of the most energetic capitalist activity today is aimed at solving the ecological problem and, of course, the social consensus supports such effort and every bright new technological fix announced by business receives the response – that's cool. Still, it is important to appreciate that capitalism inherently generates contradictions that open up the possibility for other solutions. As James O'Connor notes, the original contradiction of capitalism, between the forces and relations of production, whereby opportunities for political and social emancipation have always arisen, is now supplemented by a 'second contradiction of capitalism', whereby capitalism undermines the very *conditions of production*. To conclude this book, then, I will leave O'Connor with the last words:

> Examples of capital accumulation impairing or destroying capital's own conditions, hence threatening its own profits and capacity to produce and accumulate more capital, are many and varied. The warming of the atmosphere will inevitably destroy people, places and profits, not to speak of other species life. Acid rain destroys forests and lakes and buildings and profits alike. Salinization of water tables, toxic wastes, and soil erosion impair nature and profitability. The pesticide treadmill destroys profits as well as nature. Urban capital running on an 'urban renewal treadmill' impairs its own conditions, hence profits, for example, in the form of congestion costs and high rents. The decrepit state of the physical infrastructure in

the United States may also be mentioned in this connection. There is also an 'education treadmill', a 'welfare treadmill', a 'health care treadmill', and others. This line of thinking thus applies also to the 'personal conditions of production ... laborpower' in connection with capital's destruction of established community and family life as well as the introduction of work relations that impair coping skills and create a toxic social environment generally. In these ways we can safely introduce 'scarcity' into the theory of economic crisis in a Marxist, non-Malthusian, way. We can also introduce the possibility of capital *underproduction* once we add up the rising costs of reproducing the conditions of production. Examples include the health bill necessitated by capitalist work and family relations; the drug and drug rehabilitation bill; the vast suits expected as a result of the deterioration of the social environment (e.g. police and divorce bill); the enormous revenues expended to prevent further environmental destruction and to clean up or repair the legacy of ecological destruction from the past; monies required to invent and develop and produce synthetics and 'natural' substitutes as means and objects of production and consumption; the huge sums required to pay off oil sheikhs and energy companies, for example, as ground rent and monopoly profit; the garbage disposal bill; the extra costs of congested urban space; and the costs falling on governments and peasants and workers in the third world as a result of the twin crises of ecology and development. And so on...[102]

NOTES

Introduction

1. The distinction between front and back region was formulated by Erving Goffman in *The Presentation of Self in Everyday Life* (Harmondsworth: Penguin, 1971 [1959]). It is consistent with the kind of distinction, obliterated by post-structuralism, between surface realism and depth reality that I believe is indispensable for the critical realist epistemology to which I adhere.
2. Mark Brown, 'Underground Art – How Banksy Gave Swiss Embassy an Image Makeover', *Guardian*, 29 February 2008, p. 3.
3. Jeff Smyth and Jean Wylie, 'China's Youth Define "Cool"', http://www.chinabusinessreview.com/0407/smith.html (accessed 18 March 2008).
4. Paul Rabinow, ed., *The Foucault Reader*, Harmondsworth: Penguin, 1986 (1984).
5. Robert Farris Thompson, *Black Gods and Kings*, Bloomington: Indiana University Press, 1976 (1971), p. 1.
6. Robert Farris Thompson, *African Art in Motion*, Berkeley and Los Angeles: University of California Press, 1974, p. 43.
7. Ibid.
8. Ibid., p. 44.
9. Ibid., p. 45.
10. Ibid.
11. Richard Majors and Janet Mancini Billson, *Cool Pose: The Dilemmas of Black Manhood in America*, New York: Touchstone, 1993 (1992).
12. Paul Gilroy, *The Black Atlantic: Modernity and Double Consciousness*, London: Verso, 1993.
13. Dick Pountain and David Robins, *Cool Rules: Anatomy of an Attitude*, London: Reaktion, 2000, p. 41.
14. Ibid., p. 44.
15. Lewis MacAdams, *Birth of the Cool: Beat, Beebop and the American Avant-Garde*, London: Scribner, 2002 (2001). *The Oxford English Dictionary* has trouble dealing with a word that is used mostly in oral culture, since it always requires a written source for first usage. Originally, the earliest date the OED had

for 'cool' was as recent as 1948, but its use in a 1933 short story by Zora Neale Hurston was later discovered, and subsequently its appearance in a travelling-minstrel lyric of 1902. Since then, it has been traced back to 1884 in the interjection, 'Dat's cool!' (see Alex Games, *Balderdash and Piffle: One Sandwich Short of a Dog's Dinner*, London: BBC Books, 2007, p. 213).
16. Pountain and Robins, *Cool Rules*, p. 26.
17. See Jon Savage, *Teenage: The Creation of Youth, 1875–1945*, London: Pimlico, 2008 (2007), pp. 386–90.
18. Norman Mailer, *The White Negro*, San Francisco: City Lights, 1970 (1957).
19. Majors and Mancini, *Cool Pose*, p. xi.
20. Ibid., p. 30.
21. Cornel West, 'Nihilism in Black America', in G. Dent, ed., *Black Popular Culture*, Seattle: Bay Press, 1992, pp. 37–47.
22. David Robins, 'A Summer of Stabbings', *Prospect*, October 2007, pp. 50–1.
23. Thomas Frank, *The Conquest of Cool: Business Culture, Counterculture, and the Rise of Hip Consumerism*, Chicago: University of Chicago Press, 1997.
24. Theodore Roszak, *The Making of a Counter Culture: Reflections on the Technocratic Society and its Youthful Opposition*, London: Faber and Faber, 1970 (1968).
25. See Thomas Frank's *What's the Matter with America?*, London: Secker and Warburg, 2004.
26. Frank, *The Conquest of Cool*, p. 4.
27. Peter Biskind, *Easy Riders, Raging Bulls*, London: Bloomsbury, 1998.
28. Frank, *The Conquest of Cool*, p. 11.
29. Ibid., p. 13.
30. See Jim McGuigan, 'The Politics of Cultural Studies and Cool Capitalism', *Cultural Politics* 2 (2), July 2006, pp. 137–58.
31. Frank, *The Conquest of Cool*, p. 31.
32. Jonas Ridderstrale and Kjell Nordstrom, *Funky Business: Talent Makes Capital Dance*, London: Pearson, 2002 (2000).

Chapter 1

1. Marshall Berman, *All That Is Solid Melts Into Air: The Experience of Modernity*, London: Verso, 1982, p. 92.
2. Karl Marx and Friedrich Engels, *The Communist Manifesto*, trans. Samuel Moore, London: Penguin, 1967 (1848), p. 83.

3. See David Renton, ed., *Marx on Globalisation*, London: Lawrence and Wishart, 2001.
4. Karl Marx, *Capital: Volume One*, trans. Ben Fowkes, London: Penguin, 1976 (1867), pp. 1022–3. For a recent appreciation of Marx's most important book, see Francis Wheen, *Marx's Das Kapital: A Biography*, London: Atlantic Books, 2006.
5. Liah Greenfeld's *The Spirit of Capitalism: Nationalism and Economic Growth* (Cambridge, MA: Harvard University Press, 2001) also acknowledges the historical importance of the 'English' case in what is an excessively nationalistic account of the origins and general orientation of capitalism, particularly from the point of view of the modern-day United States.
6. Werner Sombart, *Der Moderne Kapitalismus*, 2 vols, Leipzig: Dunker and Humblot, 1902; *Economic Life and the Modern Age*, edited by Nico Stehr and Reiner Grundmann, New Brunswick, NJ: Transaction, 2001. See also, Martin Riesebrodt, 'Dimensions of the Protestant Ethic', in William Swatos and Lutz Kaelber, eds, *The Protestant Ethic Turns 100: Essays on the Centenary of the Weber Thesis*, Boulder: Paradigm, 2005.
7. See, for instance, Irving Zeitlin, *Ideology and the Development of Sociological Theory*, Englewood Cliffs: Prentice Hall, 1994, 5th edn. Zeitlin's book, first published in 1968, went through several revised editions and remains a reliable study of how academic sociology evolved in critical response to Marxism. Zeitlin himself believes that Weber's research on the 'spiritual' aspect of capitalism is actually quite compatible with Marxism but does not discount the likelihood that Weber was at least partly motivated by a political desire to offer an 'alternative' account to that of Marxism.
8. David McLellan, *Marxism After Marx*, London: Macmillan, 1979.
9. The complacency of Parsonian structural functionalism was submitted to devastating critique by, first, Charles Wright Mills in *The Sociological Imagination* (New York: Oxford University Press, 1959), and, later, by Alvin Gouldner in *The Coming Crisis of Western Sociology* (New York: Avon, 1970), both of which contributed to a break with mainstream sociology and the development of a radical sociology in a more positive relation to Marxism.
10. Max Weber, *The Protestant Ethic and the Spirit of Capitalism*, trans. Talcott Parsons, London: Unwin, 1930.
11. For instance, Max Weber, *The Protestant Ethic and the 'Spirit' of Capitalism*, trans. Peter Baehr and Gordon C. Wells, London:

Penguin, 2002; Max Weber, *The Protestant Ethic and the Spirit of Capitalism*, trans. Stephen Kalberg, Oxford: Blackwell, 2002.
12. R.H. Tawney, *Religion and the Rise of Capitalism*, Harmondsworth: Penguin, 1972 (1922/1926), p. 211.
13. Talcott Parsons, 'The Pattern Variables', reprinted from *The Social System*, New York: Free Press, 1951, as Chapter 6 of *On Institutions and Social Evolution*, Leon H. Mayhew, ed., Chicago: University of Chicago Press, 1982, pp. 106–14, and Talcott Parsons, 'Pattern Variables Revisited – A Response to Robin Dubin', in his *Sociological Theory and Modern Society*, New York: Free Press, 1967, pp. 192–219.
14. Jan Nederveen Pieterse, *Development Theory: Deconstructions/ Reconstructions*, London: Sage, 2001, p. 21.
15. See, for instance, J.E.T. Eldridge, ed., *Max Weber: The Interpretation of Social Reality*, London: Nelson, 1971.
16. Joseph Schumpeter, 'Can Capitalism Survive?' (1936), in Richard Swedburg, ed., *Joseph A. Schumpeter: The Economics and Sociology of Capitalism*, Princeton: Princeton University Press, 1991, pp. 298–315.
17. Joseph Schumpeter, *Capitalism, Socialism and Democracy*, London: Unwin Hyman, 1987, 6th edn (1942).
18. Ibid., p. 83.
19. Ibid., p. 132.
20. Ibid., p. 131.
21. Ibid., p. 139.
22. Ibid., p. 146.
23. Daniel Bell, *The Cultural Contradictions of Capitalism*, New York: Basic Books, 1996 (20th Anniversary Edition) (1976), p. xi.
24. Daniel Bell, *The End of Ideology*, Cambridge, MA: Harvard University Press, 1988 (1960).
25. Daniel Bell, *The Coming of Post-Industrial Society: A Venture in Social Forecasting*, Harmondsworth: Penguin, 1976 (1973).
26. Bell, *The Cultural Contradictions of Capitalism*, p. xx.
27. Ibid., pp. xxi–xxii.
28. Ibid., p. xxiv.
29. Ibid., p. 55.
30. Ibid., p. 21.
31. Ibid., p. 65.
32. Ibid., p. 70.
33. Tariq Ali, *The Clash of Fundamentalisms: Crusades, Jihads and Modernity*, London: Verso, 2002.
34. See Stuart Sim, *Fundamentalist World: The New Dark Age of Dogma*, Cambridge: Ikon, 2004.

35. Luc Boltanski and Eve Chiapello, *The New Spirit of Capitalism*, trans. Gregory Elliott, London: Verso, 2005 (1999).
36. Ibid., p. 3.
37. See Scott Lash and John Urry, *The End of Organized Capitalism*, Cambridge: Polity Press, 1987.
38. See, for instance, Richard Sennett's lament in *The Culture of the New Capitalism*, New Haven: Yale University Press, 2005.
39. Boltanski and Chiapello, *The New Spirit of Capitalism*, p. 10.
40. As in Manuel Castells's *The Rise of the Network Society*, Cambridge, MA: Blackwell, 2000 (1996). Also, see Jan Van Dijk, *The Network Society*, London: Sage, 1999 (1991).
41. For example, Geoff Mulgan, *Connexity: How to Live in the Connected World*, London: Chatto and Windus, 1997.
42. See Jim McGuigan, 'The Information Age', Chapter 5 of *Modernity and Postmodern Culture*, Maidstone: Open University Press, 2nd edn, 2006 (1999), pp. 115–36.
43. See Gregory Elliott, *Althusser: The Detour of Theory*, London: Verso, 1987.
44. Boltanski and Chiapello, *The New Spirit of Capitalism*, p. 24.
45. See Mike Davis, *Planet of Slums*, London: Verso, 2007 (2006).
46. Boltanski and Chiapello, *The New Spirit of Capitalism*, p. 80.
47. Ibid., p. 90.
48. Ibid., p. 97.
49. Luc Boltanski and Eve Chiapello, 'The Role of Criticism in the Dynamic of Capitalism – Social Criticism Vs Artistic Criticism', unpublished paper for the Capitalism and Its Critiques conference at King's College, University of London, 25 March 2006.
50. Boltanski and Chiapello, *The New Spirit of Capitalism*, p. 37.
51. Boltanski and Chiapello, 'The Role of Criticism in the Dynamic of Capitalism'.
52. Boltanski and Chiapello, *The New Spirit of Capitalism*, p. 199.
53. Ibid., p. 230.
54. Ibid., p. 346.
55. Ibid., p. 347.
56. Alex Callinicos, *The Resources of Critique*, Cambridge: Polity, 2006, p. 69.
57. Castells, *The Rise of the Network Society*. It is interesting to note that in the 1990s, when the rhetorics of network society and exclusion/inclusion rose to such prominence, Eric Olin Wright decided to discard his earlier model of domination and subordination to account for 'contradictory class locations' – and, specifically, the location of managers – in favour of a revived model of exploitation. Of course, this was not the model that appealed to the new spirit

of capitalism, no more than domination/subordination had done. A conception of 'losers' for which 'winners' were not structurally responsible – roughly what the model of exclusion/inclusion means in practice – was much more appealing. See E.O. Wright, 'Class Analysis, History and Emancipation', *New Left Review* 202 (first series), November–December, 1993, pp. 15–35.
58. Boltanski and Chiapello, *The New Spirit of Capitalism*, p. 353.
59. Ibid., p. 360.
60. Ibid., p. 361.
61. Ibid., p. 375.
62. Ibid., p. 379.
63. Ibid., p. 390.
64. Sebastian Budgen, 'A New Spirit of Capitalism', *New Left Review* 1 (second series), January–February, 2000, p. 151.
65. Boltanski and Chiapello, *The New Spirit of Capitalism*, p. 485.
66. Ibid., p. 486.
67. Ibid., p. 487.
68. Ibid., p. 488.
69. Ibid., p. 489.
70. Ibid.
71. Ibid., p. 490.
72. Ibid., p. 491.
73. Callinicos, *The Resources of Critique*.
74. Adolf A. Berle and Gardiner C. Means, *The Modern Corporation and Private Property*, New York: Harcourt, Brace, 1968, revised edn (1932).
75. Adolf A. Berle, *The 20th Century Capitalist Revolution*, New York: Harcourt, Brace, 1954.
76. Theo Nichols, *Ownership Control and Ideology*, London: George Allen and Unwin, 1969. See also, Robin Blackburn, 'The New Capitalism', in Perry Anderson and Robin Blackburn, eds, *Towards Socialism*, London: Fontana, 1965, pp. 114–45.
77. Ralph Miliband, *The State in Capitalist Society*, London: Weidenfeld and Nicolson, 1969.
78. James Burnham, *The Managerial Revolution*, Harmondsworth: Penguin, 1945 (1941).
79. George Orwell, 'James Burnham and the Managerial Revolution' (1945), *The Collected Essays, Journalism and Letters of George Orwell Volume 4: In Front of Your Nose, 1945–50*, edited by Sonia Orwell and Ian Angus, Harmondsworth: Penguin, 1970 (1968), pp. 192–215.
80. Raymond Williams, 'Industry', *Keywords*, London: Fontana, 1981, 2nd edn (1976), pp. 165–9. See also Mike Gane, *French Social Theory*, London: Sage, 2003.

81. Clark Kerr, John T. Dunlop, Frederick H. Harbison and Charles A. Myers, *Industrialism and Industrial Man: The Problem of Labour and Management in Economic Growth*, London: Heinemann, 1962 (1960).
82. Anthony Giddens, *The Consequences of Modernity*, Cambridge: Polity, 1990.
83. See Jim McGuigan, 'Cultural Analysis, Technology and Power', Chapter 1 of *Rethinking Cultural Policy*, Maidstone: Open University Press, 2004, pp. 7–32.
84. Peter F. Drucker, *Post-capitalist Society*, Oxford: Butterworth-Heinemann, 1993.
85. Castells, *The Rise of the Network Society*.
86. Peter L. Berger, *The Capitalist Revolution: Fifty Propositions About Prosperity, Equality, and Liberty*, Aldershot: Wildwood House, 1987 (1986).
87. In his speech at the World Economic Forum in 2008, Bill Gates adopted the term and the reasoning behind the concept of 'cultural capitalism'.
88. Jeremy Rifkin, *The Age of Access: How the Shift from Ownership to Access is Transforming Capitalism*, Harmondsworth: Penguin, 2000.
89. Raymond Williams, *Towards 2000*, Harmondsworth: Penguin, 1985 (1983), p. 93.
90. Bob Ross and Don Mitchell, 'Neo-Liberal Landscapes of Deception – Detroit, Ford Field, and the Ford Motor Company', *Urban Geography* 25 (7), 2004, pp. 685–90.
91. Rifkin, *The Age of Access*, p. 10.
92. Ibid., p. 30.
93. Ibid., p. 40.
94. Ibid., p. 45.
95. Ibid., p. 47.
96. Ibid., p. 48.
97. See Scott Lash and John Urry, *Economies of Signs and Space*, London: Sage, 1994.
98. Theodor Adorno and Max Horkheimer, *Dialectic of Enlightenment*, London: Verso, 1979 (1944).
99. Rifkin, *The Age of Access*, p. 52.
100. Ibid., pp. 7–8.
101. Ibid., p. 98.
102. Ibid., p. 115.
103. Ibid., p. 138.
104. Ibid., p. 42.

105. See Herbert Schiller, *Culture Inc.: The Corporate Takeover of Public Expression*, New York: Oxford University Press, 1989.
106. Rifkin, *The Age of Access*, p. 171.
107. Ibid., p. 247.
108. Ibid., p. 174.
109. Jeremy Rifkin, 'The Age of Access – The New Politics of Culture Vs. Commerce', *Renewal* 9 (2/3), Winter, 2001, pp. 33–48.
110. Jeremy Rifkin, 'Worlds Apart', *Guardian*, 3 July 2001, p. 15.

Chapter 2

1. Herbert Marcuse, *One-Dimensional Man*, London: Abacus, 1972; originally published in the US in 1964.
2. Herbert Marcuse, *The Aesthetic Dimension: Towards a Critique of Marxist Aesthetics*, Boston: Beacon, 1978.
3. Theodor Adorno and Max Horkheimer, *Dialectic of Enlightenment*, London: Verso, 1979 (1944). See also Ernst Bloch, Georg Lukács, Bertolt Brecht, Walter Benjamin and Theodor Adorno, *Aesthetics and Politics*, London: Verso, 1980 (1977).
4. See Raymond Williams's discussion of Emily Bronte's *Wuthering Heights* in *The Long Revolution*, Harmondsworth: Penguin, 1965 (1961), pp. 75–86.
5. See Jim McGuigan, *Rethinking Cultural Policy*, Maidenhead: Open University Press, 2004, p. 115.
6. Marcuse, *One Dimensional Man*, p. 57.
7. Ibid., p. 61.
8. See Alasdair MacIntyre's astute critique, *Marcuse*, London: Fontana, 1970.
9. Jakob Rosenberg, *Rembrandt: Life and Work*, London: Phaidon, 1964.
10. Terry Eagleton, *The Function of Criticism: From the Spectator to Post-Structuralism*, London: Verso, 1984; and his *The Ideology of the Aesthetic*, Oxford: Blackwell, 1990.
11. Elizabeth Wilson, *Bohemians: The Glamorous Outcasts*, London: Tauris Parke, 2003, p. 2.
12. Roland Barthes, *Mythologies*, trans. Annette Lavers, London: Paladin, 1973 (1957).
13. Wilson, *Bohemians*, p. 17.
14. Sharon Zukin, *Loft Living: Culture and Capital in Urban Change*, New Brunswick: Rutgers University Press 1989 (1982).
15. T.J. Clark, *Image of the People: Gustave Courbet and the 1848 Revolution*, London: Thames and Hudson, 1973; see also Clark's

companion volume, *The Absolute Bourgeois: Artists and Politics in France 1848–1851*, London: Thames and Hudson, 1973.
16. Karl Marx, excerpt from *The Eighteenth Brumaire of Louis Bonaparte*, in Lewis S. Feuer, ed., *Marx and Engels: Basic Writings on Politics and Philosophy*, London: Fontana, 1969, p. 360.
17. Clark, *Image of the People*, p. 152.
18. Alexander Sturgis, Rupert Christiansen, Lois Oliver and Michael Wilson, eds, *Rebels and Martyrs: The Image of the Artist in the Nineteenth Century*, London: National Gallery/Yale University Press, 2006, pp. 96–7.
19. Pierre Bourdieu, *The Rules of Art: Genesis and Structure of the Literary Field*, trans. Susan Emanuel, Cambridge: Polity, 1996 (1992), p. 49.
20. Pierre Bourdieu, 'The Field of Cultural Production, or: The Economic World Reversed', Chapter 1 of *The Field of Cultural Production: Essays on Art and Literature*, trans. Randal Johnson, Cambridge: Polity, 1993, pp. 29–73.
21. Bourdieu, *The Rules of Art*, p. 55.
22. Ibid., p. 60.
23. Charles Baudelaire, *Selected Writings on Art and Literature*, Harmondsworth: Penguin, 1972.
24. See Keith Tester, ed., *The Flâneur*, London: Routledge, 1994. Also, see Walter Benjamin, *Charles Baudelaire: A Lyric Poet in the Era of High Capitalism*, London: New Left Books, 1973.
25. See Jim McGuigan, *Modernity and Postmodern Culture*, Maidenhead: Open University Press, 2006, 2nd edn (1999), for a fuller discussion. Incidentally, Fantin-Latour's 1867 *Portrait of Manet* may be regarded as a depiction of the type of the *flâneur*.
26. Bourdieu, *The Rules of Art*, p. 138.
27. T.J. Clark's work is an instance of a political hermeneutics in which he reads art in relation to power struggles of the time, especially in terms of class. The kind of institutional analysis associated with Bourdieu's methodology is not incompatible with such an approach but is rather more concerned with analysing the social institutions within which art is produced and circulated.
28. For the following analysis of the significance of the Salon de Refusés in the dialectic of refusal and incorporation I am very much indebted to George Heard Hamilton's descriptive account in his *Manet and His Critics* (New York: Norton, 1969 [1954]).
29. See Paul Hayes Tucker, ed., *Manet's Le déjeuner sur l'herbe*, Cambridge: Cambridge University Press, 1998.
30. Hamilton, *Manet and His Critics*, pp. 10–11.

31. Belinda Thomson, *Impressionism: Origins, Practice, Reception*, London: Thames and Hudson, 2000, p. 148.
32. T.J. Clark, *The Painting of Modern Life: Paris in the Art of Manet and His Followers*, London: Thames and Hudson, 1985.
33. Howard Becker, *Art Worlds*, Berkeley and Los Angeles: University of California Press, 1982.
34. Thomson, *The Impressionists*, p. 122.
35. See, for instance, Pierre Bourdieu's conversations with Hans Haacke published as *Free Exchange* (Cambridge: Polity, 1995 [1994]).
36. Jay Leyda, *Kino: A History of the Russian and Soviet Film*, London: George Allen and Unwin, 3rd edn, 1983 (1960).
37. Maxim Gorky, Karl Radek and Nikolai Bukharin et al., *Soviet Writers' Congress 1934: The Debate on Socialist Realism and Modernism*, London: Lawrence and Wishart, 1977.
38. Dawn Ades, Tim Benton, David Elliott and Iain Boyd Whyte, *Art and Power: Europe Under the Dictators*, London: South Bank Centre, 1995.
39. Henry Grosshans, *Hitler and the Artists*, New York: Holmes and Meier, 1983.
40. John Berger, *The Success and Failure of Picasso*, Harmondsworth: Penguin, 1965, p. 3.
41. Ibid., p. 10.
42. Tim Hilton, *Picasso*, London: Thames and Hudson, 1975, p. 15.
43. Ibid., pp. 85–6.
44. John Berger, 'The Moment of Cubism', in *Selected Essays and Articles: The Look of Things*, Harmondsworth: Penguin, 1972, pp. 152 and 153. For a further discussion, see my *Modernity and Postmodern Culture*, pp. 5–6.
45. Berger, *Success and Failure of Picasso*, p. 40.
46. Gijs van Hensbergen's book, *Guernica: The Biography of a Twentieth-Century Icon* (London: Bloomsbury, 2004), is the main source used here on the politics and history of *Guernica*.
47. Berger, *Success and Failure of Picasso*, p. 156.
48. In his otherwise excellent study, *The Power of Art* (London: BBC Books, 2006, p. 395), Simon Schama hovers between 'the American staff [of the UN] or the media' in attributing responsibility for the cover up of *Guernica* at Powell's press conference on the invasion of Iraq in 2003. It seems unlikely that the US government actually had to request the cover up, since whoever did it was presumably 'on message' anyway. Ideological distortion on this scale tends usually to work in a tacit and depersonalised manner.
49. Quoted by Berger, *Success and Failure of Picasso*, p. 173.
50. Hayden Herrera, *Frida: A Biography of Frida Kahlo*, London: Bloomsbury, 1989 (1983), p. 132.

51. Peter Hamill, *Diego Rivera*, New York: Abrams, 1999, p. 64. Hamill's book on Rivera and Herrera's biography of Kahlo are the main sources drawn upon here on the Mexican muralist; Herrera's biography of Kahlo is an unsurpassed source on not only her life but also her work.
52. Ibid., p. 87.
53. Ibid., p. 90.
54. As Isabel Acantra and Sandra Egnolff's *Frida Kahlo and Diego Rivera* (Munich: Prestel, 2005) demonstrates, it is difficult to discuss either of these two artists without reference to the other.
55. Oriana Baddeley, 'Reflecting on Kahlo – Mirrors, Masquearade and the Politics of Identification', in Emma Dexter and Tanya Barson, eds, *Frida Kahlo*, London: Tate Publishing, 2005, p. 47.
56. Julie Taymor, *Frida*, Buena Vista Home Entertainment, 2003.
57. Edward Lucie-Smith, *Latin American Art of the 20th Century*, London: Thames and Hudson, 1993.
58. Rozsika Parker and Griselda Pollock, *Old Mistresses: Women, Art and Ideology*, London: Pandora, 1981.
59. Griselda Pollock, *Differencing the Canon: Feminist Desire and the Writing of Art's Histories*, London: Routledge, 1999, p. 97.
60. Herrera, *Frida*, pp. 96–7.
61. See Clement Greenberg, *The Collected Essays and Criticism*, Vol. 1, *Perceptions and Judgments, 1939–44*, Vol. 2, *Arrogant Purpose, 1945–49*, both Chicago: University of Chicago Press, 1986; Vol. 3, *Affirmations and Refusals, 1950–56*, Chicago: University of Chicago Press, 1993; ed., John O'Brian.
62. Quoted by Frances Stonor Saunders, *Who Paid the Piper? The CIA and the Cultural Cold War*, London: Granta, 1999, p. 253.
63. Kirk Varnedoe and Pepe Karmel, *Jackson Pollock*, London: Tate Publishing, 1999. In November 2006, David Geffen, the entertainment tycoon, sold Pollock's *No5, 1948* at the world record price for a painting of $140 million (£73.35m) to a Mexican, David Martinez, a financier who deals in Third World debt.
64. Quoted by Stonor Saunders, *Who Paid the Piper?*, p. 258.
65. Ibid., p. 1.
66. Raymond Williams, 'Advertising – The Magic System', in *Problems of Materialism and Culture*, London: Verso, 1980, p. 184; originally published in 1960.
67. Ibid., p. 190.
68. Klaus Honnef, *Andy Warhol 1928–1987: Commerce Into Art*, Cologne: Taschen, 1990.
69. Fredric Jameson, *Postmodernism, Or, The Cultural Logic of Late Capitalism*, London: Verso, 1991, pp. 6–9.

70. Walter Benjamin, 'The Work of Art in the Age of Mechanical Reproduction', in *Illuminations*, ed., Hannah Arendt, London: Cape, 1970 (1955); originally written by Benjamin in 1936.
71. Colin MacCabe, Mark Francis and Peter Wollen, eds, *Who is Andy Warhol?*, London: British Film Institute, 1997.
72. Klaus Honnef, *Pop Art*, Cologne: Taschen, 2006.
73. Todd Gitlin, 'Postmodernism – Roots and Politics', Ian Angus and Sut Jhally, eds, *Cultural Politics in Contemporary America*, New York: Routledge, 1989, pp. 347–60.
74. See David Hopkins, *Art After Modernism 1945–2000*, Oxford: Oxford University Press, 2000.
75. Alexander Alberro, *Conceptual Art and the Politics of Publicity*, Boston: MIT, 2003, p. 2.
76. Ibid., p. 13.
77. Chin-tao Wu, *Privatising Culture: Corporate Art Intervention since the 1980s*, London: Verso, 2002.
78. Herbert Schiller, *Culture Inc.: The Corporate Takeover of Public Expression*, New York: Oxford University Press, 1989.
79. John A. Walker, *Left Shift: Radical Art in 1970s Britain*, London: I.B. Taurus, 2002.
80. Angela McRobbie, *In the Culture Society: Art, Fashion and Popular Music*, London: Routledge, 1999, p. 8.
81. Rita Hatton and John A. Walker, *Supercollector: A Critique of Charles Saatchi*, London: Institute of Artology, 3rd edn, 2005 (2000).
82. Jim McGuigan, 'The Social Construction of a Cultural Disaster – New Labour's Millennium Experience', *Cultural Studies* 17 (5), September 2003, pp. 669–90. Also, see my *Cultural Analysis*, London: Sage, 2010.
83. Julian Stallabrass, *High Art Lite: The Rise and Fall of Young British Art*, London: Verso, 2nd edn, 2006 (1999).
84. Ibid., p. 60.
85. Ibid., p. 63.
86. Victoria Alexander, 'A Strange Sensation – Controversies in Art', in *The Sociology of the Arts*, Oxford: Blackwell, 2003, pp. 297–303.
87. See Hatton and Walker, *Supercollector*, pp. 42 and 55.
88. Stallabrass, *High Art Lite*, p. 271.
89. Ibid., p. 298.
90. Ibid., pp. 6 and 175.
91. Ibid., pp. 300–1.
92. Banksy, *Wall and Piece*, London: Century, 2nd edn, 2006.
93. Julia Kristeva, *Powers of Horror: An Essay on Abjection*, New York: Columbia University Press, 1982 (1980).

Chapter 3

1. *Time*, 25 December 2006–1 January 2007.
2. Ibid., p. 4.
3. Ibid., pp. 30–1.
4. Ibid., pp. 32–44.
5. Ibid., p. 48.
6. Ibid., pp. 50–6.
7. Jon Pareles, 'Express Yourself', *The Observer Review*, 17 December 2006, pp. 10–11.
8. For instance, Hans Magnus Enzensberger, 'Constituents of a Theory of the Media' (1970), in *The Consciousness Industry: On Literature, Politics and the Media*, New York: Continuum, 1974.
9. In *Freedom* (Milton Keynes: Open University Press, 1988, p. 61), Zygmunt Bauman writes: 'Costly, "panoptical" methods of control, pregnant as they are with dissent, may be disposed of or replaced by a less costly and more efficient method of seduction (or, rather, the deployment of "panoptical" methods may be limited to a minority of the population, which for whatever reason cannot be integrated through the consumer market).'
10. Yiannis Gabriel and Tim Lang, *The Unmanageable Consumer: Contemporary Consumption and its Fragmentation*, London: Sage, 1997, p. 1.
11. Abraham Maslow's 'hierarchy of needs' (distinguishing between the 'basic needs' of physiology, safety, belonging and love, on the one hand, and the 'higher needs', especially of self-activation and esteem, on the other) remains a fundamental and reasonable set of distinctions in spite of dispute over the particulars of classification. See Maslow's *Motivation and Personality*, New York: Harper and Row, 2nd edn, 1970 (1954).
12. Thorstein Veblen, *The Theory of the Leisure Class*, Mineola: Dover, 1994 (1899), p. 94.
13. Ibid., pp. 108, 109.
14. Michael Spindler, *Veblen and Modern America: Revolutionary Iconoclast*, London: Pluto, 2002, p. 37.
15. Pierre Bourdieu, *Distinction: A Social Critique of the Judgement of Taste*, trans. Richard Nice, London: Routledge, 1984 (1979), pp. 4–5.
16. Pierre Bourdieu and Jean-Claude Passeron, *Reproduction in Education, Society and Culture*, trans. Richard Nice, London: Sage, 1977 (1970).

17. Pierre Bourdieu, *Acts of Resistance: Against the New Myths of Our Time*, trans. Richard Nice, Cambridge: Polity, 1998.
18. For instance, by John Carey, *What Good Are the Arts?*, London: Faber and Faber, 2005.
19. Bourdieu, *Distinction*, p. 359.
20. Ibid., p. 87.
21. Fred Pfeil, '"Makin' Flippy-Floppy" – Postmodernism and the Baby-Boom PMC', in *Another Tale to Tell: Politics and Narrative in Postmodern Culture*, London: Verso, 1990, pp. 97–125.
22. Herbert Gans, *Popular and High Culture: An Analysis and Evaluation of Taste*, New York: Basic Books, 2nd edn, 1999 (1974).
23. Richard Dyer, *Stars*, London: British Film Institute, 1977.
24. Chris Rojek, *Celebrity*, London: Reaktion, 2001.
25. Gary Whannel, *Media Sports Stars: Masculinities and Moralities*, London: Routledge, 2002.
26. Robert Goldman and Stephen Papson, *Nike Culture: The Sign of the Swoosh*, London: Sage, 1998.
27. Walter La Feber, *Michael Jordan and the New Global Capitalism*, New York: Norton, 1999, p. 92.
28. Elmore Leonard, *Be Cool*, London: Penguin, 2005 (1999).
29. *Be Cool*, dir., F. Gary Gray, MGM, 2005.
30. Cited by Gabriel Tolliver and Reggie Osse, *Bling: The Hip-Hop Jewellery Book*, London: Bloomsbury, 2006.
31. Zenga Longmore, 'Bling-Bling', in Richard Ingrams, ed., *Bling, Blogs and Bluetooth: Modern Living for Oldies*, London: Profile, 2006, p. 19.
32. Minyah Oh, *Hip Hop's Crown Jewels*, New York: Wenner Books, 2006, p. 2.
33. For instance, Dick Hebdige, *Subculture: The Meaning of Style*, London: Methuen, 1979.
34. Paul Willis, *Common Culture*, Milton Keynes: Open University Press, 1990.
35. Tolliver and Osse, *Bling*, pp. 6–7.
36. Erica Kennedy, *Bling*, London: Arrow, 2005 (2004), p. 192.
37. Ellis Cashmore, *The Black Culture Industry*, London: Routledge, 1997, p. 1.
38. Ibid., p. 177.
39. Russell Keat, 'Scepticism, Authority and the Market', in R. Keat, N. Whiteley and N. Abercrombie, eds, *The Authority of the Consumer*, London: Routledge, 1994, p. 27.
40. Joan Robinson, *Economic Philosophy*, Harmondsworth: Penguin, 1964.

41. Jim McGuigan, 'Sovereign Consumption', in M. Lee, ed., *The Consumer Society Reader*, Oxford: Blackwell, 2000, pp. 294–9. For a fuller discussion of sovereign consumption in relation to cultural and media policy see also my 'Cultural Populism Revisited', in M. Ferguson and P. Golding, eds, *Cultural Studies in Question*, London: Routledge, 1997, pp. 138–54.
42. Karl Marx, *Grundrisse: Introduction to the Critique of Political Economy*, trans. Martin Nicolaus, Harmondsworth: Penguin, 1973, p. 91.
43. Jean Baudrillard famously rejected Marx's 'productionist' perspective in *The Mirror of Production* (St Louis: Telos, 1975 [1973]) and proposed a reorientation of critical analysis to consumption, most notably in *For a Critique of the Political Economy of the Sign* (St Louis: Telos, 1981 [1972]), where he stressed the growing significance of 'sign value' over 'exchange/ use value'. In fact, he denied the distinction between exchange value and use values that was first proposed by Adam Smith and developed influentially by Marx. That modern society has become much more oriented towards consumption and that certain kinds of commodity are sought more for their symbolic properties than for their practical usefulness is beyond dispute. However, Baudrillard went too far and, in effect, endorsed the masking over of production and the alienation associated with commodity fetishism that are so crucial to capitalism's ideological power, which is the topic of this book.
44. Stuart Hall, 'Marx's Notes on Method – A "Reading" of the "1857 Introduction"', *Cultural Studies* 6, Birmingham: Centre for Contemporary Cultural Studies, Autumn 1974, p. 142.
45. Antonio Gramsci, 'Americanism and Fordism', in Q. Hoare and G. Nowell Smith, eds, *Selections from the Prison Notebooks of Antonio Gramsci*, London: Lawrence and Wishart, 1971, pp. 277–318.
46. Michel Aglietta, *A Theory of Capitalist Regulation: The US Experience*, London, Verso, 1987 [1976], p. 82.
47. Martin Shaw, *Marxism and Social Science: The Roots of Social Knowledge*, London: Pluto, 1975, p. 20.
48. Martyn Lee, *Consumer Culture Reborn: The Cultural Politics of Consumption*, London: Routledge, 1993, p. 101.
49. Ibid., p. 108.
50. Susan Christopherson and Michael Storper, 'The City as Studio; the World as Back Lot – The Impact of Vertical Disintegration on the Location of the Motion Picture Industry' (1986), in A. Gray

and J. McGuigan, eds, *Studying Culture: An Introductory Reader*, London: Arnold, 1997 (1993), pp. 256–74.
51. See, for instance, Ash Amin, ed., *Post-Fordism: A Reader*, Oxford: Blackwell, 1994.
52. See Asu Aksoy and Kevin Robins, 'Hollywood for the 21st Century – Global Competition for Critical Mass in Image Markets', *Cambridge Journal of Economics* 16 (1), 1992; and Janet Wasko, *Hollywood in the Information Age*, Cambridge: Polity, 1994.
53. Robin Murray, 'Fordism and Post-Fordism', in S. Hall and M. Jacques, eds, *New Times: The Changing Face of Politics in the 1990s*, London: Lawrence and Wishart, 1989, p. 42.
54. Ibid., p. 43.
55. Ibid., p. 44.
56. Andrew Wernick, *Promotional Culture: Advertising, Ideology and Symbolic Expression*, London: Sage, 1991, p. viii.
57. Stewart Ewen, *Captains of Consciousness: Advertising and the Social Roots of the Consumer Culture*, New York: Basic Books, 2001, 25th Anniversary Edition (1976).
58. Ibid., p. 55.
59. Ibid., p. 108.
60. Walter Lippmann, *Public Opinion*, New York: Free Press, 1997 (1922), p. 158.
61. Larry Tye, *The Father of Spin: Edward L. Bernays and the Birth of Public Relations*, New York: Henry Holt, 1998.
62. Stuart Ewen, *PR! A Social History of Spin*, New York: Basic Books, 1996, pp. 102–27.
63. Edward Bernays, *Crystallizing Public Opinion*, New York: Boni and Liveright, 1923.
64. Lizabeth Cohen, *A Consumers' Republic: The Politics of Mass Consumption in Postwar America*, New York: Horizon, 2003.
65. For example, Vance Packard, *The Hidden Persuaders*, Harmondsworth: Penguin, 1960 (1957).
66. Ewen, *PR!*, p. 306.
67. William Leiss, Stephen Kline, Sut Jhally and Jacqueline Botterill, *Social Communication in Advertising: Consumption in the Mediated Marketplace*, London: Routledge, 3rd edn, 2005 (1986), pp. 153–9.
68. Ibid., p. 155.
69. Ibid., p. 566.
70. Ibid., pp. 566–7.
71. Judith Williamson, *Decoding Advertisements: Ideology and Meaning in Advertising*, London: Marion Boyars, 1978, p. 174.

72. Leiss, Botterill et al., *Social Communication in Advertising*, pp. 563–4.
73. Ibid., pp. 566–7.
74. See, for instance, Mica Navs (with Orson Nava), 'Discrimination or Duped? Young People as Consumers of Advertising', in M. Nava, *Changing Cultures: Feminism, Youth and Consumerism*, London: Routledge, 1992, pp. 171–84.
75. Douglas Coupland, *Generation X: Tales for an Accelerated Culture*, London: Abacus, 1992 (1991).
76. Jean Baudrillard, *The Consumer Society: Myths and Structures*, London: Sage, 1998 (1970); Daniel Bell, *The Cultural Contradictions of Capitalism*, New York: Basic Books, 1996 (20th Anniversary Edition) (1976); Colin Campbell, *The Romantic Ethic and the Spirit of Modern Capitalism*, Oxford: Blackwell, 1997; Thomas Frank, *The Conquest of Cool: Business Culture, Counterculture, and the Rise of Hip Consumerism*, Chicago: University of Chicago Press, 1997; Naomi Klein, *No Logo: Taking Aim at the Brand Bullies*, London: Flamingo, 2000.
77. Leiss, Botterill et al., *Social Communication in Advertising*, p. 517.
78. Leo Benedictus, 'Psst! Have You Heard?', *Guardian G2*, 30 January 2007, pp. 7–11.
79. Malcolm Gladwell, 'The Coolhunt', *New Yorker*, 17 March 1997.
80. Ibid.
81. Joseph Heath and Andrew Potter, *The Rebel Sell: How the Counterculture Became Consumer Culture*, Chichester: Capstone, 2005, p. 194.
82. 'Commandos of Cool', *The Money Programme*, BBC2, 19 June 2002.
83. Douglas Rushkoff, *Coercion: Why We Listen to What 'They' Say*, New York: Riverhead, 1999, p. 20. See also Martin Howard, *We Know What You Want: How They Change Your Mind*, New York: Disinformation, 2005, a book by a former marketing executive that applies Rushkoff's ideas to specific cases.
84. Conrad Lodziak, *Manipulating Needs*, London: Pluto, 1995, p. 46.
85. For instance, Guy Debord, *The Society of the Spectacle*, trans. Donald Nicholson-Smith, New York: Zone, 1995 (1967).
86. Conrad Lodziak, *The Myth of Consumerism*, London: Pluto, 2002.
87. Lodziak, *Manipulating Needs*, p. 59.

88. See, for instance, André Gorz, *Critique of Economic Reason*, trans. Gillian Handyside and Chris Turner, London: Verso, 1989 (1988); and *Capitalism, Socialism, Ecology*, trans. Chris Turner, London: Verso, 1994 (1991). Lodziak has written a book with Jeremy Tatman about Gorz: *André Gorz: A Critical Introduction*, London: Pluto, 1997.
89. John Gittings, *The Changing Face of China: From Mao to Market*, Oxford: Oxford University Press, 2005.
90. Leslie Sklair, *Globalization: Capitalism and its Alternatives*, Oxford: Oxford University Press, 2002, 3rd edn, p. 62.
91. Ibid., p. 108.
92. Jean Baudrillard, *Seduction*, trans. Brian Singer, New York: St Martin's Press, 1990 (1979).
93. Ibid., p. 158.
94. Bauman, *Freedom*, p. 61.
95. Zygmunt Bauman, *Intimations of Postmodernity*, London: Routledge, 1992, pp. 97–8.
96. Ewen, *Captains of Consciousness*, Pt 3, Ch.7, 'Consumption and Seduction', pp. 177–84.
97. Alissa Quart, *Branded: The Buying and Selling of Teenagers*, London: Arrow, 2003, p. 9.
98. Neal Lawson, 'Turbo-Consumerism is the Driving Force Behind Crime', *Guardian*, 29 June 2006, p. 31.
99. Zygmunt Bauman, *Work, Consumerism and the New Poor*, Buckingham: Open University Press, 1998.
100. Michel Foucault, *Discipline and Punish: The Birth of the Prison*, trans. Alan Sheridan, Harmondsworth: Penguin, 1977 (1975).
101. Zygmunt Bauman, 'Collateral Casualties of Consumerism', *Journal of Consumer Culture* 7 (1), 2007, pp. 25–6.
102. Karl Marx, *Capital: Volume One*, trans. Ben Fowkes, Harmondsworth: Penguin, 1976 (1967), pp. 163–4.
103. Ibid., p. 165.
104. Manuel Castells, *The Rise of the Network Society*, Malden, MA, and Oxford: Basil Blackwell, 2000 (1996); *The Power of Identity*, Malden, MA, and Oxford: Basil Blackwell, 2004 (1997); *End of Millennium*, Malden, MA, and Oxford: Basil Blackwell, 2004 (1998).
105. Manuel Castells, Mireira Fernandez-Ardevol, Jack Linchuan Qiu and Araba Sey, *Mobile Communication and Society: A Global Perspective*, Cambridge, MA: MIT Press, 2007.
106. Jim McGuigan, *Modernity and Postmodern Culture*, Maidenhead: Open University Press, 2006 (1999), Ch.5, 'The Information Age', pp. 115–36; 'Technological Determinism and Mobile

Privatisation', in V. Nightingale and T. Dwyer, eds, *New Media Worlds: Challenges for Convergence*, Sydney: Oxford University Press, 2007, pp. 5–18.
107. Raymond Williams, *Television: Technology and Cultural Form*, London: Fontana, 1974.
108. Brian Winston, 'How are Media Born and Developed?', in J. Downing, A. Mohammadi and A. Sreberny-Mohammadi, eds, *Questioning the Media: A Critical Introduction*, London: Sage, 1995 (1990), pp. 54–74; *Technologies of Seeing: Photography, Cinematography and Television*, London: British Film Institute, 1996.
109. Bobbie Johnson, 'The Coolest Player in Town', *Guardian* (Technology section), 22 September 2005, pp. 1–2.
110. David Smith, 'Why the iPod is Losing its Cool', *Observer*, 10 September 2006.
111. John Lanchester, 'Engine Trouble', *Guardian* G2, 26 January 2006, pp. 6–11.
112. Jack Schofield, 'Microsoft Struggles to Regain its Cool Amid the Upstarts', *Guardian* (Technology section), 28 September 2006, p. 6.
113. John Harris, 'Future Imperfect', *Guardian*, 30 September 2006, pp. 27–8.
114. John Kenneth Galbraith, *The Affluent Society*, London: Penguin, 1999 (1958).
115. Williams, *Television*, p. 26.
116. Williams, *Towards 2000*, Harmondsworth: Penguin, 1985 (1983), p. 188.
117. Williams, *Second Generation*, Hogarth Press, 1988 (1964).
118. Williams, *Towards 2000*, pp. 188–9.
119. Ibid., p. 189.
120. John Urry, *Sociology Beyond Societies: Mobilities for the Twenty-First Century*, London: Routledge, 2000.
121. Jim McGuigan, 'Towards a Sociology of the Mobile Phone', *Human Technology* 1 (1), April 2005, pp. 41–53. See also my 'Technological Determinism and Mobile Privatisation' and my *Cultural Analysis*, London: Sage, 2010.
122. Paul du Gay, Stuart Hall, Linda Janes, Hugh Mackay and Keith Negus, *Doing Cultural Studies: The Story of the Mobile Phone*, London, Sage, 1997.
123. Adam Burgess, *Cellular Phones, Public Fears and a Culture of Precaution*, Cambridge: Cambridge University Press, 2004.
124. George Myerson, *Heidegger, Habermas and the Mobile Phone*, Cambridge: Icon, 2001.

125. Ulrich Beck and Elisabeth Beck-Gernsheim, *Individualization: Institutionalized Individualism and its Social and Political Consequences*, trans. Patrick Camiller, London: Sage, 2002 (2001).
126. Dylan Jones, *iPod, Therefore I Am*, London: Weidenfeld and Nicolson, 2005.
127. Richard Wray, 'Mobile Phone World Meets in Search of the Next Big Thing', *Guardian*, 13 February 2006, p. 28.
128. The iPhone dispenses with buttons and has a touch screen. Over 2007, it was to be marketed first in the US, followed by the UK and then Asia in 2008. At the beginning of 2007 it was announced that the 4gb model was to retail at $499 (£257) and the 8gb model at $599 (£339) in the UK (Bobbie Johnson and Les Glendinning, 'Apple Proclaims its iPhone Revolution', *Guardian*, 10 January 2007, p. 11). In fact, when the iPhone was eventually released onto the UK market in November 2007, the 4gb model had been abandoned and the 8gb model was sold at the reduced price of £269, still £89 more than in the US ('When it Comes to the Crunch, That New Apple iPhone will cost £900', *Times Online*, 10 November 2007). There was controversy over the contract that customers were obliged to sign up to. It locked them into the O2 network for 18 months at a cost of £35 a month for the basic service and £55 a month for the full service, generally considered to be an expensive and restrictive contract. Should users break with the contract and go on to a different network, they were advised the iPhone would probably not work and if it did work they would infringe the warranty on the handset.
129. James Katz and Mark Aakhus, eds, *Perpetual Contact: Mobile Communication, Private Talk, Public Performance*, Cambridge: Cambridge University Press, 2002.
130. Gerard Goggin, *Cell Phone Culture: Mobile Technology in Everyday Life*, London: Routledge, 2006, pp. 183–4.
131. Ibid., pp. 112, and passim.
132. For instance, Geoffrey Lean, 'Danger on the Airwaves – Is the Wi-Fi Revolution a Health Time Bomb?', *Independent on Sunday*, 22 April 2007, pp. 8–9.
133. Ulrich Beck, *Risk Society: Towards a New Modernity*, London: Sage, 1992 (1986).
134. Castells et al., *Mobile Communication and Society*.
135. Joseph Wilde and Esther de Haan, *The High Cost of Calling: Critical Issues in the Mobile Phone Industry*, SOMO: Centre for Research on Multinational Corporations, November 2006, p. 8.

136. See Mike Gane, 'The *Communist Manifesto*'s Transgendered Proletarians', in M. Cowling, ed., *The Communist Manifesto: New Interpretations*, Edinburgh: Edinburgh University Press, 1998, pp. 132–41.
137. Wilde and de Haan, *The High Cost of Calling*, p. 30.
138. Jon Agar, *Constant Touch: A Global History of the Mobile Phone*, Cambridge: Icon, 2003.

Chapter 4

1. The analysis of ideology in the social sciences is an area of fierce debate and great differences of theoretical opinion. The various positions on the concept are reviewed by Terry Eagleton in *Ideology: An Introduction* (London: Verso, 2007 [1991]). A particularly notable topic of disputation is over 'the dominant ideology thesis'. Nicholas Abercrombie, Stephen Hill and Bryan Turner, in *The Dominant Ideology Thesis* (London: George Allen and Unwin, 1980), argued influentially that the persistence of capitalism does not depend on ideological domination, and in this they are probably right. However, that does not preclude the possible existence of a dominant ideology that legitimises capitalism (and other structures of domination) in the face of opposition and critique. In an otherwise important contribution to the theory of ideology, John B. Thompson, in *Ideology and Modern Culture* (Cambridge: Polity, 1990), retained the notion of a dominant ideology but claimed that this is not best defined in terms of distortion but should be understood exclusively as a matter of power, a contest between different ideological discourses. The problem with such an argument is that it tends towards relativism and dispenses with a concept of truth. Alternatively, I would argue that it is more useful analytically to retain the critical argument concerning distortion, which is not the same as saying that ideology is 'false consciousness'. Whilst ideology may distort, it need not necessarily be entirely false. For it to work, ideology must address real issues and make sense of them in a convincing manner in contest with other, perhaps truer representations of the world. This, I believe, is integral to the role of ideology in social, political, economic and cultural leadership, that is, hegemony (see Raymond Williams, 'Base and Superstructure in Marxist Cultural Theory' [1973], reprinted in *Problems in Materialism and Culture*, London: Verso, 1980, pp. 31–49).

2. Daniel Yergin and Joseph Stanislaw, *The Commanding Heights: The Battle for the World Economy*, New York: Touchstone, 2002 (1998).
3. F.A. Hayek, *The Road to Serfdom*, London: Routledge and Kegan Paul, 1944.
4. John Burton et al., *Hayek's 'Serfdom' Revisited*, London: Institute of Economic Affairs, 1984.
5. Andrew Gamble, *Hayek: The Iron Cage of Liberty*, Cambridge: Polity, 1996.
6. David Harvey, *A Brief History of Neoliberalism*, Oxford: Oxford University Press, 2005, p. 2.
7. Ibid., p. 3.
8. Ibid., p. 5.
9. Ibid., p. 11.
10. Ibid., p. 23.
11. Ibid., p. 80.
12. Thomas Frank, *One Market Under God: Extreme Capitalism, Market Populism and the End of Economic Democracy*, London: Secker and Warburg, 2001 (2000), p. 15.
13. Ibid., p. xiv.
14. Pierre Bourdieu, *Acts of Resistance: Against the New Myths of Our Time*, trans. Richard Nice, Cambridge: Polity, 1998, p. vii.
15. Pierre Bourdieu, 'A Reasoned Utopianism and Economic Fatalism', trans. John Howe, *New Left Review* 227 (1st series), 1998, p. 125.
16. See Norman Fairclough's splendid *New Labour, New Language?* (London: Penguin, 2000). The rhetoric of neoliberalism and its inscription into British politics have been a focus of critical discourse analysis over the past few years. For further references, see http://www.ling.lancs.ac.uk/staff/norman/norman.htm
17. Pierre Bourdieu et al., *La Misère du Monde*, Paris: Editions du Seuil, 1993. Translated into English by Priscilla Parkhurst Ferguson, Susan Emanuel, Joe Johnson and Shoggy T. Waryn as *The Weight of the World: Social Suffering in Contemporary Society*, Cambridge: Polity, 1999.
18. Pierre Bourdieu and Loïc Wacquant, 'NewLiberalSpeak – Notes on the New Planetary Vulgate', trans. David Macey, *Radical Philosophy* 105, 2001, p. 2.
19. Ibid., p. 5.
20. Ibid.
21. See Anthony Giddens, *The Third Way: The Renewal of Social Democracy*, Cambridge: Polity, 1998, and *The Third Way and its Critics*, Cambridge: Polity, 2000.

22. Voltaire, *Candide*, trans. John Butt, Harmondsworth: Penguin, 1947.
23. See, for instance, Lawrence Harrison and Samuel Huntington, eds, *Culture Matters: How Values Shape Human Progress*, New York: Basic Books, 2000.
24. Alan Warde, 'Production, Consumption and "Cultural Economy"', in Paul du Gay and Michael Pryke, eds, *Cultural Economy: Cultural Analysis and Commercial Life*, London: Sage, 2002, pp. 185–200.
25. Peter Anthony, *Managing Culture*, Buckingham: Open University Press, 1994.
26. Scott Lash and John Urry, *Economies of Signs and Space*, London: Sage, 1994.
27. Lord Young of Graffham, 'Enterprise Regained', Paul Heelas and Paul Morris, eds, *The Values of the Enterprise Culture: The Moral Debate*, London: Routledge, 1992.
28. Andrzej Huczynski, *Management Gurus: What Makes Them and How to Become One*, London: Routledge, 1993.
29. Peter Drucker, *The New Realities*, London: Mandarin, 1990 (1989), p. 218.
30. Rosabeth Moss Kanter, *When Giants Learn to Dance: Mastering the Challenges of Strategy, Management, and Careers in the 1990s*, London: Unwin, 1990 (1989), p. 177.
31. Thomas Peters and Robert Waterman, *In Search of Excellence: Lessons from America's Best-Run Companies*, New York: HarperCollins, 1982.
32. Tom Peters, *The Tom Peters Seminar: Crazy Times Call for Crazy Organizations*, New York: Vintage, 1994, p. 282.
33. Chris Painter, 'Public Service Reform – Reinventing or Abandoning Government?', *Political Quarterly* 65 (3), pp. 242–62.
34. David Osborne and Ted Gaebler, *Reinventing Government: How the Entrepreneurial Spirit is Transforming the Public Sector*, Reading, MA: Addison: Wesley, 1992, pp. 19–20.
35. See John Clarke and Janet Newman, *The Managerial State: Power, Politics and Ideology in the Remaking of Social Welfare*, London: Sage, 1997; and Colin Leys, *Market-Driven Politics: Neoliberal Democracy and the Public Interest*, London: Verso, 2001.
36. Nikolas Rose, *Governing the Soul: The Shaping of the Private Self*, London: Routledge, 1990.
37. Michel Foucault, 'Governmentality' (1978), in Graham Burchell, Colin Gordon and Peter Miller, eds, *The Foucault Effect: Studies in Governmentality, with Two Lectures and an Interview with*

Michel Foucault, Hemel Hempstead: Harvester Wheatsheaf, 1991, pp. 87–104.
38. Nikolas Rose, 'Governing the Enterprising Self', in Heelas and Morris, *The Values of the Enterprise Culture*, p. 141.
39. Ibid., p. 145.
40. Ibid., p. 146.
41. Ibid., p. 149.
42. Ibid., p. 150.
43. Raymond Williams, 'Social Darwinism', in *Problems on Materialism and Culture*, London: Verso, 1980, pp. 86–102.
44. Paul du Gay, *Consumption and Identity at Work*, London: Sage, 1996, p. 77.
45. Ibid., p. 116.
46. Deborah Cameron, *Good to Talk: Living and Working in a Communication Culture*, London: Sage, 2000.
47. Natasha Walter, 'What's Love Got to Do With It?', *Guardian*, 14 January 2004, p. 25.
48. Jim McGuigan, 'Apprentices to Cool Capitalism', *Social Semiotics* 18 (3), 2008, pp. 309–19. A version of this case study also appears in my *Cultural Analysis*, London: Sage, 2010.
49. Quentin Hoare and Geoffrey Nowell Smith, eds, *Selections from the Prison Notebooks of Antonio Gramsci*, London: Lawrence and Wishart, 1971.
50. Louis Althusser, 'Ideology and Ideological State Apparatuses (Notes Towards an Investigation)' (1970), in *Essays on Ideology*, London: New Left Books/Verso, pp. 1–60.
51. Stuart Hall, 'The Rediscovery of "Ideology" – Return of the Repressed in Media Studies', in M. Gurevitch, J. Curran and J. Woollacott, eds, *Culture, Society and the Media Studies*, London: Methuen, pp. 56–90.
52. Edward Herman and Noam Chomsky, eds, *Manufacturing Consent: The Political Economy of the Mass Media*, New York: Pantheon, 1988.
53. David Miller, ed., *Tell Me No Lies: Propaganda and Distortion in the Attack on Iraq*, London: Pluto, 2003; Sheldon Rampton and John Stauber, *Weapons of Mass Deception: The Uses of Propaganda in Bush's War on Iraq*, London: Constable and Robertson, 2003.
54. Jeffrey Klaehn, 'A Critical Review and Assessment of Herman and Chomsky's "Propaganda Model"', *European Journal of Communication* 17 (2), 2002, pp. 147–82; John Corner, 'Debate: The Model in Question – A Critical Response to Klaehn on Herman and Chomsky', *European Journal of Communication* 18 (3),

2003, pp. 367–75; Jeffrey Klaehn, 'Debate: Model Construction – Various Other Epistemological Concerns. A Reply to John Corner's Commentary on the Propaganda Model', *European Journal of Communication* 18 (3), 2003, pp. 377–83.

55. Jürgen Habermas, *The Structural Transformation of the Public Sphere: An Inquiry into a Category of Bourgeois Society*, trans. Thomas Burger with the assistance of Frederick Lawrence, Cambridge: Polity, 1989 (1962); Craig Calhoun, ed., *Habermas and the Public Sphere*, Cambridge, MA: MIT Press, 1992.

56. See my 'The Cultural Public Sphere', *European Journal of Cultural Studies* 8 (1), November 2005, pp. 427–43; also in Alex Benchimol and Willy Maley, eds, *Spheres of Influence: Intellectuals and Cultural Publics from Shakespeare to Habermas*, Bern: Peter Lang, 2007, pp. 243–63.

57. Jim McGuigan, *Culture and the Public Sphere*, London: Routledge, 1996.

58. Edward Herman and Robert McChesney, *The Global Media: The New Missionaries of Global Capitalism*, London: Cassell, 1997.

59. Hollywood's multiple exploitation of intellectual property is synergistic both economically and culturally, not only operating intensively at the level of the firm but also extensively at the level of the industry and by interacting with other industries such as tourism. See Nathan Vaughan, *Hollywood Synergy*, Ph.D. thesis, Loughborough University, 1997.

60. Toby Miller, Nitin Govil, John McMurria, Richard Maxwell and Ting Wang, *Global Hollywood 2*, London: British Film Institute, 2005 [2001], p. 10.

61. Ibid., pp. 7, 119.

62. Ibid., p. 123.

63. Mari Castanada Paredes, 'Television Set Production at the US-Mexico Border – Trade Policy and Advanced Electronics for the Global Market', in Justin Lewis and Toby Miller, eds, *Critical Cultural Policy Studies: A Reader*, Malden, MA: Blackwell, 2003, pp. 272–81.

64. Caroline Pauwels and Jan Loisen, 'The WTO and the Audio-visual Sector – Economic Free Trade vs. Cultural Horse Trading?', *European Journal of Communication* 18 (3), 2003, pp. 291–313.

65. See, for instance, Scott Lash and Celia Lury, *Global Culture Industry*, Cambridge: Polity, 2007.

66. David Hesmondhalgh, *The Cultural Industries*, 2nd edn, London: Sage, 2007.

67. Theodor Adorno and Max Horkheimer, *Dialectic of Enlightenment*, London: New Left Books/Verso, 1979 (1944). See also Theodor Adorno, *The Culture Industry: Selected Essays on Mass Culture*, J.M. Bernstein, ed., London: Routledge, 1991; and Shane Gunster, *Capitalizing on Culture: Critical Theory for Cultural Studies*, Toronto: University of Toronto Press, 2004.
68. Heinz Steinart, *Culture Industry*, trans. Sally-Ann Spencer, Cambridge: Polity, 2003 (1998), p. 9.
69. Bernard Miege, *The Capitalization of Cultural Production*, New York: International General, 1989.
70. Nick Garnham and Joyce Epstein, 'Cultural Industries, Consumption and Policy', in *The State of the Art or the Art of the State?*, London: Industry and Employment Branch, Department for Recreation and the Arts, Greater London Council, 1985, pp. 145–65. Garnham published a version of this paper as 'Concepts of Culture – Public Policy and the Cultural Industries', *Cultural Studies* 1 (1), January 1987, pp. 23–37; and it has been anthologised in several other publications.
71. For an extremely insightful and illuminating treatment of cultural industries/business from a managerial point of view, see Dag Bjorkegren, *The Culture Business: Management Strategies for the Arts-Related Business*, London: Routledge, 1996.
72. Simon Frith, 'Knowing One's Place – The Culture of the Cultural Industries', *Cultural Studies From Birmingham*, no.1, Birmingham: Department of Cultural Studies, University of Birmingham, 1991, pp. 134–55.
73. Geoff Mulgan and Ken Worpole, *Saturday Night or Sunday Morning? From Arts to Industry: New Forms of Cultural Policy*, London: Comedia, 1986.
74. John Hartley, ed., *Creative Industries*, Oxford: Blackwell, 2005, p. 1.
75. John Hartley, *A Short History of Cultural Studies*, London: Sage, 2003, p. 118.
76. Chris Anderson, *The Long Tail: How Endless Choice is Creating Unlimited Demand*, London: Random House, 2006.
77. Tyler Cowen, *In Praise of Commercial Culture*, Cambridge, MA: Harvard University Press, 1998.
78. Creative Industries Task Force, *Creative Industries Mapping Document*, London: Department for Culture, Media and Sport, 1998, p. 8.
79. Ministerial Creative Industries Mapping Group, *Creative Industries Mapping Document*, 2nd edn, London: Department for Culture, Media and Sport, 2001, p. 00.05.

80. Work Foundation, *Staying Ahead: The Economic Performance of the UK's Creative Industries*, London, Work Foundation/DCMS, 2007, p. 30.
81. Ibid., p. 16.
82. Ibid., p. 117.
83. Ibid., p. 18.
84. Ibid., p. 23.
85. Ibid., p. 103.
86. Ibid., p. 106.
87. Chris Bilton, *Management and Creativity: From Creative Industries to Creative Management*, Oxford: Blackwell, 2007.
88. In his criticism of *Staying Ahead*, Mark Lawson disputed that culture should be treated in such reductively business terms; see 'Culture is Not an Industry', *Guardian*, 29 June 2007, p. 40. In his reply to Lawson, the chief executive of the Work Foundation, Will Hutton insisted that it should; see 'There's No Unbridgeable Gulf Between Culture and Business', *Guardian*, 6 July 2007, p. 37.
89. Larry Elliott and Dan Atkinson, *Fantasy Island: Waking Up to the Incredible Economic, Political and Social Illusions of the Blair Legacy*, London: Constable, 2007, p. 92.
90. Frank Webster, *Theories of the Information Society*, 3rd edn, London: Sage, 2007.
91. Richard Florida, *The Rise of the Creative Class: And How It's Transforming Work, Leisure, Community and Everyday Life*, Melbourne: Pluto, 2003 [2002].
92. Nick Garnham, 'From Culture to Creative industries – An Analysis of the Implications of the "Creative Industries" Approach to Arts and Media Policy Making in the United Kingdom', *International Journal of Cultural Policy* 11 (1), March 2005, pp. 15–29.
93. Nick Garnham, 'Afterword – The Cultural Commodity and Cultural Policy', in Sara Selwood, ed., *The UK Cultural Sector: Profile and Policy Issues*, London: Policy Studies Institute, 2001, p. 458.
94. Jim McGuigan, 'Neo-Liberalism, Urban Regeneration and Cultural Policy'; chapter in my *Cultural Analysis*, 2010.
95. David Brooks, *Bobos in Paradise: The New Upper Class and How They Got There*, New York: Simon and Schuster, 2000, p. 10.
96. The original new-class theorist was Milovan Djilas, who noted the rise of a new ruling class in communist Yugoslovia, known in the Soviet Union as the *nomenklatura*, in the 1950s; see *The New Class: An Analysis of the Communist System*, London: Unwin, 1966 (1957).
97. Florida, *The Rise of the Creative Class*, p. 74.

98. Ibid., p. 328.
99. Ibid., p. 68.
100. Ibid., p. 74.
101. Ibid., p. 192.
102. Ibid., p. 166.
103. Robert Putnam, *Bowling Alone: The Collapse and Revival of American Community*, New York: Simon and Schuster, 2000.
104. Richard Florida, *Cities and the Creative Class*, New York: Routledge, 2005, p. 6.
105. Ibid., p. 19.
106. Ibid., p. 122.
107. Ibid., p. 101.
108. Ibid., p. 144.
109. Ibid., p. 171.
110. Richard Florida, *The Flight of the Creative Class: The New Global Competition for Talent*, New York: Collins, 2007.

Chapter 5

1. Quoted by Paul Mason, *Live Working or Die Fighting: How the Working Class Went Global*, London: Harvill Secker, 2007, p. 184.
2. Here I am adopting Richard Florida's categories of service and creative workers, as discussed in the last chapter. These categories are not entirely satisfactory, and the notion of a 'creative class' is especially questionable. However, part of my aim in this chapter is to explore the conditions at the lower echelons of work in rich countries like the US and Britain, particularly in the customer care and caring occupations, for which the category of service work is appropriate. I also intend to examine conditions of work in the professional-managerial class in general, and in cultural and media occupations in particular – the kind of work characterised by Florida as 'creative'.
3. Barbara Ehrenreich, *Nickel and Dimed: Undercover in Low-wage USA*, London: Granta, 2002 (2001).
4. Barbara Ehrenreich, *Bait and Switch: The (Futile) Pursuit of the American Dream*, New York: Metropolitan/Henry Holt, 2005; Richard Florida, *The Rise of the Creative Class: And How It's Transforming Work, Leisure, Community and Everyday Life*, Melbourne: Pluto, 2003 (2002).
5. Ehrenreich, *Bait and Switch*, p. 9.
6. Ibid., p. 18.

7. Richard Sennett and Jonathan Cobb, *The Hidden Injuries of Class*, London: Faber & Faber, 1993 (1972).
8. Richard Sennett, *The Corrosion of Character: The Personal Consequences of Work in the New Capitalism*, New York: W.W. Norton, 1998.
9. Richard Sennett, *The Culture of the New Capitalism*, New Haven: Yale University Press, 2006.
10. Arlie Russell Hochschild, *The Managed Heart: Commercialization of Human Feeling*, Berkeley: University of California Press, 2003 (1983), p. 3.
11. Karl Marx, *Early Writings*, Harmondsworth: Penguin, 1975.
12. Istvan Meszaros, *Marx's Theory of Alienation*, London: Merlin, 1970; Bertell Ohlman, *Alienation: Marx's Conception of Man in Capitalist Society*, London: Cambridge University Press, 1971.
13. Harry Braverman, *Labour and Monopoly Capitalism: The Degradation of Work in the Twentieth Century*, New York: Monthly Review Press, 1974.
14. Robert Blauner, *Alienation and Freedom: The Factory Worker and His Industry*, Chicago: Chicago University Press, 1964.
15. Hochschild, *The Managed Heart*, pp. 3–9.
16. See Simon Williams, *Emotion and Social Theory: Corporeal Reflections on the (Ir)Rational*, London: Sage, 2001.
17. C. Wright Mills, *White Collar: The American Middle Classes*, New York: Oxford University Press, 1951, pp. 161–88.
18. Erving Goffman, *The Presentation of Self in Everyday Life*, London: Penguin, 1969 (1959).
19. David Riesman with Nathan Glazer and Ruel Denny, *The Lonely Crowd: A Study of the Changing American Character*, New Haven: Yale University Press, 1961.
20. See, for instance, Michael Billig, *Freudian Repression: Conversation Creating the Unconscious*, Cambridge: Cambridge University Press, 1999.
21. Arlie Russell Hochschild, 'Emotion Work, Feeling Rules, and Social Structure', *American Journal of Sociology* 85 (3), 1979, pp. 551–75.
22. Hochschild, *The Managed Heart*, pp. 160–1.
23. Arlie Russell Hochschild, *The Time Bind: When Work Becomes Home and Home Becomes Work*, New York: Metropolitan/Henry Holt, 1997.
24. Arlie Russell Hochschild, *The Second Shift: Working Parents and the Revolution at Home*, New York: Viking, 1989.

25. For instance, see the special issues of *Soundings* 11, 'Emotional Labour', Spring 1999, and *Soundings* 20, 'Regimes of Emotion', Summer 2002.
26. Alan Bryman, *The Disneyization of Society*, Chapter 5, 'Performative Labour', London: Sage, 2004, pp. 103–29.
27. Nicholas Hoover Wilson and Brian Jacob Lande, 'Feeling Capitalism – A Conversation with Arlie Hochschild', *Journal of Consumer Culture* 5 (3), 2005, pp. 275–88.
28. Arlie Russell Hochschild, 'Global Care Chains and Emotional Surplus Value', in Will Hutton and Anthony Giddens, eds, *On the Edge: Living with Global Capitalism*, London: Jonathan Cape, 2000, pp. 130–46.
29. Ibid., p. 131.
30. Ibid., p. 137.
31. Ibid., p. 142.
32. Barbara Ehrenreich and Arlie Russell Hochschild, eds, *Global Woman: Nannies, Maids, and Sex Workers in the New Economy*, London: Granta, 2003 (2002).
33. For instance, Leo Panitch and Colin Leys, eds, *Socialist Register 2001: Working Classes, Global Realities*, London: Merlin, 2000; and Mason, *Live Working or Die Fighting*.
34. André Gorz, *Farewell to the Working Class: An Essay on Post-Industrial Socialism*, trans. M. Sonnenscher, London: Pluto, 1982 (1980).
35. Charles Leadbeater, *Living on Thin Air: The New Economy*, London: Viking 1999.
36. Ulrich Beck, *The Brave New World of Work*, trans. Patrick Camiller, Cambridge: Polity, 2000 (1999), p. 1.
37. Ulrich Beck, *Risk Society: Towards a New Modernity*, London: Sage, 1992 (1986). Others have also commented on individualisation, such as Zygmunt Bauman, *The Individualized Society*, Cambridge: Polity, 2001, and Anthony Elliott, *The New Individualism: The Emotional Costs of Globalization*, Abingdon: Routledge, 2006.
38. Anthony Giddens, *Runaway World: How Globalisation is Reshaping Our World*, London: Profile, 1999.
39. Ulrich Beck, *Ecological Politics in an Age of Risk*, trans. Amos Weisz, Cambridge: Polity, 1995 (1988).
40. Jonathan Rutherford, 'Zombie Categories – Interview with Ulrich Beck', in J. Rutherford, ed., *The Art of Life: On Living, Love and Death*, London: Lawrence & Wishart, 2000, pp. 35–51.
41. Ulrich Beck and Elisabeth Beck-Gernsheim, *The Normal Chaos of Love*, trans. Mark Ritter and Jane Wiebel, Cambridge: Polity, 1995 (1990), p. 6.

42. Ibid., p. 7.
43. Beck, *Risk Society*, p. 135.
44. Ulrich Beck and Elisabeth Beck-Gernsheim, *Individualization: Institutionalized Individualism and its Social and Political Consequences*, trans. Patrick Camiller, London: Sage, 2002 (2001), pp. 23–9.
45. Fredric Jameson, *Postmodernism, or, the Cultural Logic of Late Capitalism*, London: Verso, 1991.
46. Beck and Beck-Gernsheim, *Individualization*, p. xxi.
47. Alison Beale, 'From "Sophie's Choice" to Consumer Choice – Framing Gender in Cultural Policy', *Media, Culture & Society* 21, 1999, p. 442.
48. Ibid., p. 443.
49. See Stuart Hood, ed., *Behind the Scenes: The Structure of British Television in the Nineties*, London: Lawrence and Wishart, 1994; and Sue Ralph, Jo Langham Brown and Time Lees, eds, *Current Debates in Broadcasting 7: What Price Creativity? Papers from the 28th University of Manchester Broadcasting Symposium 1997*, Luton: John Libbey, 1998.
50. Todd Gitlin, 'Postmodernism – Roots and Politics', in I. Angus and S. Jhally, eds, *Cultural Politics in America*, New York: Routledge, 1989.
51. Susan Christopherson and Michael Storper, 'The City as Studio; the World as Back Lot – The Impact of Vertical Disintegration on the Location of the Motion Picture Industry', in A. Gray and J. McGuigan, eds, *Studying Culture*, 2nd edn, 1997 (1986), pp. 256–74.
52. See, for instance, Richard Patterson, 'Work Histories in Television', *Media, Culture & Society* 23, 2001, pp. 595–620; and Gillian Ursell, 'Labour Flexibility in the UK Commercial Television Sector', *Media, Culture & Society* 20, 1998, pp. 129–53, and Gillian Ursell, 'Creating Value and Valuing Creation in Contemporary UK Television – Or "Dumbing Down" the Workforce', *Journalism Studies* 4 (1), 2003, pp. 31–46.
53. On overwork in Britain generally, not only in the 'creative industries', see Madeleine Bunting, *Willing Slaves: How the Overwork Culture is Ruling Our Lives*, London: HarperCollins, 2004.
54. James Silver, 'Exploitation is More Widespread than Ever', *Guardian* (Media section), 11 April 2005, p. 2.
55. Angela McRobbie, *British Fashion Design: Rag Trade or Image Industry?*, London: Routledge, 1998.

56. Angela McRobbie, 'From Holloway to Hollywood – Happiness at Work in the New Economy', in P. du Gay and M. Pryke, eds, *Cultural Economy: Cultural Analysis and Commercial Life*, London: Routledge, 2002, p. 97.
57. Angela McRobbie, 'Clubs to Companies – The Decline of Political Culture in Speeded Up Creative Worlds', *Cultural Studies* 16 (4), 2002, p. 521.
58. Ibid., p. 522.
59. Ibid., p. 523.
60. Ibid., p. 525.
61. Tony Jefferson, ed., *Cultural Studies 7/8 Resistance Through Rituals*, Birmingham: Centre for Contemporary Cultural Studies, 1978.
62. Michel Maffesoli, *The Time of the Tribes: The Decline of Individualism in Mass Society*, London: Sage, 1996 (1988).
63. Nick Barham, *Disconnected: Why Our Kids are Turning Their Backs on Everything We Thought We Knew*, London: Ebury, 2006 (2004).
64. Madeleine Bunting, 'In Our Angst Over Our Children We're Ignoring the Perils of Adulthood', *Guardian*, 13 November 2006, p. 27.
65. Juliet Schor, *Born to Buy*, New York: Scribner, 2004, p. 47.
66. See, for instance, Gene Del Vecchio, *Creating Ever-Cool: A Marketer's Guide to a Kid's Heart*, Gretna, Louisiana: Pelican, 1997.
67. Schor, *Born to Buy*, p. 51.
68. Ibid., p. 53.
69. Alissa Quart, *Branded: The Buying and Selling of Teenagers*, London: Arrow, 2003.
70. Ed Mayo, *Shopping Generation*, London: National Consumer Council, July 2005, p. 2.
71. Julia Margo and Mike Dixon with Nick Pearce and Howard Reed, *Freedom's Orphans: Raising Youth in a Changing World*, London: Institute for Public Policy Research, 2006, p. xiii.
72. George Ritzer, *The McDonaldization of Society*, New Century Edition, Thousand Oaks: Pine Forge/Sage, 2000 (1993).
73. Financial Services Authority, *Consumer Research 44: Young People (18–24) and Their Financial Information Needs*, London: FSA, September 2005.
74. Financial Services Authority/Personal Finance Research Centre/University of Bristol, *Levels of Financial Capability in the UK: Results of a Baseline Survey*, London: FSA, March 2006.

75. An article by Denis Campbell, 'House Price Rises Lock Out Half of New Young Buyers', *Observer*, 3 December 2006, p. 7, gives figures for house prices as a multiple of annual income around Britain. In my opinion, the calculations given by Campbell underestimate the scale of the problem.
76. Anya Kamenetz, *Generation Debt: Why Now is a Terrible Time to Be Young*, New York: Riverdale, 2006, p. ix.
77. Ibid., p. 115.
78. Ibid., p. 116.
79. Robin Blackburn, *Banking on Death, Or, Investing in Life: The History and Future of Pensions*, London: Verso, 2002, p. 3. Blackburn's *Banking on Death* and his *Age Shock: How Finance is Failing Us* (London: Verso, 2002), are the major sources for what follows in this chapter.
80. It is remarkable how modest left-wing thought has become in the face of neoliberal hegemony. See Blackburn's modest proposal for a universal pension for everyone in the world: 'A Global Pension Plan', *New Left Review* 47, 2nd series, September–October, 2007, pp. 71–92. For as little as $205 billion a year everyone could have a dollar a day pension, which would of course be of much greater benefit to the poor of the world than the workers I have concentrated upon in this chapter. The comparatively wealthy might wish to forgo that particular benefit.
81. Robert Tressell, *The Ragged Trousered Philanthropists*, London: Penguin, 2004. This book, arguably the greatest of all socialist novels, was originally published in an abridged and bowdlerised form in 1914, by which time Tressell was already dead. For an excellent publishing and political history of *The Ragged Trousered Philanthropists*, see David Harker's *Tressell: The Real Story of the Ragged Trousered Philanthropists*, London: Zed, 2003.

Chapter 6

1. See Erik Olin Wright, 'Compass Points – Towards a Socialist Alternative', *New Left Review* 41, 2nd series, September–October 2006, pp. 93–124; and 'Guidelines for Envisioning Real Utopias', *Soundings* 36, 'Politics and Markets', Summer 2007, pp. 26–39.
2. Wright, 'Compass Points', p. 101.
3. *Cool Brands: An Insight into Some of Britain's Coolest Brands 2007–8*, London: Superbrands, 2007.
4. Naomi Klein, *No Logo: Taking Aim at the Brand Bullies*, London: Flamingo, 2000, p. 68.
5. Ibid., p. 77.

6. Ibid., p. 45.
7. *The Economist*, 8–14 September 2001.
8. Ibid., p. 9.
9. Steve Hilton, 'The Logo Motive', *Media Guardian*, 22 April 2002, p. 3.
10. Klein, *No Logo*, p. 206.
11. Ibid., p. 213.
12. Ibid., p. 211.
13. Ibid., p. 218.
14. Andrew Ross, ed., 'Preface and Acknowledgements' to *No Sweat: Fashion, Free Trade, and the Rights of Garment Workers*, London: Verso, 1997, p. 1.
15. Lina Rodriguez Meza, 'Testimony', in ibid., pp. 5–8.
16. Michael Piore, 'The Economics of the Sweatshop', in ibid., pp. 135–42.
17. Karen McVeigh, 'The Sweatshop High Street – More Brands Under Fire', *Guardian*, 3 September 2007.
18. Jeffrey St Clair, 'Seattle Diary – It's a Gas, Gas, Gas', *New Left Review* 238, 1st series, November–December, 1999, pp. 81–96. See also Andrew Cockburn and Jeffrey St Clair, *Five Days that Shook the World: The Battle for Seattle and Beyond*, London: Verso, 2000.
19. Naomi Klein, 'The Tyranny of the Brands', *New Statesman*, 24 January 2000, p. 25.
20. Guy Debord, *The Society of the Spectacle*, trans. D. Nicholson Smith, New York: Zone, 1994 (1967).
21. Klein, *No Logo*, p. 280.
22. Kalle Lasn, *Culture Jam: The Uncooling of America*™, New York: Eagle Brook, 1999, pp. xii–xiv.
23. Umberto Eco, 'Towards a Semiological Guerrilla Warfare', *Travels in Hyperreality*, trans. William Weaver, London: Picador, 1987 (1967), pp. 135–44.
24. See, for instance, *Adbusters* No. 45: *The Big Ideas of 2008*. As well as attacking the culture of corporate capitalism, in recent years, *Adbusters* has derided Hugo Chávez for appearing too much on and controlling television in Venezuela, which is somewhat contradictory and uncomradely since for years commercial television in Venezuela was allowed to transmit unrelenting propaganda against Chávez. The leading Venezuelan commercial channel – RCTV, one of five commercial broadcasters – was even permitted to support the attempted coup to overthrow him in 2002, long before Chávez eventually refused to renew its franchise in 2007. It was replaced with the first ever public service channel

in Venezuela's history. See Francisco Dominguez, 'Understanding Venezuela', *Soundings* 37, Winter 2007, pp. 92–104.
25. Klein, *No Logo*, p. 343.
26. Matt Haig, *Brand Failures: The Truth About the 100 Biggest Branding Mistakes of All Time*, London: Kogan Page, 2003.
27. Klein, *No Logo*, p. 347.
28. Ibid.
29. Ibid., pp. 263, 266.
30. Giovanni Arrighi, Terence Hopkins and Immanuel Wallerstein, *Antisystemic Movements*, London: Verso, 1989.
31. Paul Kingsnorth, *One No, Many Yeses: A Journey to the Heart of the Global Resistance Movement*, London: Free Press, 2003.
32. Ibid., p. 62.
33. The following are useful surveys of the anti-capitalist movement: Emma Barcham and John Charlton, eds, *Anti-Capitalism: A Guide to the Movement*, London: Bookmarks, 2001; Notes from Nowhere, ed., *We Are Everywhere: The Irresistible Rise of Global Anticapitalism*, London: Verso, 2003; Alfredo Saad-Filho, ed., *Anti-Capitalism: A Marxist Introduction*, London: Pluto, 2003; Joel Schalit, ed., *The Anti-Capitalism Reader: Imagining a Geography of Opposition*, New York: Akashic, 2002.
34. Manuel Castells, 'Mexico's *Zapatistas* – the First Informational Guerrilla Movement', in *The Power of Identity*, 2nd edn, Oxford and Malden, MA: Blackwell, 2004 (1997), pp. 72–86. See also Juana Ponce de Leon and Jose Saramago, eds, *Our Word is Our Weapon, Selected Writings, Subcommandante Marcos*, London: Serpent's Tail, 2001.
35. Jim McGuigan, 'The Public Sphere', in P. Hamilton and K. Thompson, eds, *The Uses of Sociology*, Oxford: Blackwell, 2002, pp. 81–128.
36. Jürgen Habermas, *Between Facts and Norms: Contribution to a Discourse Theory of Law and Democracy*, trans. William Rehg, Cambridge: Polity, 2006 (1992).
37. John Brady, 'The Public Sphere in the Era of Anti-Capitalism', in Schalit, *The Anti-Capitalism Reader*, pp. 55–69.
38. Simon Tormey, *Anti-Capitalism: A Beginner's Guide*, Oxford: Oneworld, 2004, p. 140.
39. Ibid., p. 76.
40. Nobel economist James Tobin suggested that a tax on the movement of capital out of financial markets could be used to fund development in poorer parts of the world.
41. See Alex Callinicos, *An Anti-Capitalist Manifesto*, Cambridge: Polity, 2003.

42. Alex Callinicos, 'At an Impasse? Anti-Capitalism and the Social Forums Today', *Absurdist Republic: A Quarterly Journal of Revolutionary Socialism* 115, July 2007, p. 2; http://my.opera.com/PRC/blog/show.dml/1137300 (accessed 8 January 2008).
43. Ibid., p. 6.
44. Ibid., p. 9.
45. Ibid., p. 16.
46. Jim McGuigan, *Modernity and Postmodern Culture*, 2nd edn, Maidenhead: Open University Press, 2006 (1999).
47. Michael Hardt and Antonio Negri, *Empire*, Cambridge, MA: Harvard University Press, 2000; *Multitude: War and Democracy in the Age of Empire*, New York: Penguin, 2004.
48. James Petras and Henry Veltmeyer, *Empire with Imperialism: The Globalizing Dynamics of Neo-Liberal Capitalism*, London: Zed, 2005, pp. 104–5.
49. Ibid., p. 27.
50. Ibid., p. 28.
51. Ibid., p. 32.
52. Gilles Deleuze and Félix Guattari, *A Thousand Plateaus: Capitalism and Schizophrenia*, vol. 2, trans. Brian Massumi, London: Continuum, 1992 (1980).
53. McGuigan, *Modernity and Postmodern Culture*, pp. 132–3.
54. Deleuze and Guattari, *A Thousand Plateaus*, p. 21.
55. Ibid., p. 25.
56. D.L. Raby, *Democracy and Revolution: Latin America and Socialism Today*, London: Pluto, 2006.
57. Richard Gott, *Hugo Chávez and the Bolivarian Revolution*, London: Verso, 2005 (2000). Incidentally, the Wikipedia entry on Chávez is well worth consulting on his life and career: http://en.wikipedia.org/wiki/Hugo_Ch%C3%A1vez (accessed 18 January 2008).
58. Philip Bounds, 'Chávez and RCTV – The Verdict After a Year', *Fifth-Estate-Online: International Journal of Radical Mass Media Criticism*: http://www.fifth-estate-online.co.uk/comment/ChávezandRCTV.html (accessed 15 June 2008).
59. Rory Carroll, 'Cheap and Cheerful – Venezualans Cling to Right for Petrol at 42p a Tank', *Guardian*, 18 January 2008, p. 29.
60. Petras and Veltmeyer, *Empire with Imperialism*.
61. See Marta Harnecker, *Rebuilding the Left*, trans. James Duckworth, London: Zed, 2007.
62. By the middle of 2008, Morales, similarly to Chávez, was experiencing right-wing rebellion and unscrupulous efforts to overthrow his legitimate regime. See Rory Carroll and Andres

Schpani, 'Bolivia Split in Two as the Wealthy Aim to Defy the Morales Revolution', *Observer*, 24 August 2008, p. 38.
63. See Tariq Ali, *Pirates of the Caribbean: Axis of Hope*, London: Verso, 2006.
64. See Pablo Navarrete's introduction, and a couple of critical articles from Venezuela on Chávez's failed referendum of December 2007, 'Por Hora No Pudimos' [We Couldn't for Now], *Red Pepper*, February–March 2008, pp. 32–5.
65. Karl Marx and Friedrich Engels, *The Communist Manifesto*, trans. Samuel Morse, Harmondsworth: Penguin, 1967 (1848, 1888), p. 120.
66. David Harvey, *The Limits to Capital*, London: Verso, new and fully updated edition, 2006 (1982), p. xxii.
67. Ibid., p. xxvii.
68. Andrew Gamble and Paul Walton, *Capitalism in Crisis: Inflation and the State*, London: Macmillan, 1976, p. 140.
69. Andrew Glyn and Bob Sutcliffe, *British Capitalism, Workers and the Profit Squeeze*, Harmondsworth: Penguin, 1972.
70. Harvey, *The Limits to Capital*, p. 191.
71. Ibid., p. 426.
72. Ibid., pp. 424–5.
73. Ibid., p. 443.
74. Robert Brenner, *The Economics of Global Turbulence: The Advanced Capitalist Economies from Long Boom to Long Downturn 1845–2005*, London: Verso, 2006 (1998).
75. Harvey, *The Limits to Capital*, p. 444.
76. Naomi Klein, *The Shock Doctrine: The Rise of Disaster Capitalism*, London: Penguin, 2007, pp. 9, 14.
77. Ibid., p. 17.
78. Ibid., p. 299.
79. Ibid., p. 301.
80. Ibid., p. 426.
81. Ibid., p. 427.
82. Andrew Glyn, *Capitalism Unleashed: Finance, Globalization, and Welfare*, Oxford: Oxford University Press, 2006, p. 180.
83. Donella Meadows, Jorgen Randers and Dennis Meadows, *Limits to Growth: The 30-Year Update*, London: Earthscan, 2005 (2004).
84. George Monbiot, *Heat: How to Stop the Planet Burning*, London: Allen Lane, 2006.
85. Bjorn Lomborg, *The Skeptical Environmentalist: Measuring the Real State of the World*, Cambridge: Cambridge University Press, 2001.

86. Bjorn Lomborg, *Cool It: The Skeptical Environmentalist's Guide to Global Warming*, London: Marshall Cavendish, 2007.
87. George Monbiot, 'The Stakes Could Not Be Higher. Everything Hinges on Stopping Coal', *Guardian*, 5 August 2008, p. 25.
88. Ulrich Beck, 'All Aboard the Nuclear Power Superjet, Just Don't Ask About the Landing Strip', *Guardian*, 17 July 2008, p. 31.
89. Arthur Scargill, 'Coal Isn't the Climate Enemy, Mr Monbiot, It's the Solution', *Guardian*, 8 August 2008, p. 32.
90. See Martin Durkin, *The Great Global Warming Swindle*, A WAG TV production for Channel 4, 2007.
91. For example, Juliet Jowit, 'Row Erupts Over Risk to Polar Bears', *Observer*, 14 October 2007, pp. 10–11.
92. Davis Guggenheim, *An Inconvenient Truth: A Global Warning*, Participant Productions, 2006.
93. Monbiot, *Heat*, p. 50.
94. Lomborg, *Cool It*, p. 216.
95. Office of Climate Change, *Stern Review on the Economics of Climate Change*, London: HM Treasury/Cabinet Office, 2006.
96. Stern, 'Summary and Conclusions', *Review of Economics of Climate Change*, p. ix; http://www.hm-treasury.gov.uk/independent_reviews_stern_economics_clima... (accessed 8 March 2008).
97. Jonathon Porritt, *Capitalism as if the World Matters*, London: Earthscan, 2005, p. 32.
98. Ibid., p. 133.
99. Joel Bakan, *The Corporation: The Pathological Pursuit of Profit and Power*, London: Constable and Robinson, 2004; Mark Aachbar, Jennifer Abbott and Joel Bakan, *The Corporation*, Picture Media Corporation, 2005.
100. Noam Chomsky, *Profit Over People: Neoliberalism and Global Order*, New York: Seven Stories, 1999 (1998).
101. Daniel Buck, 'The Ecological Question – Can Capitalism Prevail?', in Leo Panitch and Colin Leys, eds, *Socialist Register 2007: Coming to Terms with Nature*, London: Merlin, 2006.
102. James O'Connor, *Natural Causes: Essay in Ecological Marxism*, New York: Guilford Press, 1998, p. 166.

INDEX

Compiled by Sue Carlton

3GSM World Congress 125
9/11 terrorist attacks 209, 221
abjection 82
abstract expressionism 71–2, 74
Académie française 48
Acción Democrática party 214
accumulation, primitive 219
actually existing socialism 58, 129, 197, 227
Adbusters 203, 204
Adorno, Theodor 40, 45, 153–4, 200
adventure capitalism 14
advertising 104, 107–10
   and art 73–4, 77, 80
   and celebrities 93–5
   and coercion 111–12
   as creative industry 158
   incorporating critique 108, 109–10
   market segmentation (totemism) 7, 107, 108, 109
   personalisation (narcissism) 107, 108, 109
   product symbols (iconology) 107, 108, 109, 115
   product-oriented approach (idolatry) 107, 108–9
   standards 106
   see also marketing
aestheticism, (art for art's sake) 54–5, 60
Africa, and origins of 'cool' 2–3
African National Congress (ANC) 207
Aglietta, Michael 101–2

Alberro, Alexander 75–7
Ali, Tariq 21
alienation 46, 47, 112, 169, 182
Allende, Salvador 133, 221
alternative energy 224
Anderson, Chris 156–7
Anglicanism 14, 15
Anonymous Society of Painters, Sculptors, Engravers etc. 57–8
anti-capitalist movement 43–4, 203–4, 205–7
   and diversity of perspectives 208–9, 210–11
   and worldwide media 207–8
anti-war movement 209, 210
AOL-Time Warner 150, 152
Apple 124, 125, 141, 161
Apprentice, The 146–9
Argentina 216, 221
art 45–82
   and business 72–82
   and capitalism 42, 48, 80, 81
   and communism 58–72, 73
   and 'cool' 77, 79, 80–1
   form and content 46
   and incorporation 46–7, 50, 55–8, 59, 72–3, 82
   patronage 48, 53, 75, 78, 155, 157
   and rebellious autonomy 47–58
   and refusal 45–7, 50, 56–7, 58, 59, 72, 75–6, 80
artist, as entrepreneur 77, 81
Atkinson, Dan 161
ATTAC 209, 210

BA (British Airways) 161
Bacon, Francis 77
Baddeley, Oriana 67
Bakan, Joel 228
Banksy 2, 82
Barthes, Roland 49
Baudelaire, Charles 54–5
Baudrillard, Jean 109, 114
Bauman, Zygmunt 85, 114–16
BBC (British Broadcasting Corporation) 143
Be Cool (movie) 95
Beale, Alison 182–4
Beck, Ulrich 166, 175–81, 182, 225
Beck-Gernsheim, Elisabeth 166, 177–8, 179, 182
Becker, Howard 57
Beckett, Samuel 46
Beckham, David 93
Beckham, Victoria ('Posh') 93
Bell, Daniel 19–22, 37, 109, 144, 161
Benjamin, Walter 74
Berger, John 59, 61–2
Berger, Peter 36
Berle, Adolf A. 32–3
Berman, Marshall 9
Bernays, Edward 105
bio-fuels 224
biographies, individualised 178, 179
Biskind, Peter 6
Bismarck, Otto von 16, 194
Black Bloc 208
black culture 94–9
   and 'cool brands' 200
   music business and authenticity 97–8
Blackburn, Robin 193
Blair, Tony 138, 140, 143
bling 95–7, 147–8
bloggers 83

'bobo' (bourgeois bohemian) lifestyle 162, 164
Bohemia/bohemians 49–51, 53, 54, 55, 58, 68, 72, 164
Bolívar, Simón 214
Bolivia 214, 216
Boltanski, Luc 22–31, 38, 44
Botterill, Jacqueline 107, 108–9
Bourdieu, Pierre 53–4, 58, 88–90, 91–2, 137–40
bourgeoisie 9–10, 75, 89
brands 199–205
   cool brands 199–203
   defence of brand culture 200–1
   and exploitation 200
   resistance to brand culture 203–5
Branson, Richard 158
Braque, Georges 60
Brazil 207, 209, 216
Brazilian Workers Party 209
'Brazilianisation' 175–6
Breakdown (Landy) 82
Brenner, Robert 219
Breton, André 70
Britain
   and brand culture 191, 200, 203
   broadcasting 184–6
   children and consumerism 191–2
   coal industry 225
   and fashion design industry 187
   GLC socialist strategy 155
   nationalisation 132–3
   and neoliberalism 131, 141, 142, 143
Brooklyn Museum 80
Brooks, David 162, 163, 164
Brown, Gordon 143
Bruyas, Alfred 53
Bryman, Alan 172
Budgen, Sebastian 30

Bunting, Madeleine 190
bureaucracy 16, 18, 140, 141, 142
Burnham, James 33–5
Bush, George W. 21, 209, 221, 228
business
  and art 72–82
  and incorporation of 'cool' 6–7
  and politics 105
  see also corporations
business ideology 130

Callinicos, Alex 28, 31, 210
Calloway, Cab 4
Calvin, John 14
Cameron, Deborah 145
Cameron, Ewen 220
Campbell, Colin 109
Canada, transition to neoliberalism 182–4
capital
  accumulation 11, 20, 102, 113, 177, 218, 222–3, 228
  corporate 199, 201, 224
  creative 164–5
  different kinds of 227
  finance 219, 227
  and labour 10–11, 136
  limits to 218
  over-accumulation 218, 220
  social 164, 227
capitalism 9–44
  contradictions of 11, 18, 19–22, 217–18, 228–9
  and crisis 101, 217, 218–19
  and disasters 220–2
  and environment 217–18, 220, 222, 227–8
  global 21, 113, 173–4, 211
  and ideology 22, 23–4, 30
  incorporation/neutralisation of critique 38, 44, 204–5
  and legitimacy 1, 9, 22, 23, 31, 36–7, 44, 137, 217
  liberal 22, 129, 131
  limits to 198, 216–29
  Marx's analysis of 9–12
  neoliberal 8, 19, 129, 130–40, 141, 168, 217
  see also neoliberalism
  new spirit 19–31, 124
  and Protestant ethic/asceticism 9, 12–16, 20, 21, 22, 88, 124, 144
  and religious belief 16–17, 24, 129
  survival and adaptation 17–19, 34, 105–6, 197, 216, 217
  transformation of 22–31
    role of artistic critique 26, 27, 30
    role of social critique 26–8, 29
  transmogrification 31–44
  see also cultural capitalism; neoliberalism; organised capitalism; welfare capitalism
carbon capture and storage (CCS) 224, 225
carbon emissions 223, 224, 226
  emissions trading 226–7
care chains, global 173–4
Cashmore, Ellis 97–8
Castells, Manuel 23, 29, 117, 126
Castro, Fidel 201, 214, 215
Catholicism 14, 15
Cavite, Philippines 202
celebrities, and individualisation 180
Central Intelligence Agency (CIA), cultural strategy 72
Chapman, Jake and Dinos 79–80, 81
Chartism 52

Chávez, Hugo Rafael 198,
  213–16
 attempts to overthrow 214–15
 commitment to poor 213, 215
 media hostility to 215
Chen, Steve 84
Chernobyl accident (1986) 177
Chiapas 207
Chiapello, Eve 22–31, 38, 44
Chicago School of economics
  133, 221
Chile, and neoliberalism 133
China 36, 133, 165
 and capitalism 113, 127–8,
  197
 coal 225
 and 'cool' 2
 economic growth 219, 222
 and sweated labour 202
Chomsky, Noam 150
Church of Stop Shopping 207
Churchill, Winston 134
cinema 58, 67, 103, 118, 151
cities, typology 24
civil society 43, 191, 198
Clark, T.J. 52, 57
climate change 223, 225–6
 see also environmental crisis;
  global warming
Clinton, Bill 138
Club of Rome 222
coal 224, 225
Cobain, Kurt 110
Coca Cola 200
Cold War 35, 63, 72
coltan 128
'commanding heights' 132
commodity fetishism 7, 8, 115,
  116–19
communism 32, 34, 36, 117,
  132, 197
 artists and 58, 63, 67–8, 70–2,
  73
 collapse of 8, 10, 36, 129, 133,
  197
 and industrialism 206
 threat of 16, 18, 104, 136, 197
competition 130, 136, 142–3,
  157–8, 184, 186, 218
conceptual art 74, 75, 76–7
*Confederación des Trabajadores
 de Venezuela* (CTV) 214–15
Congolese civil war 128
Congress for Cultural Freedom
 (US) 72
connexity 23, 24, 29–30
consumerism/consumer culture 7,
  8, 83–128
 artists and 77, 81, 82
 children/young people and 96,
  191–2, 193, 196
 and class 86–9
 conspicuous consumption
  86–8, 92
 consumer empowerment 85,
  103, 112, 126
 'cool' seduction 108–16
 and determinancy of
  production 100–1, 103–4
 failed/flawed consumers
  115–16
 manipulation 41, 84–5,
  111–14, 145, 172–3
  see also advertising;
   marketing; public relations
 mass 20, 21, 87, 99–108
 productive consumption 85
 sovereign consumer 85,
  99–100, 145, 182
 and taste 88–91
cool capitalism 7–8, 38, 44, 98,
  109, 129
'cool'/'coolness' 1–7, 95, 190,
  199
 in advertisements 1–2
 and black style 5, 95, 96–7,
  98–9

'cool'/'coolness' *continued*
  and China 2
  origins of concept 2–3
  in post-war France 4
  and rebelliousness 190
  resistance and incorporation 5–6, 8
  in US 3–4, 190
coolhunting 110–11, 148
Coppola, Francis Ford 6
corporate social responsibility 33, 127, 128, 227–8
Corporate Watch 203
corporations
  defence of brand culture 200–1
  largest 152
  manipulation and empowerment 84–5
  separation of ownership and control 32–4
  takeover of public space 201
County Hall (London) 80
Coupland, Douglas 109
Courbet, Gustave 51, 52–3, 54
Cowen, Tyler 157–8
creative class thesis 162–5
creative destruction 18, 135, 205, 220
'Creative Economy Programme' 159
creative industries 149–65
  and cheap labour 151–2
  and dominant ideology thesis 149–52
  and economic growth 164–5
  economics of 156–7
  and information society theory 161–2
  and neoliberalism 158, 182–3, 187–8
  and subsidies 155, 157–8
  see also cultural industries; culture industry
Creative Professionals 163

credit 21, 102, 192–3
  see also debt
credit crunch (2007–08) 192, 219
Creel, George 105
critical modernists 174
Cuba 201, 214, 216
cubism 60, 62
cultural capitalism 37–44
cultural commons, exploitation of 43
cultural consumption 88–92
  and celebrity 92–5
  and class 88–91
  'pure aesthetic' and 'popular aesthetic' 89–90
cultural industries 153–5, 160–1
  and competition 154, 157–8
  see also creative industries; culture industry
culture, and politics 53–4
culture industry 152–4
'culture jamming' 204

de Haan, Esther 126–8
de-industrialisation 5, 24, 37, 155, 161–2
de-traditionalisation 179, 180
debt 39, 166, 191, 192–3
  see also credit
Deleuze, Gilles 212–13
dematerialisation 39
democracy 16, 104–5, 106, 150, 211
  and celebrity 87, 94
  consumerist 220
  digital 83–4
  and individualisation 181
  and property ownership 192
  Venezuela 213, 215
Democracy Unlimited of Humboldt County 207
Department for Culture Media and Sport (DCMS) (UK) 158, 159

deregulation 142, 183
Detroit 37
Detroit Industry murals (Rivera) 66
Detroit Institute of Arts 66
development theory 16
Diaz, Vicky 173–4
Diesel, Fifty-Five DSM range 111
disaffection, incorporation of 1, 6, 96
disaster capitalism 220–1
Disney 150, 152, 172–3
'Disneyization' 172
Dondero, George 71
Dreyfus Affair 55
Drucker, Peter 36, 141
Du Gay, Paul 144–5
Durkheim, Emile 17
Dyson vacuum cleaner 161

East Asia, growth of capitalism 219
Eco, Umberto 204
economic growth 164–5, 205, 222–3
   limits to 222
   see also capital, accumulation
The Economist 200
Ehrenreich, Barbara 166–8, 174
Elliott, Larry 161
Emin, Tracey 79
emotional labour 168–74
employment
   low wages 167
   and older people 167
Engels, Friedrich 13, 216–17
Enlightenment 15, 45
Enron scandal 33
enslavement, contemporary kinds of 198–9
enterprise culture 140–9
   and language 145–6
   and public sector 143
   and the self 144

entrepreneurship 6–7, 18, 22, 76, 77, 78, 81, 98, 141
   see also enterprise culture
environmental crisis 217–18, 222–3
   capitalist solution to 227–8
   opposing views on 223–7
   see also carbon emissions; climate change; global warming
Epstein, Joyce 154
European Social Forum 210
Ewen, Stuart 104, 106, 115
exclusion 28–9, 87, 90, 115–16, 139
existentialism 178, 181, 199
exploitation 24, 26, 27, 31, 128, 130, 151, 166, 174, 198
   and concept of exclusion 28–9
   of consumers 113–14
   in creative industries 186–7, 188
   extraction of surplus value 11, 35, 169
   of intellectual property 159, 160, 185
   outsourcing and 40
Export Processing Zones (EPZs) 127
expressionism 60–1

fashion designers 187
feminism 67, 68, 70, 71
film industry, dominance of Hollywood 150–2
Financial Services Authority (FSA) 191–2
First World War
   and art movements 60
   US intervention 105
flâneur 54–5
Flaubert, Gustave 46, 53
flight attendants, and emotion management 170–1

Florida, Richard 162–5, 167
Fonda, Peter 6
Ford, Edsel 66
Ford, Henry 102
Fordism 101–3
Foucault, Michel 143
France
  and concept of 'cool' 4
  labour flexibility 27
  and neoliberalism 138–9
Franco, Francisco 61
Frank, Thomas 6–8, 109, 136–7
Franklin, Benjamin 15
Free Trade Area for the Americas (FTAA) 207
Freewheeling (guerrilla marketers) 111
Freeze exhibition (1988) 77–8
French Communist Party 63
French Revolution (1789) 45, 51
Freud, Sigmund 170
Frida Kahlo and Diego Rivera (Kahlo) 67
Frida (movie) 68, 70
Friedman, Milton 133, 141
Frozen Assets (Rivera) 63

Gabriel, Yiannis 85
Gaebler, Ted 142–3
Gamble, Andrew 218
Gans, Herbert 92
Gap 203
garment industry, and sweated labour 203
Garnham, Nicholas 154–5, 162
Gates, Bill 30
GATS (General Agreement on Trade in Services) 152
generation crisis 188–96
Genoa, anti-capitalist protest (2001) 207
Gentileschi, Artemesia 68–9
Germany 13, 15, 16, 219
  Nazi Germany 33, 34, 153

Giant Wireless Technology 128
Giddens, Anthony 35, 140, 176
Giotto 64
Giuliani, Rudi 80
Gladwell, Malcolm 110–11
global capitalism 21, 113–14, 173–4, 211
global justice movement 199, 206
  see also anti-capitalist movement
global warming 222, 224, 225, 226
  see also climate change; environmental crisis
globalisation 10, 19, 26, 130, 132, 139, 156, 219
  and employment 175, 183, 205
  and imperialism 211–12
  and individualisation 180
Glyn, Andrew 218, 222
Goffman, Erving 170
Goggin, Gerard 126
Google 84, 119
Gordon, DeeDee 110
Gore, Al 225
Gorz, André 112, 175
Gott, Richard 213
governmentality 143–5
graffiti artists 82
Gramsci, Antonio 101, 146
gratification, deferred and instant 15, 21, 124, 147
Great Depression 18, 66, 102
Greater London Council (GLC) 154, 155
Greenberg, Clement 71
Greenwald, Rachel 145–6
Guatemala, coup (1954) 105
Guattari, Félix 212–13
Guernica 61–2
Guernica (Picasso) 62–3
guerrilla marketing 110, 111
Guevara, Ernesto 'Che' 214

H&M 203
Haacke, Hans 80
Habermas, Jürgen 208
Hall, Stuart 101
Hamill, Pete 64–5
Hamilton, George Heard 56
Hardt, Michael 211, 212
Hartley, John 156
Harvey, David 134–6, 217–19, 220
Harvey, Marcus 79
Hatton, Rita 80
Hayek, Freidrich von 133–4
Heath, Joseph 111
hedonism 4, 5, 8, 21, 38, 88, 109, 144, 166
Hegel, G.W.F. 12, 51
hegemony theory 149
Herman, Edward 150
Herrera, Hayden 68, 69
Hewlett-Packard 141
Hill & Knowlton (China) Public Relations Co. Ltd. 2
Hilton, Steve 200–1
Hilton, Timothy 60
Hindley, Myra, painting of 79
hip-hop culture 96
Hirst, Damien 77–9, 81, 82
Hivech Startech Film Window 128
Hochschild, Arlie Russell 166, 168–74
Hollywood 6, 92, 96, 103, 118, 150–2
Hopper, Dennis 1–2, 6
Horkheimer, Max 40, 45, 153–4, 200
house prices, rising 192
Hume, Gary 79
Hurley, Chad 84
Hussein, Saddam 209

ideology
  and capitalism 22, 23–4, 30
  and misrepresentation/distortion 131–2
  and political doctrine 130–1
impressionists 55, 56, 57–8
India
  mobile phone industry 128
  sweated labour 203
Indian Ocean coastland, tsunami 221
indignation 26, 27, 29, 30, 54
individualisation 166, 175–88
  and ecological politics 181
  and globalisation 180
  institutional individualism 179
  and neoliberalism 179, 181–7
  and risk-taking 176–8, 183, 187
  and sub-politics 181
  typology 179–81
  and work in creative industries 182–8
industrialism/industrialisation 35–6, 45, 66, 154, 176–7, 179
  and environment 206, 227
  managerial revolution 33–5
information and communication technologies (ICTs) 117, 156–7
information society 36
Institute for Public Policy Research (IPPR) 191
intellectual property 40, 159, 160, 185
Intergovernmental Panel on Climate Change 225
International Labour Organisation (ILO) 214
International Monetary Fund (IMF) 133, 220
Internet 19, 83–4, 119, 124
  anti-capitalist movement and 207
  'User-generated content' 84

invisible hand 222
iPhones 125
iPod 119, 122, 124, 161
Iraq, invasion and occupation of (2003) 62, 150, 209, 210, 211, 220, 221
ironic detachment 4–5, 111
ititu 3, 95
Ive, Jonathan 125

Jackson, Michael 98
Jameson, Fredric 74, 181
Jhally, Sut 107–8
Jobs, Steve 119, 125, 141
Jordan, Michael 93–5
Joseph, Keith 133, 134

Kahlo, Frida 46, 59, 65, 67–71
Kamenetz, Anya 192–3
Kanter, Rosabeth Moss 141
Keat, Russell 99
Kennedy, Erica 97
Keynesianism 102, 133, 181–2
Khrushchev, Nikita 71
Kingsnorth, coal-fired power plant 224
Kingsnorth, Paul 206–7
Klein, Naomi 109, 199–200, 202, 203–5, 220–2
Kline, Stephen 107–8
knowledge society 36, 175
Koons, Jeff 77
Kosuth, Joseph 77
Kristeva, Julia 82

La Feber, Walter 94
laissez-faire 131, 182
Lal, Mohan 166
Landy, Michael 82
Lang, Tim 85
Lasn, Kalle 204
Lawson, Neal 115
Lee, Martyn 102–3
Leiss, William 107–8

Lenin, V.I. 66, 132
Leonard, Elmore 95
lifetime value (LTV) 41
Lippmann, Walter 104–5
Livingstone, Ken 215
Lloyd George, David 194
Lodziak, Conrad 112
Lomborg, Bjorn 223–4, 225–6
Longmore, Zenga 95
Longshore Workers Union 204
Lovelock, James 224–5
Lucas, Sarah 79
Lucie-Smith, Edward 68
Lucky Strike 105
Lula da Silva, Luiz Inácio 209
Lutheranism 14, 16
Luxemburg, Rosa 220

McGee, Alan 158
Macmillan, Harold 142
McRobbie, Angela 77, 187–8
Mailer, Norman 5
Majors, Richard 5
management
  managerial revolution 33–5
  separation of ownership and control 32–3
  survey of French texts 25–6
Mancini Billson, Janet 5
Manet, Edouard 55, 56, 57
Marcus Garvey Park 147
Marcuse, Herbert 45–7
market mechanism
  limits to efficiency of 129–30
  natural monopolies 130, 135
market research 110–11, 125, 138, 147
  see also coolhunting; marketing
market values 129–65
  see also enterprise culture; neoliberalism
marketing
  and 'cool' 108–16, 190–1
  viral marketing 110, 115, 191
  see also advertising

Marx, Karl 9–13, 15, 16, 18, 23, 46
  and commodity 116–17, 171
  and limits to capitalism 216–17, 218
  production and consumption 100–1
  on Revolution of 1848 (France) 51
  working conditions 127, 168–9
Marxism/Marxists 12–13, 16, 32, 34, 153
  alienation 169
  and art 46, 59, 65–6, 72
  capital accumulation 222–3
  and consumer culture 101
  decline in rate of profit 218
  limits to capitalism 34, 198, 217
  military expenditure 220
  revolutionary proletariat 175, 212
Matalan 203
Matisse, Henri 66
Means, Gardiner C. 32–3
media corporations, concentration of ownership 149, 150
Methodism 14
Mexican Communist Party 65, 70
Mexican Revolution (1920) 64
Meza, Lina Rodriguez 202
Microsoft 40, 119, 152
Miege, Bernard 153–4
Millennium Dome expo 78
Miller, Toby 150–1
Mills, C. Wright 170
Mitterrand, François 138–9
mobile phone industry
  outsourcing 127–8
  structure of 127

mobile phones 122–3, 125–7
  and 'citizen-reporters' 126
  and developing countries 126
mobile privatisation 119–26
modernisation 16–17, 135
Modernism 20–1
Monbiot, George 223, 224–5
Le Monde diplomatique 209
Mont Pelerin Society 133
Morales, Evo 216
Mothercare 203
motor cars 121
  manufacturers 152
Motorola 127, 128
Movimento dos Trabalhadores Rurais Sem Terra (the Landless Rural Workers' Movement-Brazil) 207
mp3 devices 124
Mueck, Ron 79
Mulgan, Geoff 155–6
multinational corporations (MNCs), relations with nation states 211–12
multitasking 27
multitude 212
murals/muralists 63, 64, 65–7, 69, 72
Murdoch, Rupert 84
Murray, Robin 103
Museum of Modern Art (MOMA) (New York) 62, 63, 71
MySpace 84

narcissism 4, 107, 108, 109
National Association of Manufacturers (NAM) 106
National Consumer Council (NCC) 191
Nederveen Pieterse, Jan 16
negative equity 192
Negri, Antonio 211, 212

neo-Fordism 186
neoconservatism 19, 46, 137–8
neoliberalism 130–40, 179,
    181–2, 205, 214, 216
  and British broadcasting 184–5
  and creative industries 158,
    182–3, 187–8
  definition of 134
  and environmental crisis 226–7
  and generational crisis 119
  as ideological project 136
  and individualisation 179,
    181–7
  opposition to 206–7, 209
  and pension provision 194
  and popular consent 136–7
  and regulation 136
  and role of state 132, 134–5
  and women 182–4
  see also capitalism, neoliberal
networks/networking 23, 24, 30,
    31, 180, 182, 188
  network economy 39–40, 42
  network society 29, 36, 117
  'network-extender' 30
New Deal (US) 34, 66, 102, 194
New Economic Policy (NEP-
    Soviet Union) 132
New International Division of
    Cultural Labour (NICL)
    151, 152
New International Division of
    Labour (NIDL) thesis 151
New Labour (UK) 28, 140
'New Neurotic Realism' 80
New Orleans 221
New Workers School 66
New York 71, 75
'NewLiberalSpeak' 139–40
newly industrialising countries
    (NICs) 36, 37, 113, 127,
    163
News Corp 84
news media, and propaganda 150

NHS (National Health Service)
    143
Nigeria, and origins of 'cool' 2–3
Nike 40, 93–5
Nokia 127
North American Free Trade
    Association (NAFTA) 182,
    183, 207
nuclear power 177, 224–5

Obregón, General Alvaro 64
O'Connor, James 228–9
Ofili, Chris 79, 81
Oh, Minya 95
oil companies 152
organised capitalism 6, 25–6,
    102, 132, 133, 138, 182,
    206, 217
  and art 75
  separation of ownership and
    control 32
  and socialistic features 23, 24,
    26, 32, 129, 168, 194
  transition to neoliberal
    capitalism 8, 132, 141, 168,
    184, 193
Orwell, George 34–5
Osborne, David 142–3
Osse, Reggie 96
outsourcing 27, 39–40, 93,
    127–8, 162, 172, 185, 201

Packard, Vance 106
Palacio de Bellas Artes (Mexico
    City) 66
Paris Commune (1871) 53, 57
Paris Exposition (1937) 61–2
Parreñas, Rhacel 173
Parsons, Talcott 13–14, 16
pension funds 33
pension provision 193–5
performative labour 172–3
Peters, Tom 141–2
Petras, James 211, 212, 216

Philip Morris 76
Picasso, Pablo 46, 59–64, 66, 71
Pietism 14
Pink Fairies 208
Pinochet, Augusto 133
P.L.A.Y. (Participate in the Lives of American Youth) 94
polar bears 225–6
Pollock, Griselda 68–9
Pollock, Jackson 71–2
pop art 74–5, 76
Porritt, Jonathon 227–8
post-Fordism 103, 186
post-industrialism 36, 37, 132, 142, 152, 161, 175, 179
postmodernism 74, 91, 181, 206
poststructuralist theory 153
Potter, Andrew 111
Pountain, Dick 3–5
Powell, Colin 62
Prado 61
Presbyterianism 14
privatisation 130, 133, 135, 142, 214
production
  control over the means of 34
  determining consumption 100–1, 103–4
profit rate 218, 219
projective city 24, 25, 30
proletariat 51, 89
  revolutionary 175, 212
propaganda 72, 80, 106, 109, 145, 150, 199, 220
public relations 75, 76, 90, 91, 93, 104–5
public space, corporate takeover of 201
Punks 5
Puritanism 14, 15, 21, 124
  see also capitalism, and Protestant ethic/asceticism
Putnam, David 158
Putnam, Robert 164

al Qaida 212–13
Quart, Alissa 115, 191

R (relationship) technologies 41
radiation, from mobile phones 126
Rafelson, Bob 6
Rap 98
RCTV 215
Rebuck, Gail 158
Reclaim the Streets 203
Reebok 110
Reform Act (1832) (Britain) 51–2
regulation 136, 142, 143, 185
  and environment 221, 224, 226
  self-regulation 144
Rembrandt, Harmenszoon van Rijn 48
retail industry 103, 144–5
retirement age 195
Reverend Billy 207
Revolution of 1848 (France) 51
Revolutionary Bolivarian Movement (MBR-200) 213–14
rhizome, concept of 212–13
Riesman, David 170
Rifkin, Jeremy 37, 38–44
risk-taking 176–8, 183, 185, 187
'risk society' 176–7
Rivera, Diego 46, 59, 63–7, 68–9, 70–1
Robins, David 3–5
Rockefeller Centre (New York) 66
Rockefeller, Nelson 62, 66, 71–2
Rojek, Chris 92
Romanticism 45, 49, 61
Roosevelt, Franklin D. 18, 34, 66, 102, 106, 194
Rose, Nikolas 143, 144
Ross, Andrew 202
Rothko, Mark 71

Royal Academy (London) 79
Royal Academy of Painting and Sculpture (France) 55–6
Rushkoff, Douglas 111
Russia, after collapse of communism 221
Russian Revolution (1917) 58, 71

Saatchi, Charles 77, 78–9, 80–1
Saatchi, Maurice 78
Salon des Refusés 56–7
Salon, the 51, 52, 54, 56, 57
San Cristobal de las Casas 207
Sartre, Jean-Paul 55
Saville, Jenny 79
Scargill, Arthur 225
Schneider, Bert 6
Schor, Juliet 190, 191
Schumpeter, Joseph 17–19, 23
scientific management 102
 see also Fordism
Seattle protest (1999) 203–4, 206–7
Second World War 106
self, commodification of 171
Sennett, Richard 166, 168
Sensation exhibition (1997) 79–80
shareholders 11, 32, 33
 shareholder value 228
Shenzen 128
shock therapy 220, 221
Siegelaub, Seth 75–6
Silver, James 186
Situationists 26, 204
Sklair, Leslie 113
slavery 3–4, 97
Smith, Adam 15, 141
Smith, Paul 158
social art 54, 60, 82
social democracy 8, 71, 129, 143, 194, 197, 208
Social Exclusion Unit 28

social regulation/control 85, 102, 114
 see also Fordism
socialism 18–19, 21, 34, 201, 217
 actually existing 58, 129, 197, 227
 and environmental crisis 227
 and market values 131, 132
 revolutionary 207
 socialistic features of capitalism 23, 24, 26, 32, 129, 168, 194
 South America 197–8, 213, 216
 threat of 16, 104
Sombart, Werner 12
SOMO (Centre for Research on Multinational Corporations) 126, 128
Sony 147, 152
Sony Walkman 123–4
South America, resurgence of socialism 197–8, 213, 216
Soviet Union 34, 63, 65, 71, 106, 197
Special Economic Zones (SEZs) 127–8
Spindler, Michael 88
stakeholder dialogue 228
Stalin, Josef 58, 63, 70, 71
Stallabrass, Julian 79, 80, 81
Stanislaw, Joseph 132, 133, 136
Stern Review on the Economics of Climate Change (2006) 226
Stern, Sir Nicholas 226
Stewart Report (2000) 126
stock-market crash (1929) 102
Stonor Saunders, Frances 72
students, and debt 193
Sugar, Alan 146
Super Creative Class 163
Superbrands 199

surplus value 11, 35, 169, 217
surrealism 61
Sutcliffe, Bob 218
sweated labour 201, 202–3, 205

Tate Modern 80
   Kahlo exhibition 67
Tawney, R.H. 15
Taylor, Frederick 102
technology 45–6
   communication technologies 117–28, 151, 164, 177
   and 'supervening social necessity' 118
   technological determinism 117–19
telephone call centres 172, 173
television 118, 119, 122, 125, 148
   advertising 107, 184
   and mobility 120
   neoliberalism 184–5
Thailand, mobile phone industry 128
Thatcher, Margaret 78, 131, 133, 134, 136, 155
Thatcherism 80, 141, 161, 185
Thompson, Robert Farris 2–3
Thomson, Belinda 57
Time magazine, Person of the Year 83–4, 85
Tobin tax 209
Toddington Manor (Gloucestershire) 81
Toffler, Alvin 142
Tolliver, Gabriel 96
Tönnies, Ferdinand 17
Tormey, Simon 208
trade unions 23, 26, 27, 102, 204
   attempts to overthrow Chávez 214–15
   membership decline 175
   and sweated labour 202

TRIPS (Trade-Related Intellectual Property Rights) 152
Trotsky, Leon 65, 71
Truman, Harry S. 71
Trump, Donald 146, 147–8
Turner prize 78

unemployment 27, 105, 175, 180, 182
Union National des Trabajadores (UNT) (Venezuela) 215
UNITE (garment workers union) 202
United Nations Building (New York) 62

Van Gogh, Vincent 74
Vasconcelos, Kose 64
Veblen, Thorstein 87–8, 92
Veltmeyer, Henry 211, 212, 216
Venezolana de Televisión (VTV) 215
Venezuela 213–15
   and oil 215–16
   see also Chávez, Hugo
Viacom 150
Virgin Atlantic 161
Voltaire 55

Wacquant, Loïc 139–40
Wal-Mart 152, 167
Walker, John A. 80
Walter, Natasha 145–6
Walton, Paul 218
war on terror 209, 221
Warhol, Andy 74, 77
Washington consensus 133
Waterman, Robert 141–2
'Web 2.0' 84
Weber, Max 12, 13–17, 22, 129
Weimar constitution 16
welfare capitalism 23, 136, 138, 141
   see also organised capitalism

welfare state 23, 76, 102, 181–2
Wernick, Andrew 104
West Papua, tribal resistance 207
Whannel, Gary 93
White Bloc 208
Wightman, Baysie 110
Wilde, Joseph 126–8
Wilhelm, Kaiser 16
Williams, Raymond 37, 46, 73, 118, 119–21
Williamson, Judith 108
Willis, Paul 96
Wilson, Elizabeth 49–51
Winston, Brian 118
women
   careers in broadcasting 186
   and consumer seduction 115
   and exploitation 168–9, 173–4
   and neoliberalism 182–4, 186
   and smoking 105
Woods, Tiger 94
Work Foundation, *Staying Ahead* report 159–61
World Bank 133, 220
World Economic Forum 209
world music 43
World Social Forum (WSF) 198, 207, 209–10
World Trade Organisation (WTO) 133, 152, 211
   Seattle protest (1999) 203–4, 206–7
World's Fair (New York-1939) 106

Worpole, Ken 155–6
Wozniak, Steve 141
Wright, Erik Olin 198
Wu, Chin-tao 76

Yergin, Daniel 132, 133, 136
Yorubaland 2–3, 95
Young British Art 46, 75, 77, 79–80, 81–2
Young, David, Baron Young of Graffham 141
young people and children
   and consumerism 96, 109–10, 115, 190–1, 196
   in creative industries 187–8
   and economic problems 192–3, 196
   and financial education 191–2
   and generation crisis 188–96
   and housing costs 192
   and McDonaldisation of work 191, 193
   and mobile phones 122, 123
   and pension provision 193–4, 196
   and rebellion 189–90, 204
YouTube 84

Zapatista Landscape (The Guerrilla) (Rivera) 64
Zapatista uprising (1994) 206, 207
zazou subculture 4
Zola, Emile 55
Zukin, Sharon 49